WHEN MARYS WERE KINGS!

VOLUME TWO OF THE 'KINGS OF THE RECS!' SERIES

LADY CHATTERLEY, THE BEATLES, ARNOLD ST MARYS FC
AND MUCH, MUCH MORE...

ROGER RANN

- - - - -

ISBN 978-0-9557305-1-1

PUBLISHED BY
JAMES HAWTHORN
EAGLE CLOSE
ARNOLD
NOTTINGHAM
NG5 7FJ

© ROGER RANN 2008

FIRST PUBLISHED OCTOBER 2008

FOR CHARLIE, AND FOR OLIVER, AND FOR EMMA

Printed by Fineprint (Nottingham) Ltd.

www.FineprintLtd.com
Tel: 0115 9111 700

CONTENTS

SUBSCRIBERS

A big, big thank you to everyone listed below who reserved a copy of the book. A lot of you did the same for KOTR! and I am grateful to you all for your support.

MARK BUTLER

DAVID MATTHEWS

MARTIN WILLIAMS

GRAHAM TAYLOR

JOHN AND PAM LAMB

ANDY NOWAK

STEVE RANN

IVOR AND STEPH HOLLAND

DERRICK AND BERYL BARNES

ALF AND ANNE ASKEW

DAVID HOLLINGSWORTH

RICHARD PANTER

MICK GRETTON

KEITH PARNILL

STUART J PYKETT

ANDREW AND PENNY MILLWARD

BILL COLLEY

JOAN JONES

RICHARD LANE

ANDY KEETLEY

MALC PENNYCOOK

THOMAS HUDSON

TONY HUDSON

ROY HILL

NICK HAMILTON

GERARD KELMAN

JOHN R PARR

CHRISTOPHER PARR

DOUG DALE

DENIS KEETON

BRIAN HOWES

PATRICIA AND RODGER ARMITAGE

BOB TAIT

STUART WILSON

JOHN HINES

STEVE HOLLAND

ALEC CASTERTON

TOMMY MIDDLETON

TOM MIDDLETON

GLENN MIDDLETON

GARY MIDDLETON

DEREK LANGSDALE

GEOFF SUBDEN

ROY HOPKINSON

MIKE DERMODY

KEN CARLIN

DEREK WALLIS

GARRY LEE

STUART ASTILL

MEL HART

PAT HENDERSON

CHRIS MARSH

IAN PARKER

MICHAEL PRIDGEON

ANDREW SINGLETON

GWEN RANN

IRENA NOWAK

LARRY AND HAZEL FLEMING

DANEK AND LUCY PESZYNSKI

MARTIN BOLUS

KEITH WARSOP

JOHN DAY

TREVOR BICKNELL

ALAN HICKMAN

ACKNOWLEDGEMENTS

Before the specific 'thank yous' below, might I begin by saying that if you're not mentioned by name then please accept my sincere apologies for the oversight.

Many thanks to those unsung members of the library staffs at Belper (Paul), Newark (Tim), Nuneaton (Joana), Stamford (Denise), and Retford (Alison), who not only provided me with key pieces of information from their local newspaper archives but on each successful occasion reinforced my desire to find even more.

Thanks also to the ever-helpful Enid Doona at Arnold library for her much appreciated assistance.

Thank you again to Philip Meakin of the Nottingham Post Group Ltd for organising a letter of access re their copyright publications.

A big thank you to Andy Smith of Sky Sports' 'Futbol Mundial' for his great encouragement, ideas, and support.

My grateful thanks to Maryrose Robinson (nee Staples), whose family lived opposite ours in my pre-teen years. On meeting her for the first time in goodness knows how long she helped jog my memory with her own vivid recollection of the countryside bordering our estate.

Thank you to Martin Williams, Mark Butler, and everyone at the Arnold Town FC Supporters' Club for your invaluable help.

Once more I owe a very great debt of gratitude to Martin Dermody, whose support and enthusiasm has been constant and way above the call of duty. Who else would have walked around Waterstones moving stray copies of KOTR! into more prominent positions? Martin, if you ever require a reference as a shelf-stacker, or more rather as a point-of-sale merchandiser to give it its politically correct title, I'm your man.

Last but certainly not least my heartfelt thanks to my wife Anna. All of you who have read or seen KOTR! will probably know of her problem with MS and I am pleased to say that another year on she is as full of fight as ever. She is also still taking her responsibilities as official proof-reader rather too seriously for my liking, defacing my draft of WMWK! with her blue correcting pen in a style all too reminiscent of one or two of the more sadistic teachers that I had the misfortune to cross paths with back in my school days. As always I take all responsibility for any mistakes that have slipped through her net and my own second reading. One final thing; as was the case with KOTR! all the net proceeds of WMWK! will wing their way to the MS Society, so don't just buy yourself a copy, get one for a relative or friend. That way a cure for Anna's pernicious condition, one she shares with eighty thousand people in this country and millions worldwide, will be that little bit nearer.

INTRODUCTION

(I) 'KINGS OF THE RECS!'

Those of you already familiar with KINGS OF THE RECS!, the first volume in an intended series that I hope will eventually provide a pretty comprehensive overview of the history of football in Arnold, will know that it covers the seasons 1945-46 to 1957-58. This, Volume 2, begins with season 1958-59 and so picks up the story where KOTR! ends.

Quite a number of the players, supporters, and administrators referred to between these covers made their first appearance in Volume 1, and I have assumed that the majority of readers of this follow-up will already be acquainted with their names, exploits, and achievements, at least up until 1958. However, if you haven't already done so, and without wishing to make it appear like a blatant sales pitch, I would heartily recommend that you read KOTR! before starting this volume.

I had, of course, been unsure as to how my very first attempt at a book would be received, so I was extremely pleased when the first print sold out in just four weeks and equally as delighted that only a handful of the second print still remain. Whilst the number of copies that were being snapped up was extremely gratifying, I was even more enthused by the kind words that I received from a variety of readers in the form of letters and e-mails, a selection of which, in addition to those on the cover, I unashamedly include below:-

> *Have reached page 20 and am hooked. Even a Blackburnian is finding Austerity Period Arnold football fascinating.*
> Nigel Anderton, ex-Arnold Kingswell player

> *Congratulations on an excellent read. The book also provides a good social history of the time and your description of the proprietor of the sweet shop on Nottingham Road is spot on. My personal favourites were pineapple chunks and banana flavoured palm bars. I can't wait for the next instalment.*
> Bill Colley, ex-Arnold Rovers and Arnold Kingswell player

> *I am thoroughly enjoying the read, so nice to have some social history in with the football, and I congratulate you on a really absorbing book. Put me down for Volume 2 !!!!*
> Richard Lane, Newark football historian

> *I wish to convey my congratulations to you on your superbly written book. I am reading through one fascinating chapter every Sunday.*
> Martin Williams, Arnold Town Supporters Club

> *Congratulations! Thank you for the pleasure given over the past few weeks. I marvel at the amount of research and the effort that must have been put in to getting all those facts and figures. I look forward to the next edition.*
> Ivor Holland, Arnold Town Supporters Club

> *I enjoyed the book and am now reading it for the third time. Thank you for the wonderful memories.*
> John Anthony, ex-Arnold football follower now resident in Australia

I enjoyed reading your 'international' best seller over Xmas this year. It was clearly a labour of love, and I admire your patience and tenacity for taking on such a task. I know that it brought back very fond memories for my dad.
Andy Greensmith, son of Rovers' stalwart Franny Greensmith, now resident in New Zealand.

Of course Andy's reference to the book's success was made with tongue firmly planted in cheek, but John Anthony's e-mail made it two from the Antipodes, and copies have also found their way to France and Denmark, so maybe he has a point. Who would have thought that a publication primarily about the exploits of Arnold's footballers back in the forties and fifties, or anything about little old 'Arna' for that matter, might become an 'international' best seller!

(II) WRITING 'WHEN MARYS WERE KINGS!'

Again, those of you who have seen the Introduction to KOTR! will know that, for me, the most daunting element of getting this project into the public domain was the actual process of writing, and the situation didn't really change the second time around. Before I'd begun the main body of the book, I was in very much the same predicament as the originator of the following quote.

"I'm writing a book. I've got the page numbers done." [Steven Wright]

Of course, as befits a stand-up comedian, he was making a joke of it, but it's no laughing matter when the information in one's head refuses to make that short journey to those fingertips hovering expectantly over the keyboard.

Sometimes, even when a few words have managed to make their belated appearance on screen, the problem isn't necessarily over. Thankfully, according to the following anecdote, this happens to even the most esteemed of writers.

James Joyce was sitting disconsolately in his study when a friend dropped by.

"I've only written seven words today", Joyce told him.

"But James", his friend said reassuringly, *"seven words is a good day for you".*

"I know", replied Joyce, *"but I don't know which order they go in".*

As it transpired, there were days when even seven words in any order would have been an improvement on what I'd managed, or rather not managed, but fortunately those occasions became fewer as I warmed to the task.

The thanks for this must inevitably go to all those people who gave their time to speak with me and reminisce about life back in the late fifties and early sixties. My efforts were made so much easier by their contributions and as with the first volume I owe them a debt of the greatest gratitude.

(III) LEN ROCKLEY

One of those guys who gave me a tremendous amount of help with KOTR! was Marys' goalkeeper from 1952 to 1963, Len Rockley. In fact, it was his comment about the relative merits of Marys and Rovers some two years before it eventually came out that was to prove to be the inspiration behind the first book.

It was inevitable that when I came to begin my research for WMWK! the first person I turned to was Len. After all, he was the only surviving player to have featured in every one of the five seasons I intended to cover. We dutifully arranged our first meeting, I had the digital recorder all ready to go, and all that was needed was Len and his excellent power of recall.

When he hadn't turned up at the appointed time of two-thirty on that Thursday afternoon I began to think that maybe I'd made a mistake with the date of our meeting. After all Len, like so many of his generation, was a stickler for time-keeping, never late for any of our previous appointments. Just when I'd decided I was reaching that age where I'd better start writing things down and not trust an obviously disintegrating memory, he arrived.

Unfortunately, he wasn't quite the Len I was used to. His tremendous recollection of events from some fifty years ago was beginning to desert him, and he was having difficulty in answering even the most straightforward of questions. It was obvious he was experiencing some physical and mental distress, and we both agreed that it was best that we call it a day. I made sure that he managed to drive back home safely, the least I could do in the circumstances, but it didn't stop me worrying about his condition. Later that evening I spoke with his lovely wife Maureen and she told me that he'd been admitted to hospital. He never came out.

His funeral at St Marys Church was standing room only, the congregation filled with members of his family, including his young Granddaughter Kirsty who ought to have been given a medal for the wonderful speech she made in memory of her Granddad. Goodness knows where she got the strength to stand up in front of so many strangers to deliver it so beautifully, but she did. Then there were his ex-work colleagues, his fellow singers from the Bestwood Male Voice Choir, those who knew him from his days at Arnold Baths as a member of the Swimming Club and Water Polo teams, his golfing mates and of course his ex-colleagues and adversaries from the football arena. No wonder the church was full.

I never did get the chance to click the ON button of my digital recorder that day of our last fateful encounter and I'm glad that I didn't. It wouldn't have been the real Len Rockley. The one who, through my attempts at writing, I wanted to be remembered, along with all his contemporaries, as someone who, through their footballing achievements for their local clubs, contributed something good, worthwhile, and lasting to the community he loved. It goes without saying that his passing has left a void, but if he's casting a glance down on my efforts any time now, I hope he realises his absence made my task that much tougher.

Roger Rann
Arnold, Nottingham, October 2008

THE INTERVIEWEES

The best part of getting KOTR! into the public domain was the chance to wander down memory lane with all those players, committeemen, and supporters who I managed to get to meet in person or speak to on the telephone. I'm very pleased to say, but not at all surprised, that the process has been just as delightful the second time around.

INTERVIEWEES

SA	SAM ARCHER	*Player*
AB	ALAN BALL	*Player*
PB	PETER BURTON	*Player*
MD	MARTIN DERMODY	*Supporter*
BE	BILLY ENGLAND	*Player*
FG	FRANNY GREENSMITH	*Player*
EI	ERNIE IREMONGER	*Player*
GK	GEOFFREY KING	*Supporter*
AM	ALBERT MOORE	*Committeeman*
AO	ARTHUR OLDHAM	*Player*
GP	GEOFF PARR	*Player*
LR	LEN ROCKLEY	*Player*
DS	DAVID STAPLES	*Player*
ET	ERIC THOMPSON	*Supporter, Committeeman*
RT	ROY THOMPSON	*Supporter*
FW	FRANCES WHITT	*Supporter*
PW	PETER WILLIAMS	*Player*

He'd probably done it hundreds of times before but when the referee put his whistle to his lips and blew for time on this particular occasion he was not only signalling the end of the game, and one which happened to be the last match of the season, he was also bringing down the curtain on a whole era.

Not that the majority of the two thousand or more people milling around the King George V (KGV) playing field in the heart of a small East Midlands town would have realised it on that spring evening in 1958. It was Saturday 3 May and they had just seen the town's two best teams battle it out against each other in the final of the Central Alliance Division Two Cup, with Arnold St Marys eventually edging the contest with a two-nil victory over their keenest rivals Arnold Rovers. It was the sixteenth time the two sides had met during a heady few years where 'football fever' was a common headline in the local newspapers, and there was no reason to suspect that there wouldn't be many more great nights like this ahead.

After all, Rovers may have lost the match, but they had already been crowned champions of the Second Division of the Central Alliance and football in the town seemed set fair for this great rivalry to continue. However, even as the trophy was being awarded to Marys' captain Ron Hinson out on the pitch, the ambition and drive of the movers and shakers behind the scenes in the maroon and gold half of the town, together with an unforeseen stroke of administrative misfortune soon to befall Rovers, would contrive to ensure that, sadly, this latest head-to-head clash would also prove to be the very last. As both sets of fans set off from Gedling Road to either celebrate or commiserate at any one of the numerous pubs and clubs around town Walter 'Kegga' Parr and Syd Gray, leading lights on Marys' committee, were already thinking about the future, all the while plotting to take their beloved club ever onwards and upwards. If this future didn't involve having to pit their wits against their local rivals on a regular basis, then so much the better.

Ostensibly there was automatic promotion to the Central Alliance Division One, which was split into two sections, North and South, and when the final tables for the season were published, the top looked like this:-

	P	W	D	L	F	A	P
Arnold Rovers	32	23	4	5	96	53	50
Sutton Town Res	32	23	3	6	123	60	49
Kimberley Town	32	23	3	6	122	60	49
Ilkeston Town Res	32	21	3	8	113	45	45
Arnold St Marys	32	20	4	8	121	64	44

To all intents and purposes, the top two should have gone straight up, especially considering that Sutton Town's first team had been admitted to the Midland League, thus allowing their second string to take their place. But then came the first of the summer's shocks. For reasons detailed more fully in 'Kings of the Recs!', it was announced that Rovers weren't champions at all, and the league table was revised accordingly:-

	P	W	D	L	F	A	P
Sutton Town Res	32	23	3	6	123	60	49
Kimberley Town	32	23	3	6	122	60	49
Arnold Rovers	**32**	**22**	**4**	**6**	**93**	**54**	**48**
Ilkeston Town Res	32	21	3	8	113	45	45
Arnold St Marys	**32**	**20**	**4**	**8**	**121**	**64**	**44**

This amendment now meant that Kimberley Town had taken the second automatic promotion place, and Rovers were destined to remain in Division Two with Marys.

However, in one of those 'how did that happen?' episodes, the Saints somehow leapfrogged not only Rovers but Kimberley Town too to take up a spare place in the top division as it expanded its number of teams from seventeen to eighteen. Quite exactly how Marys' committee, despite seeing their team finish as low as fifth, succeeded in convincing the management of the Central Alliance that they were worthy of promotion to the top division remains open to conjecture, but succeed they did.

Maybe Kimberley were asked and passed up the opportunity, maybe Rovers were invited and declined too; who knows? The league's close season appeared to be riddled with the same administrative confusion that had scuppered the red and whites' authentic right to the championship a couple of months earlier and it was only once the dust had settled that it finally became clear that the two Arnold clubs' futures would no longer be so inextricably linked as in the past. And where once there was little or nothing to choose between the two sides, on this occasion, well away from the playing field, there was no doubt who were the winners and losers. So whilst Rovers remained where they were, their oldest rivals began to plan for the future at a more elevated level, and the first thing they did was to adopt an ambitious recruitment plan, one that hinged around Syd Gray's powers of persuasion.

COLIN COLLINDRIDGE IN HIS FOREST DAYS

(Courtesy Football Post)

Syd was the Club Secretary and he and the committee had identified a couple of guys who'd played League football and who it was felt had the experience required to help take the club to the next level. They were Colin Collindridge and Sid Thompson, team mates at Forest a few years earlier. Both were now at the veteran stage of their careers, in fact Colin, a versatile forward equally comfortable on the wing, at inside forward, or even wearing the number nine shirt, was approaching his thirty-eighth birthday. He'd racked up over three hundred league games for Sheffield United, Forest and Coventry City, scoring over a hundred goals. Sid, by comparison, was a mere youngster at thirty years of age. He was a skilful wing half cum inside forward who'd had a couple of dozen first team games in his time at the City Ground.

I'm sure that the two of them would have loved to have come to Gedling Road for the football alone but the clincher was that Syd Gray, who worked as a bricklayer in the Maintenance Department at Calverton Colliery, put in a good word for them with the management, with the result that Marys' two new signings were also the beneficiaries of a steady job over at the pit.

Having captured the two ex-Reds, the only other newcomer to the ranks was right back Barry Molyneux, snapped up from fellow Alliance outfit Ransome and Marles, which meant that when the new season began, the club had kept faith with eight of its cup winners. Now it was only a question of whether the Saints would prove themselves worthy of their surprise advancement, or whether it had been a step too far.

In many ways Marys' progress had been mirrored in the first half of 1958 by developments in a number of areas, locally, nationally, and globally, all far removed from the playing arena. Arnold, now with a population of around twenty three thousand people, was about to be given a much needed facelift with the local council's announcement of a five year slum clearance programme, with Front Street being nominated as a 'Development Area'. One of the first buildings in this brave new architectural world was the TSB branch which opened in March. Still situated today at the junction of Front Street and Ravenswood Road, it replaced the old prefabricated building, known locally as the 'ugly duckling', that had been opened on a temporary basis back in 1947 but which had somehow succeeded in hanging around for a decade or more.

I'm not sure whether the TSB, the bank that would sometime in the future be the one that used to say it liked to say 'yes', had a thriving line in mortgages back then, but less than a week after its official opening ceremony a canny investor, with or without financial assistance, acquired a block of six houses on Duke Street for only fourteen hundred and fifty pounds, less than two hundred and fifty quid apiece.

Not all was sweetness and light in the district however as the unacceptable face of vandalism began to rear its ugly head. Just a month earlier two 'Teddy Boys', aged eighteen and nineteen, had been found guilty of smashing glass in a Westdale Lane telephone kiosk, provoking the following hand-wringing editorial piece in the Nottingham Advertiser under the heading

"Are We Going Soft?"

"Despite what statistics claim to prove there is not much doubt that crime is on the increase. Hardly a week passes without some ruffians robbing a bank or cars containing wages, stealing mailbags, or lorry loads of cigarettes and so on. Youngsters have been known to cause wanton damage at the Beeston Youth Centre, while only last week a couple of Teddy Boys were fined £5 for malicious damage to a telephone kiosk. I understand that at least one motor car is stolen every day in the City of Nottingham. I was one of the victims recently and after two days the vehicle was recovered from some waste land at Basford. How and when is there going to be any diminution in crime? Full employment was at one time thought to have been the answer but that has failed. Perhaps I am old-fashioned but my view is that there is far too much bunkum spoken of the benefits of psychology and far too little about the deterrent of the birch and the cat. I have seen smirking youths leaving police courts joking about the fact that they got away with the 'punishment' of a £5 fine. They were heroes in the eyes of the 'gang'. There was a time when parents, school teachers and even policemen could cuff a youngster without being hauled up for assault and the reintroduction of the cane might prove more efficacious than a magisterial wigging. For persistent wrongdoers the birch and the cat would certainly do more good than probation or a meagre fine. In any case the present method of doling out justice seems to have failed and decisions by the Bench should be punishment in the real sense of the word."

Fifty years later his words remain eerily and unfortunately relevant, but at least his column didn't attempt to point the finger at contemporary music, which at the time had seen the craze for skiffle groups reach its zenith. The supposed relationship between popular music and juvenile delinquency had always been a poorly researched one but was nevertheless often wheeled out by sloppy journalists as a major reason for declining standards of behaviour amongst the young. I'm not sure whether any members of the numerous local skiffle outfits such as the Attic Boys, the Streamliners, the Grasshoppers, and the Black Jacks loved the sound of breaking glass enough to want to put a foot through a telephone kiosk but groups like them sure made a hell of a racket with their ensemble of basic and often home-made instruments.

Glaswegian Lonnie Donegan was the most successful popular music star in Britain up to the arrival of Cliff Richard later in 1958. He was the undisputed King of Skiffle, the craze that had swept the country over the previous couple of years and which enabled anybody with a tea-chest, a broomhandle, and a washboard to perform popular songs. He had taken his revved up versions of American folk songs like Cumberland Gap to the very top of the charts and spawned any number of wannabe amateur imitators. The beauty of skiffle was that it was cheap. Even the most expensive instrument, the guitar, could have been bought for less than the standard fine for vandalism. Four guineas (four pounds, four shillings or £4.20 in decimal jargon) would have even bought a model that basically played itself. For this sum, every budding front man in the district could equip himself on a Saturday afternoon with the latest Auto-chord guitar from Jack Brentnall's emporium on Goldsmith Street, sold with the tag lines 'Anyone Can Play', 'No Practice', and 'Press Button', and be wowing the ladies with his musical proficiency a few hours later down at the local village hall or youth club. A great night guaranteed for all, just as long as the crowd frenzy stopped short of laying waste to the building.

Her Majesty The Queen might have been the subject of a certain degree of vitriol courtesy of Johnny Rotten and the Sex Pistols in another era of do-it-yourself music twenty years later, but there was no chance of her being affronted at the summer's annual presentation of debutantes at Court. Not that that stopped her from doing away with this remnant of upper class social privilege and ritual, one for which the term 'coming out' had an entirely different meaning to its current usage. It's quite possible that the Monarchy was realising that, as in the wider world, change was inevitable. After all, it was only the previous Christmas that Elizabeth II had been persuaded to use the medium of TV for the very first time in her annual Speech to the nation, and if things were in a state of flux at home, matters of an international nature were also pointing the way to a rapidly changing future.

Following the signing of the Treaty of Rome the previous March, the European Economic Community (EEC) had become effective on January 1. Britain wasn't a founder member but the influence of what was known as the 'Common Market' would soon begin to make an impact beyond the borders of its original six states, but for the time being it was to Eastern Europe that most people were casting anxious glances, as the Soviet Union continued to match the USA in the nuclear arms race.

That the world was moving into a faster, more violent age was evidenced by a series of fatal accidents involving RAF Vampire Jets. The previous year, children in a playing field near Newark had to dive flat on their faces when they saw one of the jet aircraft from RAF Swinderby screaming straight towards them, but the plane crashed in a beet field just before reaching them. The pilot had already plunged to his death. A second fatality occurred when Flying Office Crossley of 501 Squadron decided to fly a Vampire at 450mph under the Clifton Suspension Bridge. He succeeded, but then crashed into the Gorge and was killed instantly.

The third instance of danger in the skies came much nearer home on the second day of 1958 when two Vampires collided over Colwick. Unsurprisingly, four airmen lost their lives in the horrific crash, but this time there were consequences on the ground too. Wreckage from one of the aircraft careered through a roof at the local Dye Works of Spray and Burgass, resulting in the death of a Carlton woman. With Manchester United's Munich air crash only over a month away, it was hardly a great spell in the annals of aviation, but whilst they were still burying the bodies of the victims of that famous disaster, it was the notion of mass annihilation via the airways that was focusing the minds of a large and growing number of people in the country.

On February 17, a collection of like-minded and worried citizens, brought together under the banner 'The Campaign for Nuclear Disarmament' (CND), held its inaugural public meeting at Central Hall, Westminster. Five thousand people attended and afterwards a number of them marched to Downing Street, thus starting a trend of mass peaceful demonstrations that firmly caught the eye of the public at large at the beginning of April. To the sounds of a skiffle group playing 'When The Saints Go Marching In', three thousand people marched past the gates of the Atomic Weapons Research Establishment at Aldermaston and called for Britain, Russia, and the United States to stop the manufacture, testing, and storage of nuclear weapons. CND claimed that twelve thousand supporters attended the final rally and that six hundred hardcore members had walked the entire fifty miles from London. At one point, the marchers forgot their peaceful manifesto and attacked a car containing a few dissenters who had accused them, through a loudspeaker, of 'playing Khrushchev's game'.

Nikita Khrushchev, the Soviet Premier, had been in power for less than a couple of weeks since taking over the reins from Nikolai Bulganin, but his name would soon become familiar to everyone in this country and the western world as a whole. The fact that the Kremlin felt the need for a change at the top a mere three days after Elvis Presley had been inducted into the US Army has always been assumed to be just a coincidence.

With 'Ban The Bomb', the iconic slogan of the era, resonating in their ears, the humble folk of Arnold might have been forgiven for thinking that the doom-mongers had been right all along when, in the middle of summer and without even a four minute warning, the town began to rumble and shake. Fortunately the end wasn't nigh, this time at least; it was merely an earth tremor.

Shortly after, on the footballing front, Brazil claimed the World Cup for the first time, beating hosts Sweden five-two and launching a young seventeen year old, Edson Arantes do Nascimento, better known by his nickname Pele, onto the world stage. Television viewers back in the UK were overawed by the exploits of the precocious Brazilian youngster and his audacious ability, and one of his two goals in the final, where he flicked the ball over a covering defender and volleyed it past the despairing dive of the Swedish goalkeeper, will live forever in the memory of those privileged to see it.

Samba football and the distinctive yellow shirts of the Brazilian side had introduced themselves to an unsuspecting but enthusiastic public, but the party was soon spoiled, at least in the UK, when yellow became the colour used to identify something far less welcome in the psyche of the British public, the dreaded and despised 'no waiting, no parking' lines along the roadside. Introduced between spring and summer of 1958, along with parking meters and parking tickets, the resulting 'Assault on the Motorist' headlines in the newspapers could have been written fifty years later.

Of course, as a nine year old, most all of these events, the football stuff apart, happened in that parallel universe known as the adult world. School, in my case the Richard Bonington County Primary on Calverton Road, was out for the summer and life, apart from the fact that my first true love, the Magpies of Notts County, had been relegated into the old Third Division, could hardly be more idyllic.

Admittedly, I was a lucky child insofar as nothing particularly bad happened in our family, apart from my Auntie having a short spell in hospital one time. All my four grandparents were hale and hearty, the family's health was good, and even though my Mum miscarried between my arrival and that of my brother Stephen five years later I never found this out until I was much older. Of course this propensity to filter out all the bad stuff is part and parcel of what might be called good parenting, even if it does mean that childhood is spent in a sweetly distilled version of life.

Still, there'd be no complaints from me. If I didn't find out until much later in life that what I'd thought of as a 'normal' growing up wasn't quite as widespread as I'd reckoned it to be, that families hid terrible secrets, I don't think the lack of such information was in any way a disadvantage. Our own Killisick Estate might have had its secrets, but for me it was no more than the biggest playground I'd ever see. The fact that when we arrived it was still only half-built meant that there were even more opportunities for adventure than a child could have hoped for.

The first bricks had been laid back in September 1947, but even with two or three local building firms working at the same time, progress had been slow; in fact the last house wouldn't be finished until eight years later in 1955. Apart from Killisick Road itself, all the other thoroughfares on the estate were named after trees; Ashdale Road, Beechwood Road, Birchfield Road, Cedar Grove, Chestnut Grove, Elm Grove, Firbeck Road, Hawthorn Crescent, Oakdale Road, and Pinewood Avenue. As it turned out the road signs were the only place where trees actually made an appearance on the estate, at least during our tenancy. There were plenty of shrubs and bushes and hedges, but no trees.

Not that they were greatly missed by most of the kids around, there were loads of them in the open countryside around the estate, but if you fancied a bit of a climb then what was better than a half built house in the days when building sites weren't fenced off at the end of the day's shift. Our own house was about a third of the way up Hawthorn and work-in-progress was still going on no more than a few doors away for ages after our arrival. It was a far cry from the sanitised climbing frames of modern playgrounds, and even those are probably under threat from a combination of the overzealousness of the health and safety police and the naked greed of the beneficiaries of the 'have you suffered an injury in the last three years?' ambulance-chasing compensation-culture industry. Back then a long plank of wood balanced precariously on a couple of bricks and leading to an upstairs window opening was too much of a temptation for most of us but if you or the plank started to wobble and you ended up in a pile of rubble as a result, it was no good blaming anyone other than yourself.

Accidents can and did happen, but the ones I remember most didn't result from misadventure on the building site but from thrills and spills on or about the road outside our house. My father was a panel beater by trade and a fine one at that, by all accounts. For my third birthday he made, from scratch, a pedal car that wouldn't have looked out of place in Hamleys, and he personalised it by giving it the number plate RJR 3. For a few years it remained just what it was, a vehicle for pedalling, but as I got a bit older it was used for rather less sedate journeys than a tour of the back garden or a trip up and down the drive. In reality, the pedals might as well have been removed for what use they were when the machine became one of the best downhill racers in our immediate vicinity. In reality, I was actually getting a bit too big to get my legs under the steering wheel anyway, so I didn't bother. I used to push the car up the hill four or five houses above ours and then position myself, bum in seat but feet up on the bonnet, for the start of an exhilarating experience that could probably only be bettered on the Cresta Run. Control of the vehicle was tenuous to say the least, but at least the first fifty or so yards was pretty straight, whether on the corsey (pavement to those not acquainted with English as spoken in Arnold fifty years ago) or the road itself.

Now it might be best to explain that Hawthorn Crescent around the early to mid nineteen fifties was not exactly overpopulated with private vehicles. In fact I believe that anybody looking back would have been hard pressed to recall more than the odd one, with the accent firmly on the 'odd', so us kids weren't exactly taking our life into our hands when we gave a passable imitation of a kindergarten version of Stirling Moss, but you did have to look out for the stray human being or the occasional delivery van. It was normally on such occasions, especially if they coincided with that bit of the Crescent that took a sharp turn right about thirty yards down past our front gate, that spills got the better of thrills.

A quick application of the brake might have saved a lot of bother, but there was one slight problem; there was no brake. It was jam down sole of foot on ground and pray. For obvious reasons shoes didn't look their Sunday best for very long and so a common sight around our way was plimsoll shod kids. Now unlike today's trainers that come with flashing lights and built in wheels, a plimsoll came in only two colours, black or white, and two styles, elasticated slip-on or lace-up. Even the ultra-cool Dunlop Green Flash hadn't been thought of yet.

Actually, single occupant cars or even the mythical orange box cart with wheels and ropes for steering weren't nearly as exhilarating as the next two things we devised in our search for the ultimate bit of daredevilry. First came the accompanied ride, which entailed a good, or basically plain stupid, friend sitting on the bonnet between your feet. This was almost insane because the driver now couldn't see where he was going and the guy obliterating his view had no control of the contraption he was sitting on. Whatever excitement youngsters of today get from their Nintendo Wii and Xbox360, they'd be hard pressed to improve on the heart in mouth experience that that was, but my own favourite and that of many of our gang was the downhill run that required the least equipment.

One roller skate and an old Dandy or Beano annual was all that was needed. Place book on skate, sit on book, lie back, and think of England. Then pray that this wasn't that one time that any vehicle capable of travelling at more than twenty miles per hour uphill made a rare appearance. I think the reason why this early variant on skateboarding was so thrilling was that firstly there was no protection. Armbands, kneebands and protective headgear were for wimps, and anyway, they hadn't been invented yet. Secondly, to increase speed the scientific need for streamlining came into the reckoning. The lower the body position you could assume, the faster you went. Unfortunately, the lower the body position, the less you could see as well, unless you had eyes on stalks.

I think that Germolene must have been the best selling product on our estate, especially if the number of grazes and abrasions that I picked up were anything to go by, but the worst incident that I can recall involved a lamppost and my own brother Stephen this very summer of 1958 when he was trying to emulate his elders and those that knew better – ha, ha – and managed to pick up a three inch gash above his ankle. Being five years his senior I'm sure I would have told him about the dangers. Then again, kids, they never listen, do they?

Shortly after Steve's unfortunate altercation with the street lighting, the second best day of the year finally arrived after what seemed like an eternity of waiting but had only been the three months or so of the close season. Surpassed only by December 25 in my affection, and even better than my birthday, the eagerly awaited first day of the new football season was with us at last, our appetites refreshed for another season of hope and glory, or as a veteran supporter of Notts now for three years, anguish and worry. Still, at three o'clock on Saturday August 23, every team in each division was equal, with all to play for, and with school not set to start for ages too, how better could it get?

Well, a victory for Notts would do for a start, so the usual family entourage of me, Dad, Granddad and Uncle, all headed down to our normal spot in the County Road stand. It was reassuring to reacquaint ourselves with all the regulars standing in the same spots that they'd occupied in times past, but if I had to recall one abiding memory from the years I spent in that old rickety wooden stand it would be this; that strangely beguiling blend of aromas wafting up through the wooden boards beneath our feet and emanating from the adjacent Cattle Market where our car was usually parked and the roofless men's urinal that was situated directly below our vantage point. I realise now that there must have been an awful lot of nervous livestock and men around then, and with the Magpies only succeeding in taking a point off Accrington Stanley in a one-all draw in front of almost fifteen thousand ever-hopeful fans, there would no doubt be a lot more fretting to come as the season unfolded.

Forest came off even worse, losing five-one against Wolves. The Reds went behind to the current League Champions after just two minutes, were three down after twenty, and never recovered. Nottingham's third local outfit, Mansfield, were even poorer than that, losing six-one at home to Southampton in the same division as Notts. And, in another sign of the different times, Preston beat Arsenal two-one in the top division, whilst Liverpool, hosting

Grimsby in the second tier, could only manage a three-all draw. Top of the hot shots on a high scoring opening day were Middlesbrough who ran up nine without reply at home to Brighton in Division Two.

With such a poor display from the area's full time professionals, it was left to Marys to try and rescue a little bit of local pride, but they faced a tough test over at Derby where their opponents were Wilmorton & Alvaston. The Saints' hosts had finished sixth the previous season and were certainly expected to provide a good example of the gulf in class between the First and Second Divisions of the Central Alliance. Although the league now covered fifty five teams spread over an impressive eleven counties, it was a relatively short trip down the A52 for the opening match. Travel fatigue was therefore no excuse when the maroon and golds found themselves two goals in arrears before the break, thanks in no small measure to defensive lapses that had gifted the home side a penalty and a free kick just outside the box, both chances being gleefully converted. Happily, the second period saw a massive improvement and the combination of established players and newcomers began to gel. Geoff Parr obliged with two goals from the left wing to help the Saints run out clear winners by four goals to two and register what the Football Post called a 'triumphant senior debut'.

Seven days later Marys were back in Derbyshire, this time over at South Normanton. The hosts, who were destined to finish fifth at the end of the season, provided another severe test of the Saints' ability to cope at the higher level, but the visitors weren't to be found wanting. New signing Sid Thompson opened the scoring with a twenty yard drive after only ten minutes but the home side equalised before half time. The game developed into a closely fought contest in the second period with neither side able to break the deadlock. Then, when it looked like a point would have to suffice, up popped Geoff Parr with the winner. With four points from two away games, both against decent sides, Marys could be well pleased with their efforts in the opening eight days of the season and it was no surprise when the Football Post reported that they were 'well worth promotion from Division II'.

Elsewhere on the second Saturday of the new campaign Forest had made amends for their previous week's drubbing and gone nap themselves, hitting five without reply against Portsmouth. In fact it was a day of seriously high scoring in the top division with two more fives, a six, and a seven from West Ham against Aston Villa. The half-dozen were rattled in by Chelsea, who thrashed Wolves six-two, greatly assisted by five from a single player, a certain eighteen year old by the name of Jimmy Greaves.

The only discordant note in an otherwise exciting opening to the season concerned Manchester United. The club, obviously still recovering from the trauma of Munich back in February, had been generously given what would now be called a 'wild-card' entry into the new season's European Cup. It was a fine gesture by the European football authorities and United had been drawn against Young Boys of Berne, the Swiss champions. Unfortunately, the dead hand of the Football Association made its mark on proceedings when it announced the following:-

> "The Consultative Committee of the Football Association has considered an
> application by Manchester United FC under FA Rule 18B for consent to take
> part in the European Champion Clubs' Competition during season 1958-59.
> The Committee is of the opinion that, as by its name, this is a competition of
> champion clubs, Manchester United FC does not qualify to take part in this
> season's competition. Consent is, therefore, refused."

Back in 1958, amateur officials still ran the Football Association (FA), and many would say that the situation hasn't changed much today even if the suits in charge are now more than handsomely remunerated, but their call on this issue clearly showed a rift between them and the professional game. It also showed them to be clearly unaware, or even dismissive, of public opinion. This regrettably wasn't the first, and certainly not the last, occasion when they demonstrated that they were so out of touch with the sensibilities of the man, and woman, in the street.

The years of the First World War between 1914 and 1918 had instilled in the nation's population a yearning to live life to the full, and with so many of the male population killed, missing, or injured, women assumed a more prominent role in society, a role which even extended into the male preserve of the world of football.

When it first appeared in 1920, Women's football immediately attracted great interest amongst both sexes and on Boxing Day that year, fifty-three thousand spectators watched a game between two of the country's leading sides. Arnold even had a ladies' team of its own, with one of its players being Mrs Amy Moore, mother of the well-known footballing Moore brothers Charlie, Keith and Albert. In fact Mrs Moore was a bit of a terror in her later years as a spectator following her sons' careers, so goodness knows what she was like kitted up.

Of course, the Football Association, knowing a good thing when they saw it, immediately banned the distaff side from playing the sport on the grounds that 'the game of football is quite unsuitable for females and ought not to be encouraged'.

Quite at odds with Oscar Wilde's famous quote that 'football is all very well as a game for rough girls, but is hardly suitable for delicate boys'.

This was probably the first but not the last occasion on which the actual meaning of the initials FA were called into question. This august body would have everyone believe it stood of course for the Football Association, but the man in the street could hardly be criticised for thinking that in fact they stood for a group of old duffers that knew sweet.......sorry, knew very little.

The irony in the Manchester United case is that the European Cup that they were refused entry into but so gloriously won ten years later has now been re-branded by the money men as the Champions League. Now this money soaked competition might be many things, but a league it most certainly isn't and nor evidently is it the sole preserve of 'champion clubs'. Yet it's not solely these distinctions that truly draw a parallel with events from 1958, but rather the change in attitude of the men at the top of the FA. When Liverpool unexpectedly won the European Cup / Champions League in 2005, they'd been slightly neglectful in domestic competition and had only managed to finish fifth. With no automatic right for the Cup Winners to defend their title, Liverpool were scheduled to sit out the following season's tournament. Until of course a little bit of power broking amongst the European and English football authorities came up with an eleventh hour solution. Yes, it was a 'wild-card' entry, pretty much the same as that denied United, and of course, on this occasion, the FA were prominent amongst the banner-wavers for 'justice'. Their Executive Director at the time, David Davies, said:-

> "We understand EUFA's situation, but we believe that for sporting reasons and for the wider interests of European Football Liverpool should get a special exemption."

Far be it for me to even suggest that anything but fair play was behind Mr Davies' pronouncement, but whenever a decision is based on 'wider interests', you can be sure that a loud 'ker-ching!' sound isn't far away.

Times have certainly changed, and even as Marys were rattling off those couple of early away wins, events were unfolding back in Nottingham that would have a profound effect on social behaviour for many years to come. Just as those Saints' players out having a Saturday evening pint to celebrate their opening victory would have heard the ringing of the 'last orders' bell, a serious altercation was kicking-off a mere three miles away in St Ann's, one of the most economically disadvantaged districts in the whole of the City. Largely a white working class area, it was also home to an increasing number of economic migrants from the West Indies.

Unfortunately, by 1958, the post-war demand for labour had started to diminish and there was increasing competition for jobs. Tension and ill-feeling between whites and 'coloured people', as they were referred to then, had begun to escalate, leading to confrontations between individuals on a number of occasions. As recently as February, a fracas on an early morning service leaving the old Mount Street bus station had made the headlines of the local papers. The set-to resulted in the driver and conductress, a Long Eaton man and his wife, being summoned along with a 'coloured' woman passenger to appear at the Shire Hall.

The cause of the disturbance had apparently started off as handbags at six paces with both the ladies giving as good as they got over a 'misunderstanding' regarding directions. Then it turned ugly and verbal insults were traded, with the highly original comments of 'black bastard' and 'why don't you go back where you came from?' both being given a good airing. This then turned to pushing and shoving, then slapping and kicking, until the driver got involved. The upshot was the court case where all three participants in the mayhem were bound over or fined. The conductress, when offering her defence, had stated that she 'did not dislike coloured people' at all and 'was always prepared to help them'. As it happened, on that first Saturday night of the new football season there were certainly quite a few members of the local black community who could have benefited from such generous assistance.

More than a thousand people went on the rampage in St Ann's that night with the Nottingham Evening Post reporting that 'the whole place was like a slaughterhouse'. According to the Chief Constable's account of proceedings, the first notification of trouble came with a 999 call from a public house on St Ann's Well Road at 22:21 BST. Such was the mayhem that the police did not declare the area safe until 00:35 the next morning. Eye witness reports confirmed numerous instances of blood being spilled on both sides of the colour divide, although the exact cause of the riot remains unclear. However, most theories agree that there had been a simmering discontent in the district over relationships between West Indian men and a number of the indigenous white female population. There seemed to be a general consensus too that the aggravation and violence was fomented in the main by the younger male members of the white community and then returned in kind by their immigrant counterparts.

Seven days later, on the evening of Saturday August 30, the crowds gathered again in St Ann's. Reports put their number at around four thousand, but the West Indian fraternity were conspicuous by their absence. A TV crew had turned up, possibly hoping for a repeat of the previous weekend's mayhem, and it appeared that a cameraman had lit a magnesium flare in an attempt to reconstruct the first riot. Quite what the intentions of the media were is not certain, but their actions turned what was a non-event up until then into something even more serious than the first altercation. With no visible black target the white youths in the crowd turned on themselves and also clashed with the police. Dozens were arrested, including an Arnold man, and five of them ended up being imprisoned.

The disturbances are often remembered as the 'teddy boy riots', a reference to the young men involved who were part of the first real manifestation of white working class youth culture, but what was as disturbing in its way was the fact that the terrible events were somehow viewed with a degree of levity totally inappropriate in the circumstances. The fact that the TV crew did what they did was bad enough, but an enterprising but totally misguided local bus company even offered tours of the riot-torn streets, leading to the Lord Mayor of Nottingham appealing to people not to go to St Ann's 'for sightseeing purposes'.

If there was an air of misplaced flippancy up here in Nottingham, events down in Notting Hill, London, were already beginning to assume far more ominous proportions. This particular district was the capital's equivalent of St Ann's, home to an increasing number of West Indian immigrants. Again, tensions had apparently reached a head over inter-racial relationships. One in particular, between a Jamaican man and his young Swedish wife, was subsequently well publicised in the media and the woman herself, Majbritt Morrison, even managed to write a book about her experiences, albeit heavily fictionalised, called 'Jungle West 11'.

There was nothing made up about the ferocity of the violence itself however. Iron bars, butchers' knives, leather belts weighted with projecting nuts and bolts, open razor blades and a petrol bomb were the armoury of choice, and the disturbances, unlike their East Midlands precursors, continued night after night until they finally petered out on September 5. Over a hundred people were charged with offences ranging from grievous bodily harm to affray and riot and possessing offensive weapons, and at the Old Bailey exemplary sentences of four years each were handed down on nine youths, all white.

Senior Metropolitan Police officers at the time tried to play down the racial aspects of the civil disobedience claiming that it was nothing more than hooliganism, the work of 'ruffians, both coloured and white'. However, when access was allowed to previously closed confidential files at the Public Record Office some forty-four years later, the finger of blame was pointed, as in Nottingham, at the young of the white working class. Youths dressed in Edwardian-type clothing and openly defiant of the police presence were conspicuous both by their dress sense and their numbers.

When calm finally returned to Notting Hill and Nottingham it was apparent that the general public had been jolted into an uneasy appreciation that the potential for racial conflict, then a way of life in the southern states of the USA, had now come to Britain. It only needed a wrong word here or a wrong look there, especially where black and white were rubbing up against each other in poorer neighbourhoods, for the violence to flare up again.

Not that aggression amongst the young was limited to clashes between people of different colour, but whenever it occurred it seemed that 'Teddy-boys' were fairly adjacent to proceedings. An image as peace-loving citizens helping old ladies cross the street wasn't quite the one that had been portrayed by the media. Every vandalised phone box, smashed shop window, and trashed youth club seemed to be attributed to these strangely garbed delinquents. Maybe it made a better headline, easier to explain to a bemused readership who might otherwise be totally confused if the damage had been caused by a couple of kids in their Sunday school best.

There was no doubt however that the 'Teds' represented the first identifiable face of British youth culture, whether their parents liked it or not. With post-war austerity finally drawing to a close and with young people now having a decent disposable income of their own, it was inevitable that some of this spare money would be spent on items designed to cause a frown or two from the older generation, especially music and clothes.

The sounds were inevitably those of rock n' roll, although time and scholarship has more correctly identified this particular genre as 'rockabilly', basically rock n' roll as played by poor white folk, or 'hillbillies'. Elvis Presley was the King, of course, but there were any number of performers who had a decent run of success; Bill Haley, Carl Perkins, Jerry Lee Lewis, Gene Vincent, and Eddie Cochran, to name but a few. In fact this last gentleman's enormously popular hit, 'Summertime Blues', became a hit smack bang in the middle of the British rioting season, August 25, and while the young American sang about problems of a more personal and financial nature, in the circumstances the title seemed pretty apt over here as well.

However, no matter their musical preferences, it was the Teds' abiding love of the dramatic when it came to sartorial elegance that lives longest in the memory. A standard outfit consisted of a long, Edwardian style, drape jacket, often with a velvet collar trim, narrow 'drainpipe' trousers, brightly coloured socks, and suede shoes with thick crepe soles, known as 'brothel creepers'. Beneath the jacket would be a smart shirt and a 'Slim Jim' or 'bootlace' tie, and for the really snappy dresser a brocade waistcoat. The crowning glory was, of course, the hairstyle, which was invariably styled into a greased-up quiff at the front, with the side hair combed back to form a DA (Duck's Arse) at the back. Put together as a whole, the hair and the gear certainly combined to give the wearer a striking look; some older folk might even have called it threatening.

Whatever the viewpoint, there were certainly many dedicated followers of that fashion amongst the young men of the time even if not too many of them lined up for Rovers and Marys, especially when the teams met for the very last time back in May 1958. A quick glance at the team photos shows only two players sporting anything remotely resembling a quiff. Given that the one of Saints' right-winger Mick Cripwell seems to be the product of careful grooming rather than an excessive use of Brylcreem, the indisputable winner as 'King of the Quiff' has to go to centre-forward Dennis Wheat. Which was quite apt in the circumstances; after all, any number nine worth his salt in those fierce local derbies was expected to be at least striking and threatening. Then again, his opposing centre-half Bill Whitt, taking his first look at him, would probably have agreed that with the hairstyle, Dennis had also added 'menacing' to his list of attributes.

DENNIS WHEAT : 'KING OF THE QUIFF'

(Arnold Library Collection)

Just as an uneasy peace was being restored to St Ann's, a conflict of sorts was taking place on the high seas. On September 2, Iceland had declared its intention to treble its fishing limits from four to twelve miles off its coast, and Britain, it seemed, was powerless to do anything about it. The country, already engaged in the Cold War, now found itself embroiled in the Cod War too.

Marys had a battle of their own the next day when Heanor Town were the visitors for the first home game of the season. The Derbyshire outfit were the current Central Alliance champions and were expected to provide a stern test of the Saints' worthiness at the higher level. They did, handing the home side a four-two defeat, but Marys still showed signs during the game that they could hold their own with the best the division could offer.

The following Saturday saw the Saints travel the short distance to Lenton to play Nottingham Forest A. Whilst they were trying to get back on the winning trail, I was down at Meadow Lane watching the Magpies tread water with another one-all home draw, this time against the less than brilliant Newport County, but the highlight of my day had already come and gone.

Earlier I'd been amongst the audience as the Metropole cinema in Sherwood celebrated the tenth anniversary of the ABC Minors, an exclusive 'club' for kids attending the matinee every Saturday. This was a specially scheduled programme consisting usually of a cartoon, news item, a film, and a serial to finish. The main feature always seemed to be a western, more than likely a B-movie, but the real excitement on the silver screen came with the climax to the morning's proceedings which, in the classic cliff-hanger tradition, would have Flash Gordon about to meet a grisly end at the hands of Ming the Merciless, Emperor of the planet Mongo.

Miraculously, come the following Saturday, Flash had conjured up yet another improbable escape, and the scriptwriters had achieved their aim in bringing us all back for another episode. With their Minors' club ABC did their own bit to encourage us to part with our tanners on a weekly basis too. First there was the 'anthem', sung with gusto by hundreds of squeaky voices and which ended '…we're all pals together, we're Minors of the A! B! C!', then the various badges to be collected, but best of all was the interval where all those kids whose birthday it was that week were invited up on stage and given an assortment of goodies. The only proviso was that you had to bring one of your birthday cards with you to show that you weren't pulling a fast one, but the verification process wasn't that rigorous. There were one or two urchins from our estate at Killisick who would have had to have been in their twenties or thirties if their number of appearances on stage had ever been totted up.

Now, whilst I was doubly worried about Flash's latest predicament and Notts' performance against Newport, Marys were having a much better time of things, overcoming Forest's youngsters quite easily by three goals to one. When they followed this up with an excellent victory over at the Manor Ground on the following Wednesday, edging out hosts Ilkeston Town by the odd goal in five, the defeat against Heanor was well behind them. In fact, when the champions surprisingly lost at home to Wilmorton & Alvaston, the Saints were second only on goal average to the Derbyshire club. With only five games played it was certainly early days yet, but the top of the table made pleasant viewing nonetheless:-

	P	W	D	L	F	A	P
Heanor Town	5	4	0	1	14	9	8
Arnold St Marys	5	4	0	1	14	10	8

Whilst Marys had got off to a pretty decent start, Rovers, suffering a severe hangover from the tumultuous events of the close season, were languishing below half way in Division One with a mere four points from their five games. Not a disaster by any means but a real anticlimax by comparison with their deeds of the previous season. Worryingly, with old Spartan League rivals Aspley Old Boys as their next opponents on the same day that the Saints were due to meet the second eleven of Southern League side King's Lynn, a perceptible gap in status, as well as performance, was beginning to appear.

The fact that Rovers beat the Old Boys in a typically close game three-two was completely overshadowed by Marys' own victory by five goals to two, Geoff Parr adding to his season's tally with a brave header that saw him injured in the process. Ironically, he had been the cause of some physical distress himself a few minutes earlier when he'd unleashed a thirty yard pile-driver that had ended up with the visiting keeper needing the trainer's attention. Geoff had built up a reputation for unleashing the occasional thunderous shot from way outside the box. In fact his goal at South Normanton in the season's second game was scored from long distance, earning him the nickname in one of the local Derbyshire papers as 'Cannonball Parr'.

The King's Lynn game hadn't been for points, instead it was a first round tie in the Central Alliance Division One Cup, open to sides from both North and South sections. The Norfolk side had got off to a decent start in their Southern section league campaign with seven points out of a possible ten, so the Saints' victory was pretty impressive. Unfortunately, it didn't put them through into the next round because this stage of the competition was scheduled to be played over two legs and it would be another four weeks until the return fixture took place.

Back in the league seven days later Marys' good form continued with yet another win, albeit this time by the closer score of three goals to two against Langwith Miners' Welfare but still sufficient to see them hit the heady heights of top spot in the table. The Football Post waxed lyrical about the Saints' performance, saying that '...to get there in their first season in Division 1 North was a magnificent achievement and one which has added considerably to the prestige of Arnold football.' And they'd achieved it with a schedule that had seen them play only two games at home. Sadly, their stay at the summit was short-lived as Ollerton Colliery brought them down to earth with a defeat by the odd goal in five at Gedling Road in the last midweek game of the year.

It wasn't the best time to lose a game, especially when the strong Matlock Town side were the visitors just three days later. Despite a fairly even first half in which a Phil Smith header made it one-all at the break, the Derbyshire team carried too much fire power for Marys in the second period and ended up comfortable three-one winners. In the space of a few days at the end of September, the Saints had slipped to fourth place, courtesy mainly of a home record at odds with their splendid away form. In the four matches staged so far at KGV, they'd lost all but one of them.

Thankfully, Goose Fair Saturday saw them back on their travels, again breaking new ground with a trip to Staffordshire to meet Burton Albion Reserves. This was Marys' second meeting with a reserve eleven of a Southern League club, the first being against King's Lynn of course, and yet again the maroon and golds had no problem in seeing off the opposition by the convincing margin of five goals to two, a fifth straight away victory that lifted them back into second place.

Given their tremendous form away from Gedling Road the Saints, together with several bus loads of supporters, headed off for the second leg of their League Cup tie the following week in good spirits. Holding a three goal advantage over King's Lynn from what had been their best home performance of the campaign, there seemed little chance that Marys would slip up. However, after twenty minutes and with the Saints doing all the attacking, the hosts took a surprise lead and it wasn't until just before the half time whistle that the scores were levelled. On the resumption Marys decided to make a game of it by conceding twice more and ended up hanging on to win by the slenderest of margins, six-five on aggregate. Still, a win is a win and when the draw for the second round of the cup was made, the Saints had the luck of it, being awarded a bye straight into the third round. As this wasn't scheduled to take place until February of the following year, Marys could now totally concentrate on establishing their credentials in the league over the next three months.

PROGRAMME FRONT COVER : KING'S LYNN RESERVES v MARYS, 11 OCT 1958

(Geoff Parr Collection)

The remaining fixtures in October were against two Miners' Welfare sides, Clay Cross at home and Langwith away. The first game was won quite comfortably by three goals to one, with Saints' wingers, Mick Cripwell and Geoff Parr, both getting on the scoresheet. These two flankmen had been prolific the previous season, scoring twenty five and twenty three goals respectively, and had had no difficulty in continuing their good form in front of goal despite the step up in standard. The following week's game at Langwith was a much closer affair but with Mick notching again and new centre-forward Ray Wilkinson joining him on the scoresheet, the Saints edged it by the odd goal in five. The win gave Marys their first double of the season but even more importantly lifted them back to the head of the table.

Their achievement in regaining top spot was given the full headline treatment in the Football Post.

Arnold St Marys Shock Team Of Central Alliance

"When [Arnold St Marys] applied for Division 1 membership during the close season … there were misgivings among some clubs. Would they be struggling among the bottom clubs and adding nothing to the premier division either in strength or prestige?

In addition, few clubs outside junior circles now carry church names. Would they be so glamorous as if, for instance, they had been known as Arnold Town? The faith of those who pushed St Marys' claims, however, has been fully justified by events.

They have proved attractive visitors by reason of their go-ahead brand of football, which has brought results. Now it remains to be seen whether the Saints can maintain the hot pace they have set themselves."

With the season still only eleven games old, the *caveat* was justified, but with five league matches scheduled for November, Marys had a golden opportunity to cement their position at the head of the table. A third miners' side, Creswell Colliery, were the Saints' visitors on the first day of the month and, like seven days previously, the game developed into another tight contest. With nothing between the two sides Marys finally managed to hang on to a slender lead to clinch victory by three goals to two.

Elsewhere in the Central Alliance it was a day of contrasting fortunes. Rovers, struggling to find a settled side following the disappointments of the close season, visited Midland Amateur Alliance side Wollaton in the Notts Senior Cup. The Arnold side were clear favourites and raced into a two-nil lead by the break, only to allow the home side right back in it in the second half. With the score two-all after ninety minutes, the match entered extra time. It soon became obvious that the game's momentum had changed entirely; there was only one team in it, and it wasn't Rovers. At the final whistle, Wollaton had claimed a resounding win by five goals to two.

Over at Heanor, it was the current Central Alliance champions who found themselves cast in the role of underdogs as they entertained Midland League Scarborough in the fourth qualifying round of the FA Cup, one step away from the draw with the big boys from the Football League. Putting up a great fight they held their East Coast visitors to a two-all draw, and then went one better four days later by beating the Seadogs on their own ground. As reward for their sterling efforts they were drawn to host Carlisle United in a fortnight's time.

Unfortunately for the Saints events in Arnold would prove to be considerably less exciting than those over at Heanor. Whilst temporary stands were being assembled for the thousands of spectators expected to jam into the Town ground, Marys were fixtureless on the second Saturday of the month. Then, whilst not having quite the attraction of the first round of the FA Cup taking place the same day, they were hosts to the high flying juniors of Nottingham Forest. Taking advantage of the Saints blank day, both Matlock Town and the young reds had closed the gap, leaving all three sides level on eighteen points from twelve matches, so the clash at Gedling Road was a genuine four-pointer.

Despite it being the middle of November the sun was shining at kick-off and, when Marys took the lead through Dennis Day after twenty five minutes, all looked set fair for a pleasant afternoon for the Saints' players and supporters alike. The home side's prospects improved further when they added a second after the break and with less than ten minutes to go it looked as though the points were in the bag. Unfortunately Mother Nature then took a hand. As if from nowhere a dense fog blanketed Gedling Road and despite everyone's best attempts to carry on, the referee decided to call it a day. There were only four minutes left to play.

Marys' disappointment at seeing a near certain victory snatched from their grasp in such an unusual fashion was slightly tempered by the fact that Matlock were otherwise engaged in a cup tie, leaving the Saints still heading the table on goal average. Over at Heanor, the Derbyshire club could have been forgiven for wishing that the bad weather had visited them in such a manner. Having famously taken the lead after just five minutes, they were then powerless to prevent Carlisle from demonstrating the difference in ability and fitness between the two sides as the visitors knocked in five goals without reply. The major consolation for the Alliance side was the tremendous crowd of 6,511 who'd packed into the enclosure, a record which remains to this day, and if they'd been unable to pull off a shock then the cup had still witnessed a genuine act of giant killing with the surprise defeat of Third Division Bournemouth by three goals to one at the hands of Isthmian League side Tooting and Mitcham United. Up till then many football followers in the East Midlands might have been unfamiliar with the team from South West London, but events closer to home would soon change all that.

In the meanwhile, Marys' game the following week succeeded in lasting the whole ninety minutes. Yet again it was a close fought match against a pit based side, this time Ollerton Colliery, and on this occasion the Saints prevailed by the odd goal in three on the miners' ground. Seven days later the maroon and golds closed out the month with a tough point in a one-all draw against Sutton Town Reserves courtesy of an eighth minute goal from Dennis Day, despite Gedling Road once more being shrouded in mist. Luckily the dense fog that caused the abandonment around the half hour mark of Mansfield Town's home game just up the A60 at Field Mill stayed away long enough for Marys' match to reach its natural conclusion. Other Alliance teams weren't so lucky either, with matches at Ilkeston, Langwith, Creswell, South Normanton, and Burton all being lost to the atrocious weather.

Those were of course still the days of pea soupers, those long ago days when any decent fog caused the Nottingham Corporation to cancel all bus services soon after lunch, with the result that thousands of city based workers were faced with a long trek back home to the suburbs and outlying districts on foot. Ironically, even as the inclement conditions were slowing matters down locally in those early days of winter, the pace of life was certainly increasing with developments further afield. Back in October the British Overseas Airways Corporation (BOAC) had launched the first scheduled transatlantic passenger jet service, and the beginning of December saw the appearance of the first motorway in Britain, the Preston By-Pass. This eight mile road was the first section of the sixty three mile long north-south M6 and was opened by no less a dignitary than the Prime Minister himself, Harold Macmillan.

The very same day, December 5, an even greater authority, Queen Elizabeth, had herself been instrumental in quickening the means of contact between A and B. As the country's senior politician was cutting the ribbon up in Lancashire, her Majesty was making a telephone call from the Bristol Central Telephone Exchange to the Lord Provost of Edinburgh, over three hundred miles away. She was heralding the Subscriber Trunk Dialling (STD) service whereby telephone callers could make long distance calls automatically without the aid of the operator. Considering that the year had also seen the development of the Hovercraft, aimed at reducing crossing times between English ports and their European counterparts across the North Sea and English Channel, there seemed little doubt that life was speeding up.

However, twenty four hours after the momentous changes to the swiftness of the country's transport and telecommunication networks, Marys' team bus could still be found threading its way towards its next destination at a rather more sedate pace. In 1958 there was no quick way from Arnold to Matlock, as many a visitor to the nearby tourist resort of Matlock Bath would confirm, but the eager anticipation amongst the Saints' players and supporters as they made the trip into the Derbyshire hills to take on their biggest rivals in the league was as high as that of any week-end day tripper. Marys' point against Sutton had meant that they had maintained their position at the head of the division but, as can be seen from the table below, their hosts at Causeway Lane had a game in hand and only trailed the Saints by a single point.

	P	W	D	L	F	A	P
Arnold St Marys	**14**	**10**	**1**	**3**	**37**	**27**	**21**
Matlock Town	13	9	2	2	34	23	20

Once the game was underway Marys, unchanged for the fourth game in a row, were soon into their stride. Despite the greasy conditions underfoot the match was being played at a fast pace and after ten minutes the Saints deservedly took the lead when Geoff Parr cut in from the left wing to add the finishing touch to a smart move down the opposite flank. Unfortunately their lead lasted merely three minutes and from then there were narrow escapes at either end as both sets of fans were treated to a contest packed with entertaining football, as befitted the top two sides in the section. The only surprise was that neither side could add to their tally in the first period; Marys had an effort disallowed for offside and then minutes before the break goalie Len Rockley pulled off a spectacular save to keep the scores level.

On the resumption the pace didn't slacken and the Saints' formidable form away from Gedling Road began to tell on the opposition. Not to be outdone by his fellow winger, outside right Mick Cripwell got his own name on the scoresheet with a little over ten minutes left and then added another six minutes later from the penalty spot. There was no way back for the home side, especially when they were reduced to ten men following an injury to their goalkeeper, and Marys ended up with a famous victory, their eighth consecutive league win on the road. It had been the sternest test yet of the Saints' championship credentials and they hadn't been found wanting. The win was sweet revenge too for the three-one defeat inflicted on them by Matlock at KGV back in September.

It was a pity that Marys were fixtureless the following week, but at least the break would have given them plenty of time to prepare for the hectic times ahead. In a schedule that would make the modern day player blanch, they were due to play three games in as many days over the Christmas period, as well as entertain the second eleven of Southern League Nuneaton Borough on the Saturday before the holidays. Not that the Warwickshire side were expected to provide that many problems, after all they'd just been thrashed seven-one on their own ground by a Matlock side still smarting from their defeat by the Saints. When Colin Collindridge gave them an early lead, Marys looked to be well on the way to extending their unbeaten run to seven games, but the poor ground conditions were proving to be somewhat of a leveller. Despite a second goal from Mick Cripwell, the visitors fought back in a manner at odds with their previous performances to claim an improbable victory by three goals to two.

The playing surface at KGV continued to give serious cause for concern. Right from it being laid two and a half years earlier, there had been a considerable and ongoing problem regarding its poor drainage, especially in the winter months. Marys had rightly become renowned throughout the Alliance for their fast, attacking, and attractive football, yet their efforts were being severely undermined at their own HQ. The contrast between the Saints' home and away results in the league certainly made for interesting reading.

	P	W	D	L	F	A	P
Home	8	3	1	4	17	19	7
Away	8	8	0	0	25	12	16

Despite the setback against Nuneaton, Marys still held top spot going into the Christmas programme. In the tradition of the times, back to back games against the same opposition were usually played over the holiday period, and occasionally a combination of the calendar and fixture demands led to the extremely testing schedule now facing the Saints. They were set to face Belper Town at home on the Thursday morning of Christmas Day, then travel to Derbyshire twenty four hours later for the return fixture on Boxing Day, and finally conclude proceedings at KGV with the visit of Shirebrook Miners Welfare on the Saturday. It was a daunting task, to say the least, especially as Belper, despite lying only sixth in the table, had dropped the fewest points in the league so far and were genuine championship contenders.

With Christmas presents barely unwrapped and their good ladies left at home preparing the festive lunch, Arnold's menfolk packed into Gedling Road for the ten thirty kick off. All that was needed to make a pleasant day even more memorable was for Marys to overcome their home hoodoo and put on a show for their biggest crowd of the season; which they did in some style. Despite the pitch again being sticky and muddy, the Saints coped with the difficulties underfoot far more convincingly than the visitors. With the quick tackling Marys' defence marshalling the opposition forwards with some ease, the maroon and golds' own front line took advantage of the team's superior possession and ran the Belper rearguard ragged. In particular centre-forward Ray Wilkinson was having a game to remember, and by the final whistle had contributed four of the maroon and golds' nap hand in a season's best victory by five goals to one.

MARYS OUTSIDE THE CHANGING ROOMS AT ARNOLD BATHS PRIOR TO THE GAME AGAINST BELPER TOWN, CHRISTMAS DAY 1958 : Back Row (l to r); B Molyneux, N Gough, L Rockley, R Hinson, D Parr. Front Row; W Archer, - -, C Moore, S Thompson, M Cripwell, - -, D Day, - -, R Wilkinson, C Collindridge, G Parr, - -, W Parr, S Gray. In front; T.Gray (Mascot). (Geoff Parr Collection)

It was an extremely happy congregation that filed away from the ground that morning, no doubt stopping at a pub or club for some liquid refreshment on the way home. Lifting up a pint glass, sharpening a knife and carving the turkey would be the most exercise a lot of them would have on this particular day. Feet up after lunch, a nice long snooze, and then a family party that evening. At least that's how I remember many a contented Christmas Day back in the fifties.

Even though we were by now well established up at Killisick, my favourite day of the year was spent back at my grandparents' home on James Street, where the whole family and quite a few neighbours too would assemble for a bit of a festive 'do'. Nominal head of the household then was my Granddad George, a miner at Bilsthorpe Colliery who inherently preferred the quiet life and was as successful as anyone I've ever known in achieving his aim. He was a man of very few words too but whenever I nipped around to see him and my Nan he would usually pop his head up from behind one of his Wild West novels that he always had on the go just long enough to enquire as to how I was.

"Ok, serree?"

"Yeah, fine Granddad, and you?"

"All rayt, serree."

That was a long conversation, too

**GRANDDAD GEORGE
HAVING A HARD TIME**

As it happened, his desire to avoid a stressful situation was never better displayed than this particular Christmas Day of 1958. He'd been along to see the Saints beat Belper and had no doubt dropped in 'for a half' at the Liberal Club on the way back with his old pal Walter 'Doddem' Archer, Marys' trainer, but the day's excitement wasn't confined to Marys' win.

The scene was the evening card school around the table in the front room, the air thick with smoke and tension, like you might see in a *film noir*. The game being played was innocuous enough though. We knew it as 'three ha'penny life' and this day there had been so many wanting to play that two packs of cards had to be used. The essence of the game was that each player started with three ha'pennies and the loser of each round put one of his coins in the 'pot' until there was only one person left with any money. They were duly declared the winners, and the 'pot' was theirs. The winnings weren't exactly a king's ransom as the ha'penny, or more correctly the halfpenny, was the second lowest value coin, twice that of the humble farthing, in circulation at the time.

The game had been going for well over an hour and there were now only three players left in, Granddad being one of them. I'd been making sure that the table didn't run out of bottles of pale ale, and everyone who had already lost their money gathered closely around with increasing interest in the eventual outcome. A couple more rounds were played and each player was left with but a single coin. The pressure was certainly on now. Cigarettes were disappearing at an extremely unhealthy rate as the next round was dealt. Everyone was in and the first card played. All of a sudden, and totally unexpectedly, Granddad jumped to his feet, threw his cards across the table and said "I'm not rackin' my brains for a ha'penny!" With that, he headed off in the direction of the back room for a drag on a Woodbine, leaving the rest of us barely able to stifle our laughter.

Of course, technically, he'd got his sums wrong, the 'pot' being worth a lot more than one half pence, but that wasn't really the point. It was the dramatic way that his participation in the game came to an abrupt end that lives in the memory. For a guy who made an art out of being undemonstrative, this little cameo was completely out of character. But it did sum up his approach to the stresses of life; avoid them wherever possible, and if that fails, leave them to someone else.

The following day he, I, my father and my uncle all suffered stress of an avoidable nature in the form of another miserable trip down to Meadow Lane where the Magpies, with only three wins in twenty three outings and giving a very passable imitation of a team in freefall, lost three-one to the less than mighty Bradford City. The fact that County's only goal came from regular left-half Bert Loxley, standing in temporarily at centre-forward, indicated that there was a real crisis at the club. When they lost the return the next day by an even bigger margin, four-one, I began to fear the worst.

Marys too, in their own return game at Belper, went down by the same score, losing their one hundred percent away record in the process, but at least they put up a fight. The easily flooded Christchurch Meadow, home of the Derbyshire side, was in just as bad a condition as Gedling Road, but early exchanges were even despite the mud. The game turned midway through the first period when the home side scored three times in four minutes, and despite a successful penalty converted by Mick Cripwell, Belper restored their three goal lead and were full value for their final victory by four goals to one.

Both games had proven gruelling and seasonal goodwill had been conspicuous by its absence. After Belper had effectively killed the game as a contest with their three rapid strikes, player conduct deteriorated and the match became what the Belper News called 'probably the roughest of the season'. The Saints' keeper, Len Rockley, normally as mild mannered as they come, got involved in a pushing and shoving altercation with the Nailers' number nine and ended up getting booked for his troubles. The local newspaper also remarked that following that set-to the referee ought to have taken sterner measures with misbehaving players rather than just speaking with them, concluding that 'it was a miracle that there were no serious injuries'.

As they reported to the ground the following day, Marys' players may still have had their limbs just about intact, but there was no doubt that they were tired ones too, and they can't have viewed the prospect of a third match in a tad over forty eight hours with any great enthusiasm. As it turned out, there wouldn't be another energy-sapping ninety minutes this time around; the pitch, almost inevitably, was unplayable.

Despite the two great victories over Matlock and Belper, the defeats against the Nailers and the reserves of Nuneaton Borough were quite a set-back. Although they were in second place, the Saints had dropped more points than any of their closest rivals. The top of the Central Alliance was dominated by Derbyshire town sides, with Marys the only viable challenger outside that county's borders.

	P	W	D	L	F	A	P
Matlock Town	17	12	2	3	52	27	26
Arnold St Marys	**18**	**12**	**1**	**5**	**48**	**36**	**25**
Ilkeston Town	17	10	4	3	46	26	24
Belper Town	16	10	3	3	60	41	23
Heanor Town	14	11	0	3	52	22	22

If the year had ended on a flat note for Marys' fans, it was nothing compared to the disappointment suffered by my parents when the only record that I could ever remember them buying was knocked off the top of the hit parade by Conway Twitty. The object of their affection had been 'Hoots Mon!' by Lord Rockingham's XI on an old 78rpm disc, the nearest we ever got to rock n' roll in our house. It was a novelty instrumental that featured snatches of Scottish dialect and I quickly grew sick and tired of hearing 'there's a moose loose aboot this hoose' every time it was played. As a number one hit my mum and dad obviously weren't the record's only devotees but my mates at school, whose parents had 'cooler' musical tastes, still weren't impressed when I told them we'd got it. Their houses were home to Elvis and the Everly Brothers, 'Jailhouse Rock' and 'All I Have To Do Is Dream', not an ensemble put together by bandleader Harry Robinson and featuring jazzer Benny Green on saxophone.

If my mum and dad weren't that switched on when it came to modern sounds in popular music, it was because they'd still got a soft spot for the music of their courting days, my father in particular being a fan of the sound of Glen Miller. He'd been a drummer in a wartime band called the Top-Hatters, and would take every opportunity to practice, most noticeably just before he began his Sunday lunch. I'd sit dutifully still whilst the set routine was adhered to; dad carving, mum plating everything up, and when it was finally time for the long awaited feast to start, what better way to announce that proceedings could begin than by a drum roll? Armed with only a knife and fork, my father, much to the dismay of his darling wife, would treat us to a tremendous display of his stickmanship, producing a dazzling combination of paradiddles and flam triplets around the edge of his plate, stopping only when he received the usual admonishment of "That's enough Jack" from his long suffering spouse. Funnily enough, they'd met whilst he was making an appearance in a band playing a dance at the old Drill Hall on Arnot Hill Road, she the local girl, him the musician up from the smoke, or at least close by. It was love at first sight, if not first sound.

Mr Twitty had struck paydirt with a stirring ballad entitled 'It's Only Make Believe' but even as he admitted in the song's lyrics that the chances of him being with his girl were nothing more than a pretence, massive numbers of television viewers were indulging in a bit of fantasy of their own. At the end of the year 'Quatermass and the Pit' began to be shown in serial form on the BBC. It was the last in a trilogy of science fiction stories based around the character of Professor Bernard Quatermass. I had been too young to watch the first two serials when they had been shown back in 1953 and 1955, but by the time of the third and last I had recently turned ten and persuaded my Mum and Dad to let me watch.

The final episode of the second series had attracted nine million viewers and, even though three years had elapsed, there was again great interest as the new story was trailed in the media. Each of the six shows was scheduled for the 8pm slot on Monday evening and I would snuggle down on the sofa, wedged between my parents, and prepare to be scared witless.

As soon as the suitably doom-laden theme music played over the opening credits, I slid further down the settee so that the cushion on my lap was strategically placed immediately below my line of sight, ready to 'accidentally' slip upwards and shield my gaze should the tension became too great, which it did; often. As with all the best of these types of production, the scary bits were more imagined than real, but there was one standout moment when the aliens at the centre of the story were first shown, rather than hinted at. Actually they were as dead as dodos, but they still looked horrible and threatening, and just when I thought it was safe to reappear from behind my cushion, one of them moved without warning. I jumped right out of my skin, my reaction not being helped by the fact that one of the oldest tricks in the cinematic book had caught my parents unawares too. It was all too much for me. I abandoned the cushion and the settee, at least the seating part, and decided that it would be best if I viewed the rest of the series from behind it instead of on it.

The viewing figures for the final episode were given as eleven million, a tremendous number for the time, but I'm sure that many of them didn't actually watch it from start to finish. Like me, they'd probably realised that the portentous announcement, aired before each episode, that the programme was considered unsuitable for 'children and those of you who may have a nervous disposition', had been aimed at them.

If Quatermass wasn't scary enough the plight of the Magpies at the beginning of 1959 was also capable of giving me sleepless nights. On the opening Saturday of the year they managed to scrape a point in an unlikely four-all draw at home to Halifax but only after giving the visitors a three goal start before half-time. The Meadow Lane pitch was in almost as bad a condition as that at Gedling Road, where the ever present mud was made even more treacherous by a heavy frost that hadn't totally cleared by kick-off. Marys' opponents were Notts Alliance side Lenton Gregory, the game a fourth qualifying round tie in the Notts Senior Cup. The difficult surface wasn't conducive to the Saints' normal high tempo style and despite the majority of the possession they couldn't breach the visitors' last line of defence until the second period. A flurry of late goals shared across the forward line, with only Colin Collindridge missing out, gave the maroon and golds a comfortable four-nil victory.

Back at KGV a fortnight later they repeated the scoreline with a win in the league over bottom markers Anstey Nomads and two weeks later, and again at home, closed out the month with a steady two-nil victory over another Notts Alliance outfit Ericsson Athletic in the Quarter Final of the Senior Cup. The clean sheet against Gregory was, surprisingly, the very first of the season and then, as in the old adage about London buses, along came two more in quick succession.

Still, it was a good habit to get into, one that had no doubt been instilled into the players with the arrival at the club of new coach Noel Simpson. Noel was a former league player of some experience, having played well over three hundred games for Forest, Coventry City, and latterly Exeter City, who he had been with as recently as the previous season. A native of Mansfield, he had returned to the district following the end of his career as a full-time professional and was now passing on his advice to Marys' squad at their twice weekly training sessions at two local schools. Stamina building circuit training had been organised by Mr Shapland, PE teacher at Robert Mellors, but with the introduction of Noel and his classes at the Redhill School gymnasium, equal emphasis was now being given to improving players' skills and technique.

NOEL SIMPSON COACHING MARYS' PLAYERS : 1959   (Courtesy Football Post)

Equally spaced in amongst Marys' three wins in the month had been two blank Saturdays, a direct result of the arctic conditions that blanketed the country and made it the coldest January in Arnold since 1945. There were mass postponements of matches and quite a few were saved from the atrocious weather only by the most enterprising of endeavours. With the Saints having to sit it out, rivals Matlock Town arrived for their game against Shirebrook only to find that eight inches of snow lay over the ground. Out came a motor roller to flatten the snow to a more respectable height whilst a committeeman popped down to the local dyeworks to pick up enough green dye to mark out the pitch. The hard work was rewarded with a five-nil victory to the league leaders. However, of all the games seriously compromised by the awful conditions, it was probably a match involving Forest themselves that dominated the headlines and is still remembered today.

Entering the FA Cup at the third round stage along with the rest of the first and second division sides, they had been drawn to play away at the previously mentioned amateur club Tooting and Mitcham United who, having beaten Bournemouth in the first round, had added the scalp of Northampton Town in the second. The Isthmian League champions played at Sandy Lane, somewhat of a misnomer on the day of the match with the rutted pitch frozen hard and covered with a sprinkling of snow. Despite the fact that the London side were reckoned by many to be the equivalent of a top third division outfit, there was little doubt that the farcical state of the playing surface contributed to an even further narrowing of the gap between their ability and that of the Reds. The Football Post reported that 'players were moving as though on a skating rink' but even Torvill and Dean would have struggled to keep their balance that day.

At the same time I was in my normal spot in the County Road stand as the Magpies were, for a change, looking like a team that could actually play. Up against fourth placed Reading Notts were good value for their two-nil half-time lead and the tea from the family flask had never tasted better. All of a sudden a roar went around the ground as the half time scores from matches around the country were posted up; incredibly, Forest were losing two-nil! Personally I had no ill feeling towards the Reds, in fact I've always wanted them to be successful apart from in head to head clashes with Notts, but the sentiment was obviously not shared by the majority of the other ten thousand spectators at Meadow Lane that afternoon.

Over at the not so Sandy Lane, Forest had conceded goals from errors they wouldn't normally have committed had the surface been decent, but lady luck was definitely with the Reds in the second period and they escaped with a two-all draw thanks to an own goal and a Billy Gray penalty. With Notts ending up winners by three goals to one it had been a good day. A pity then that Rovers' waning importance back in Arnold was cruelly emphasised when they were trounced eight-one by Alfreton Miners Welfare at KGV, their biggest ever home defeat.

A fortnight after their fright at Tooting, and following two postponements because of the icebound state of the City Ground pitch, Forest finally had a chance to redeem themselves. This time, albeit with the surface far from perfect, the difference in class told and the Reds, despite their last goal coming in the final minute, were good value for their three-nil victory. In the days when the FA Cup still had a magical air about it and giant killing feats were the stuff of legend, the Isthmian League side had captured the public's imagination to such an extent that a remarkable crowd of 42,362 headed for the banks of the Trent to see for themselves what the fuss was all about.

Despite playing just a single game for points in the first month of the New Year, Marys had succeeded in remaining amongst the league leaders in third place. If it was getting a bit congested at the head of the Central Alliance table at the beginning of February there was certainly 'Room at the Top' at the Metropole in Sherwood where the film adaptation of John Braine's novel was being shown. Trailed as 'a savage story of lust and ambition' and starring Laurence Harvey in the title role as the upwardly mobile Joe Lampton, the movie was given an 'X' rating and the nearest I got to it as a ten year old was when I pressed my nose up against the film's poster on display in the cinema foyer where I was queuing for my ABC Minors' ticket.

As well as winning two Oscars, 'Room at the Top' had a significant impact on the British film industry and was a huge hit at the box-office. Cinema goers had shown that they had an appetite for adult storylines, 'kitchen-sink' realism, and political comment, especially when the plot contained a reminder of the ever contentious class divide that was still a scar on post-war British society. The following year Nottingham's Alan Sillitoe would adapt his own novel 'Saturday Night and Sunday Morning' for the big screen, a film that would make actor Albert Finney, in his portrayal of the main character Arthur Seaton, a household name. Working-class issues were again at the core of the movie, a large part of which was actually filmed in and around Nottingham, including the Raleigh Bicycle Works, and it still influences artists today, even those in a different medium. The words 'Whatever people say I am, that's what I'm not', uttered by Arthur, were used by the Sheffield band The Arctic Monkeys as the title of their massive selling debut album almost fifty years later.

Even as local film fans were watching Joe Lampton's attempts to climb the social ladder, Marys were on their way to a place where many members of the upper classes, both past and present, had whiled away their time for a pleasant three years or so of higher education before taking up their pre-ordained position as part of the Establishment; the university city of Cambridge. Of course the Saints weren't making their longest journey of the season in pursuit of intellectual improvement, they were there to see whether they could make progress in the Central Alliance Cup. Standing in their way was the reserve team of Southern League Cambridge City, one of the most progressive non-league clubs in the country. Winger Geoff Parr recalls his impressions of the visit.

GP : I was very impressed with Cambridge City then because they'd got one or two rich men on their committee and they'd got floodlights, one of the first teams to get them. The dressing rooms were under the stand, they were brilliant. They'd got treatment tables for you to lay on, really excellent.

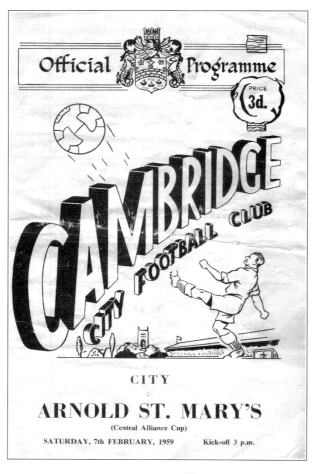

CENTRAL ALLIANCE CUP 3RD ROUND PROGRAMME 7 FEBRUARY 1959

Geoff's memory was spot on. Constituted as a limited company, the club had two future Mayors of Cambridge amongst its board of directors as well as a renowned author and a Cambridgeshire cricketer. The floodlights were brand spanking new and hadn't even been used yet. Ted Fenton, West Ham United's manager, had promised to bring his full first team for the first game under the lights just a couple of weeks later.

As Geoff and the rest of the boys enjoyed their rub downs in the luxurious surroundings, the news came through that it wasn't only the Hammers who would have a strong side on show at Milton Road. Because their first team was fixtureless that first Saturday in February, City would be using ten players against Marys who'd played in the senior side that season, including ex-Notts goalie Gordon Bradley. In the circumstances, it wasn't the best idea to concede a penalty inside the first ten minutes but fortunately the effort struck the bar and the Saints heaved a collective sigh of relief. Even so, pressure from the home side continued and just before the twenty minute mark they took the lead. For the remainder of the first period City had most of the possession but couldn't increase their lead and right on the stroke of half time Colin Collindridge, seizing onto a loose ball, cracked in the equaliser. It had been the perfect time for a response and after the break, with their confidence increasing all the time, Marys had as much of the play as their more illustrious opponents and were unlucky to only come away with a two-all draw.

The Saints didn't have to wait too long for a second shot at the southerners because the replay was scheduled for the following Saturday. When the Cambridge boys arrived in Arnold it must have been a bit of a culture shock; a parks pitch, no stands, no floodlights, and the changing rooms situated two or three hundred yards away at the town's public baths. The difference in status of the two clubs couldn't have been more marked. If the surroundings were less than plush City would also have to contend with the loss of a number of the players who had turned out in the first tie because they'd been called back up into the senior side for their Southern League Cup match against Kings Lynn whilst Marys' only problem of note was the continuing unavailability of cup-tied centre-forward Ray Wilkinson.

MARYS v CAMBRIDGE CITY RESERVES, 14 FEBRUARY 1959 : Back Row (l to r); R Wilkinson, B Molyneux, N Gough, S Gray, L Rockley, K Moore, W Parr, D Parr, S Thompson, L Rockley Snr, L Peck. Front Row; W Archer, M Cripwell, D Day, T Gray (Mascot), G Kitson, C Collindridge, G Parr.   (Geoff Parr Collection)

Even though it seemed that the advantage was very much with the Saints, the game was by no means a St Valentines Day massacre, in fact Cambridge were as dogged as Marys had been in the previous encounter and at the end of the regulation ninety minutes the teams were locked together at two apiece. It was only in extra time that the maroon and golds finally got the upper hand, ending up winning by the rather flattering scoreline of five goals to two with Geoff Parr netting twice from the left wing.

Marys' reward was a place in the Quarter Finals and a further home tie seven days later against yet another reserve eleven of a Southern League club, the fourth they had met this season; Kettering Town. The only change to the previous week's side was the introduction, after almost four months absence, of Phil 'Piddy' Smith in the troublesome number nine shirt. Despite the success the club had had in the competition, none of the stand-ins for Ray Wilkinson had lasted more than one game each in the cup run and 'Piddy' now became the fifth centre-forward to be tried in what had otherwise been a remarkably settled squad.

Despite the change, the Saints had the bit between their teeth right from the get go. Geoff Parr opening the scoring in the very first minute and the visitors' right back then headed a certain goal off the line with the goalie well beaten. Colin Collindridge added a second on the forty minute mark and when 'Piddy' Smith scored twice in a minute on the stroke of halftime, it was looking as though Ray Wilkinson would have a struggle getting back in the side. However, a second half incident put paid to any thoughts of a question mark regarding selection policy. Geoff Parr recalls:

GP : I was going down the wing and this full back came running over straight into me and I hit the steel rope round the ground. I couldn't pick my arm up, I was in severe pain. The rope caught me across the top of my arm and I was in pain all the time and couldn't carry on. I went to the General Hospital on the Sunday morning and they said it was ligaments, but I still couldn't pick my arm up at all. The club got me in with Forest and physiotherapist Bob Davies, and I went down there and Bob used to look after me. I'd be in the hot bath and he got me lifting a brush across my chest with both arms, but I could only get the arm up so far. It took seven weeks before we got the arm right.

Whilst Geoff was up to his neck in hot water at the City Ground, there was a distinct cooling down in Anglo-Soviet relations over in Moscow where Prime Minister Macmillan was being given short shrift by the Soviet Premier Nikita Khrushchev. Talks aimed at easing tensions between the east and west regarding the catastrophic potential of nuclear arms had begun cordially enough but had disintegrated into a stand-off that was reported as signalling a 'new chill' in the Cold War.

Just as the downcast Macmillan and his entourage were preparing to pack their bags and come home, the last Saturday in February saw Marys making a return of their own down at Gedling Road, back to league football for the first time in six weeks. In fact the fixture against South Normanton was only their second game for points since the Boxing Day defeat at Belper. Unfortunately, and very much contrary to pre-match expectations, the Saints lost to this Derbyshire side as well, going down by the odd goal in three to their mid-table visitors.

Marys' tremendous success over the past couple of months in both the Central Alliance and Notts Senior Cups had masked an indifferent spell in the league and the gaining of only four points in five matches had meant they'd slipped to fifth in the table as February drew to a close:-

	P	W	D	L	F	A	P
Matlock Town	22	15	2	5	66	38	32
Heanor Town	18	14	0	4	67	34	28
Ilkeston Town	21	11	6	4	57	33	28
Belper Town	18	12	3	3	78	41	27
Arnold St Marys	**20**	**13**	**1**	**6**	**53**	**38**	**27**

Of course it wasn't only the Saints whose league programme had been interrupted by a combination of poor weather and a good run in the various knockout competitions but they still faced testing times ahead with at least sixteen games to cram into a nine week spell. The only saving grace was that they were only scheduled to play two games in the run-in against teams currently above them in the league, so there was a good chance that they could take advantage of any of their immediate rivals' slip-ups when fixture congestion kicked in properly a few weeks hence.

In the event all five league matches that Marys played in March were against teams below them in the table and, despite being on the road for four of them, they took full advantage, running up an impressive one hundred percent record whilst scoring seventeen goals in the process and conceding only three. The team also remained unchanged during that spell with Ray Wilkinson back leading the line, 'Piddy' Smith taking the number ten shirt, and Colin Collindridge moving out to the left-wing where he'd spent the majority of his professional career.

If things were looking good on the pitch, there was another development off it that showed that the club's desire to progress was burning as bright as ever. An application to erect a spectators' stand at KGV, originally submitted back in November to the Arnold Council, had finally come back approved.

There was one other game played that month, and a rather historic one at that. Easter Saturday saw the visit of Rushden Town in the Semi Final of the Central Alliance Cup, the very first time that Marys had played a competitive match against a club with any Football League connections, past, present, or future. Of course the Northamptonshire club's spell there was a long way in the future, wouldn't last long, and would only be as one half of the awkwardly monikered Rushden and Diamonds following a merger with their neighbours from Irthlingborough, but nevertheless the Saints' dalliance with the 'bigger boys' had to start somewhere and this was it.

Geoff Parr, still being treated at the City Ground and obviously some way from being fully recovered, was brought in for the ineligible Ray Wilkinson, and another large crowd saw a very even contest with Rushden's quick tackling defence thwarting Marys' much vaunted attack. Just when it looked as if half-time would arrive goalless, Geoff's brother Dennis handled in the area and the visitors scored from the resultant penalty. Up against one of the better sides from the Southern section the Saints struggled for an equaliser but unfortunately their opponents stretched their lead and the game slipped from the maroon and golds' grasp. It finished up three-one, which was no disgrace, but having been so dominant in previous rounds, it was a big disappointment to players and supporters alike to go out of the competition a mere step away from the final.

A cup run that was attracting as much interest in Arnold as that of Marys', and certainly a far greater degree of attention in and around Nottingham, was Forest's own success in arriving at the semi final stage of the rather more famous FA Cup. Following their scare against Tooting back in January, the Reds had seen off Grimsby Town, Birmingham City, and Bolton Wanderers on their way to a Hillsborough showdown with Aston Villa. On the Saturday before their trip to Sheffield, Forest were hosts to Birmingham in a league match. Considering that the Reds, in those way off days before penalty shoot-outs had been invented, had needed three attempts to see off City in the Cup, this was the fourth meeting between the two sides in only three weeks. A combination of familiarity, poor weather, and the cost of following their side on the Wembley trail, led to the crowd against the West Midlanders numbering less than nineteen thousand, a season low up to then. It would have been three less had I not been cajoled by an older friend into making a rare trek with him to the City Ground.

Michael Fox lived with his parents and younger brother Peter almost opposite us at Killisick. He was three years older than me and I'd tagged along behind him quite a lot when we were kids growing up on the estate. He was the *de facto* leader of our 'gang' at a time when the term was rather less threatening than it is today. We were cast more in the image of the Beano comic's Bash Street Kids rather than the Jets and Sharks of contemporary West Side Story fame, although on reflection, Michael did look more like a Riff than a Smiffy. Two or three of us would often gather in his bedroom and listen in awe as he told us things that thirteen year-olds knew that ten year-olds didn't; or shouldn't. Things like fishing, the advent of puberty, and girls. I was enthralled and fascinated; what Michael didn't know about maggots wasn't worth knowing.

On the day of the Birmingham match Peter and I dutifully trailed behind him, happy to have the protection of someone older in what was unfamiliar territory to us both. The afternoon passed off quietly, unless you include the fireworks on the pitch where the Blues took merciless advantage of a weakened Reds' outfit and thrashed the cup hopefuls seven-one; hardly great preparation for the following week's clash against Villa. We hung around for a while after the match, hoping to get an autograph or two, but finally gave it up as a bad job. We sloped off over Trent Bridge and headed off up Arkwright Street through the Meadows, the district of Nottingham between the ground and the city centre. We'd not been walking long when we arrived at a newsagents. Michael said that he was just going inside to get something but I knew we only had enough money between us for the fare back home from the Market Square, which is why we were walking where we were walking. Still, we did as we were told and hung around on the pavement. All of a sudden he burst through the door with a sharp instruction to 'move it, quick' and we did, without question and with nary a backwards glance. Walking as fast as we could without actually running, we put a bit of distance between us and the shop before our leader signalled that it was okay to slow down.

It had all seemed rather exciting and I sensed that Peter and I were about to find out why we were asked to 'stand guard' outside the shop and then follow it with a hasty getaway. The penny finally dropped when Michael whipped a packet of cigarettes from his jacket pocket. I remembered then that he'd mentioned something earlier about 'dying for a fag' but I hadn't paid it too much mind. I certainly never expected that he was going to steal some. He showed us his ill gotten gains, ten Park Drive Tipped, second only to Woodbines, apparently, as the most disgusting cigarette ever invented by man. If they'd had health warnings on the packet in those days, it would have needed to have been so big there'd have been no room to identify the product.

The remainder of the walk along Arkwright Street was done at snail's pace, as we took two or three steps, a quick drag, two or three more steps, another furtive suck, and so one. By the time we arrived at the bus terminus on Long Row, I was already struggling a bit, and the climb up the stairs of the number fifty-two bus when it eventually arrived was a bit of an effort, too. We must have looked a right sight, huddled together on the back seat as the conductor came for our money, but we managed to smoke another cigarette between us before we arrived back at Killisick. I thought that I was going to be sick on the bus but somehow managed to hang on. Between the bus stop and our houses was a large open recreation area which we called the lammas. I was walking along the normal worn bit towards our road that I'd walked along hundreds of times before when I knew that I could walk no further. My respiratory system had given up on me. I lay down on the grass, stretched out like a small version of the Angel of the North, and gazed blankly up at the sky. Dark or not, I was seeing stars. Michael was shouting at me "Come on, or we'll all cop it!", but I couldn't move for what seemed like an eternity but was probably no more than half an hour. When eventually I realised that I wasn't going to die, I climbed gingerly to my feet, and, aided by my fellow miscreants, walked unsteadily the last three hundred yards or so home. When I eventually crept in the backdoor, my Mum asked, "Was it a good game; anything exciting happen?" "Nah, nothing special" I wheezed.

If I learned something from this little episode it was this. Don't nick fags, or anything else for that matter; and don't smoke nicked fags, or any other kind either, especially Park Drive Tipped. So I didn't; never; ever. As for Michael, he later emigrated to Zimbabwe when it was still Rhodesia and, with an irony not lost on those of us who knew him back then, joined the Salisbury Police Force!

Forest recovered sufficiently from their pasting against Birmingham to overcome Villa the following week, a single goal in the sixty fifth minute from Johnny Quigley being sufficient to guarantee victory and a place in the final where they would be meeting another unfancied side, Luton Town. For the Reds it was now only a matter of seeing the league programme through safely during the run-in to their date at Wembley, whilst for Marys, their five straight wins in March had seen them jump back up into second place in the Central Alliance and, together with their continuing involvement in the Notts Senior Cup, still with everything to play for.

	P	W	D	L	F	A	P
Matlock Town	27	18	3	6	83	46	39
Arnold St Marys	**25**	**18**	**1**	**6**	**70**	**41**	**37**
Ilkeston Town	26	13	8	5	68	40	34
Heanor Town	22	16	1	5	78	43	33
Belper Town	21	14	4	3	90	48	32

The traditional showery weather signalled the arrival of April and the Saints began the month with a couple of comfortable victories, three-nil at Clay Cross where Mick Cripwell converted a first minute penalty and Len Rockley saved one at the other end only a few minutes later, and six-two at home to Shirebrook. Next up were third placed Ilkeston Town, a team that was certainly expected to provide a much sterner test than the last two opponents, even in front of a partisan crowd at Gedling Road. Urged on by the large number of their own supporters the Robins went ahead as early as the ninth minute and with the rain and a driving wind behind them held onto their lead at the break. In fact it wasn't until the hour mark that Marys gained an equaliser when Mick Cripwell scored directly from a corner. It wasn't a fluke either because he'd already had a similar effort headed off the line earlier. When Ray Wilkinson added another a minute later the game's momentum had critically switched to the home side and it was no surprise that they doubled their tally before the end.

As well as seeing off Ilkeston's challenge for the title and completing a notable double over the highly rated Derbyshire outfit, the Saints' four-one victory drew glowing praise in the press, with particular attention being paid to right winger Mick Cripwell's unusual facility with corners from both sides of the pitch. The basic fact was that Marys' number seven was equally adept with both feet when a corner had been awarded and, by accident, design, or sheer good practice, could deliver an inswinging corner of great accuracy with amazing consistency. The Football Post even regarded him as 'the most dangerous taker of corner kicks in the competition'.

If this wasn't problematic enough for Central Alliance opposition, the next week left back Norman Gough managed to score from just over the half way line. Playing over in Leicestershire in a rearranged game against lowly Anstey Nomads, the Saints again found themselves a goal down by the ten minute mark and although 'Piddy' Smith was unlucky with a shot that struck the woodwork, it wasn't until the twenty fifth minute that Marys' number three improbably levelled the scores. After that it was a bit of a canter and despite a rather slipshod performance in defence, the maroon and golds ran out easy winners by six goals to three.

By the middle of the month fixtures were coming up thick and fast and the Saints faced a schedule of three games in slightly under five days. All of them, on paper at least, were winnable, and in two of them Marys did exactly that, even though they went behind yet again to an early goal, this time against the youngsters of Nottingham Forest A who had a left winger by the name of Bobby Tait in their line-up. Bobby would go on to have a decent career in the Football League, including a spell in Nottingham, albeit with the Magpies rather than the Reds, before spending three highly successful seasons at Gedling Road.

The first of the victories had been against Wilmorton & Alvaston at KGV and had marked the Saints' tenth consecutive league win. Unfortunately that game had taken place on the Tuesday and only forty eight hours later Marys were down to play away at Shirebrook. Normally this would have been a match the maroon and golds would have anticipated picking up maximum points from, after all they had beaten the same opponents convincingly a fortnight earlier. The problem was that it always proved difficult for amateur players to get time off their day jobs back then to enable them to properly prepare for matches with evening kick-offs, especially twice in one week and particularly when travel was involved. Even the eighteen or so miles to the pit community north of Mansfield would have added getting on for three quarters of an hour to proceedings in those early evenings of 1959. Suffice to say that a combination of these difficulties and the tired legs associated with the demands of nine games in just over three weeks conspired to limit the maroon and golds to a single point in a one-all draw.

Everyone associated with the club fervently hoped that it wouldn't prove critical, but it would have been a very unreasonable person who sought to criticize a side that had just completed its eleventh straight unbeaten game, dropping only a single point. In fact the side had been unchanged during that tremendous spell and the same eleven recovered quickly from their setback at Shirebrook and went on to beat the young Reds by the odd goal in three on the Saturday and then take Ransome & Marles apart at KGV a few days later by a season's best scoreline of nine goals to two. The players could hardly have done better; in eight games in April they had won seven and drawn one, scoring thirty four times whilst conceding eleven.

With only a single league game left, this relentless success had seen off three of Marys' closest rivals who, through a variety of circumstances, hadn't handled the run-in with the same efficiency as the Arnold club. Unfortunately, one of them had, and although they were some six points behind the Saints when the Football Post printed the league table in its final edition of the 1958-59 season, with four games in hand the title was still Belper Town's to lose rather than the maroon and golds' to win.

	P	W	D	L	F	A	P
Arnold St Marys	**33**	**25**	**2**	**6**	**104**	**52**	**52**
Belper Town	29	21	4	4	123	59	46

Marys' excellent run of form in the past month had been achieved despite the fact that it had been Arnold's wettest April since 1935 and it seemed rather apt that as the Saints were climbing back up to the top of the table, the classic Buddy Holly song 'Raining In My Heart' was heading up the charts on its way to giving the Texan his only number one hit. It would also be the first posthumous chart topper in Britain as the singer had met an untimely death in an air crash back in February, a tragedy that also claimed the lives of fellow performers Ritchie Valens and J P 'The Big Bopper' Richardson. Holly was a great influence on the British pop music scene in the years to come and his legacy remains to this day. The other side of his number one record was 'It Doesn't Matter Anymore', written by Paul Anka, and for poor old Buddy I guess that it didn't.

It was different down at Gedling Road where the prospect of ending up with a league and cup double certainly did matter. First up in May was a clash with old rivals Gedling Colliery, Walter Kirk and all, in the semi final of the Notts Senior Cup at Meadow Lane on the evening of the FA Cup Final. Following on from the Reds' famous victory that afternoon at Wembley, it could have easily have been a case of 'after the Lord Mayor's show' but both teams were at the top of their form and the game provided excellent entertainment. Gedling were uncatchable at the top of the Notts Alliance and heading for their fourth straight title, their eighth in ten years. Of course gone were the days when they had an automatic ascendancy over Marys but they were still quite capable of matching their old rivals when it mattered, and this evening was no exception. With the scores level after ninety minutes the tie went to extra time but even a further half hour couldn't separate the two sides and it finished two apiece. The replay couldn't be slotted in during the following midweek owing to prior fixture commitments so the game was scheduled for the following Saturday back at Meadow Lane, the original date and venue for the final itself.

Before they could even think about that match, the Tuesday evening saw the Saints travel to current champions Heanor Town for their last, and crucial, Central Alliance game of the season. The Derbyshire side were the only club that Marys hadn't beaten in the league so far and the two points were essential if they were to keep the pressure on Belper in the race for the title. Unfortunately, having recently hosted seven games in as many days, the state of their opponents' pitch left a lot to be desired, especially with so much at stake. Then there was the issue of fatigue. The Saints' side that night was not only the same eleven who'd played in the two hour epic against Gedling but the one that had also racked up an incredible fifteen straight league games unchanged. Winning certainly helps but there was little doubt that as they lined up for the kick-off there were plenty of players carrying those niggling injuries that were common currency at this hectic stage of a long and hard season.

However, cheered on by a large contingent of fans who'd made the twelve mile trip over from Arnold, Marys' players made light of any discomfort they might be suffering and took a first half lead courtesy of left winger Colin Collindridge. Heanor hadn't reached the first round of this season's FA Cup because they were a poor team and even though they'd had a tough run-in themselves they let the Saints know they were in a game. Fortunately, the visitors' defence put in a solid performance to keep the home side at bay and the maroon and golds hung onto their solitary goal lead to clinch two precious points.

PROGRAMME FOR FINAL LEAGUE GAME OF 1958-59

(Stan Wilton Collection)

With Belper still catching up with their own outstanding fixtures all that Marys could do now was to wait and see whether the Derbyshire side would drop the three points that would allow the Saints to clinch the championship at the first time of asking. Two points lost might even be enough for the Saints to sneak it because at the time goal average, rather than goal difference, was used to split teams who were level on points. Goal average was calculated by dividing the number of goals a side had scored by the number they had conceded and here Belper marginally held the upper hand, 2.08 to Marys' 2.02.

Ultimately of course the Saints' league fate was now completely out of their hands but this wasn't the case with the Notts Senior Cup the following Saturday when they faced Gedling in the replayed semi final. It went without saying that the 'Magnificent Eleven' lined up against their Notts Alliance opponents, putting Colin Collindridge up against the Colliery's fearsome right back for the second time in a week. Ernie Iremonger, Gedling's goalie and a future Marys' player himself, recalls the clash.

EI : Walter Kirk, 'The Assassin'. Nobody messed with Walter. If a winger got past him a couple of times he didn't get past him a third. Walter took his legs. But in that semi final 'Collo' gave him a bit of a run around. With his lanky frame and his legs up in the air he made Walter keep missing him.

Whilst Marys' left winger was winning his own personal duel the rest of the team fared better this time around too and despite Gedling pushing them hard all the way, the Saints' narrow one-nil victory was enough to secure them a place in the Senior Cup final for the very first time in the club's history.

THE MAGNIFICENT ELEVEN : THE MARYS' LINE UP THAT REMAINED UNCHANGED FOR FIFTEEN LEAGUE GAMES FEB-MAY 1959 : Back Row (l to r); B Molyneux, N Gough, L Rockley, K Moore, D Parr, S Thompson. Front Row; W Archer (Trainer), M Cripwell, D Day, R Wilkinson, P Smith, C Collindridge. In Front; T Gray (Mascot)   (Courtesy Football Post)

The influence of ex-Forester Colin Collindridge in his first season at Gedling Road was hard to overstate. An ever-present in the side since November, he'd missed just six matches to date, a fine testament to the fitness levels he'd maintained despite being in his thirty-ninth year. Geoff Parr was certainly one of those impressed by the veteran, both on and off the pitch.

*GP : He was a great player, Colin. He helped everybody, he wasn't selfish at all. He had a good brain, I thought he was the bee's knees, really. He was very versatile, could play centre forward, drop back, be on the wing. I felt quite young alongside 'Collo' with his bit of curly hair and neckerchief! He was a real character. He had a moped and after a game once they reckoned he took Dennis Day **and** Dennis Wheat home on the back! He used to have records in Russian and other languages, probably because his dad was a union man, a top man. He even got a job at RAF Newton as a chef! During the war he was stationed at Syerston, he was air crew. He used to get the row boat across the Trent to the Star and Garter at Hazelford.*

Colin was generous of spirit too, best exemplified by a gesture he made before the Senior Cup final.

GP : My injury meant I hadn't played in the run-in but for the Senior Cup final Colin decided that he would step aside and let me play instead. He was a bloody good lad.

Not many players, then or now, would give up their place in the side with a cup winners' medal in the offing, but it was a measure of the man that he did. Of course, Geoff's presence hardly weakened the side. He'd been in fine goalscoring form before his unfortunate and very painful altercation with the boundary rope and was well on the way to emulating his previous campaign's twenty-plus goal tally. Now, thanks to his friend's benevolence, he had a chance to end the season on a high.

Standing in his and his team's path in this last match of the season were Retford Town, Yorkshire League champions and another one of Marys' opponents this season whose players were all on professional contracts. Not that the Saints' were in awe of any side, paid or not, especially considering that they had been so successful themselves whilst still retaining their amateur status. A status, incidentally, that at the outset of the campaign had been used to promote the view that they didn't belong amongst the likes of Ilkeston, Heanor, and Matlock. Now, having finished higher than all of those so-called bigger teams, it had come to be regarded as a shining tribute to those running the club.

Of course Marys' committee were wise to the ways of the world, especially that of local football, and had always had a reputation for 'looking after' their players discretely. Given that four thousand spectators, the majority from the Arnold district, turned up at Sutton Town's ground at Priestsic Road for the final, I reckon that Syd Gray and Charlie Moore would have made sure that some of the club's share of the gate money found its way, in the time honoured fashion, into the players' boots.

The wet weather of April was a thing of the past and, on the third Saturday in May, the game kicked off in conditions more suitable for cricket, a point elaborated upon quite amusingly by the local Retford paper: 'Sutton's long-suffering pitch – there had been six games on it last week before Saturday's match – was as hard as a dance floor and dry as a Texan dust-bowl. The weather was perfect – for sunbathing...' Their reporter at the game, who sounded like he also doubled as the paper's TV correspondent, even went on to suggest that 'football on such a warm evening would have 'creased' Cheyenne Bodie and 'The Lawman', tough characters as they reckon to be'. Now, as all lovers of Nineteen Fifties' Westerns will know, the latter show's stirring theme tune began with the words 'The Lawman came with the sun, there was a job to be done...' and, as the two sets of players eyed each other up across the half way line and the referee blew for the start of the game in temperatures more suited to flaming June than mid-May, there was indeed a job to be done, even if only one of the sides was getting paid to do it.

Urged on by their fans, who heavily outnumbered their Retford counterparts, it was the 'play for fun' Marys who had the better of the opening skirmishes with centre forward Ray Wilkinson causing the Shamrocks' defence all manner of problems. It came as no surprise when as early as the twelfth minute the Saints took the lead and, in real 'Roy of the Rovers' fashion, the scorer was none other than Geoff Parr, latching on to a rebound to fire a cross shot into the far corner of the net. On the odd occasion that Retford threatened, their forwards found Len Rockley in commanding form, but they were mostly penned inside their own half as the maroon and golds maintained their grip on proceedings.

Half time arrived with the score unchanged and on the resumption Retford began with only ten men. Minutes before the break their right winger had been forced to leave the field for treatment for a suspected broken nose and he was still back in the dressing room as the second half got underway. With their one goal advantage and their opponents a man short, Marys sensed that they had a great chance to put the game beyond the Shamrocks' reach and stepped up the attacking pressure. Geoff Parr had a chance saved by the keeper and then shortly afterwards came an opportunity that could have won them the cup. A fine move amongst the forwards ended with Geoff slipping a pass into the path of Ray Wilkinson a few yards from goal but the centre forward snatched at his effort and the chance went begging.

It was effectively the last time the Saints threatened. Almost immediately Retford were back to full strength and twenty minutes after returning to the fray their number seven showed that he was suffering no ill effects from his injury by driving home the equaliser. Thankfully, Marys' defence proved resolute in the closing stages of normal time and the game went into an extra period. As is often the case the additional thirty minutes were a non-event with both sides feeling the effects of the energy sapping conditions and seeming happy to settle for a replay; the game ended one-all. The Retford reporter called it a fair result, nominated right half Keith Moore as the Saints' best player, and informed his readers that the replayed fixture would have to be held over until the evening of Wednesday August 19, this time at Meadow Lane, when it would be played as a curtain raiser to the new season, due to commence three days later.

It was frustrating to players and fans alike that having come so close to clinching the trophy Marys would now have to sit out the close season before having another crack at Retford but the real disappointment came with the official confirmation that Belper had finally caught up with their fixture backlog and gathered sufficient points to pip the Saints for the Central Alliance championship. The fact that in the final analysis the title had indeed been settled on goal average only made the news that much harder to take.

In truth, the maroon and golds could hardly have done more to bring silverware to Arnold in a season that had exceeded all expectations. Despite the odd hiccup earlier in the season as they were acclimatising themselves to life in the top division, their form in the latter part of the campaign had been nothing but exemplary, as can be seen by this comparison:

	P	W	D	L	F	A	P
First 20 games	20	13	1	6	53	38	27
Last 14 games	14	13	1	0	52	14	27

They also had an incredible away record too, dropping only three points in their seventeen league games on the road, losing only to champions Belper in that set-to in the mud back on Boxing Day. Additionally, and in keeping with the fast, attacking football that the club were becoming well known for, the Saints had also managed the difficult task of scoring in every one of their forty five matches to date, both league and cup. That they'd done all this with a core group of just thirteen players was probably the most impressive achievement of them all. Len Rockley, Norman Gough, Dennis Parr, and Mick Cripwell were ever-presents whilst Barry Molyneux was absent only the once with Sid Thompson missing a couple.

Of course Marys' exploits were somewhat secondary, even in Arnold, to Forest's headline grabbing run and ultimate triumph at Wembley in the FA Cup. On the Monday evening following their two-one victory over Luton Town an open-top coach parade was organised for the Reds. As die-hard Magpie fans it was only a last minute decision to pop down town to try and catch a glimpse of the legendary trophy and the nearest we could get was the Goose Fair roundabout at the end of Gregory Boulevard. As the coach approached the cheers of the crowd reached a crescendo but even as I stood wedged by the side of the road between my Dad and my uncle my thoughts still invariably wandered back to the plight of poor old Notts. They'd begun the season poorly, got even worse as it progressed, and by the end of the campaign were, in the words of the Football Post, 'completely devoid of skill and intelligence'. They were lacking too in enough points to save them from the ignominious drop into the basement, the fourth division of the Football League, then quite bluntly and properly known as 'Division Four'.

Less than five thousand hardly souls, including me, had braved the elements to watch Colchester United perform the last rites on the penultimate day of the season. It was painful to watch but by then I was past caring anyway, I only went to complete my programme collection for the season. At the final whistle I folded the treasured possession neatly and put it inside my jacket pocket to protect it from the driving rain. We filed out of the ground, picked our way through the sodden Cattle Market to where our car was parked and edged our way out of the large metal gates and off down Meadow Lane. We'd got stuck at one of the many level crossings that always seemed to bar our way home through Sneinton when out of the car radio came the reassuringly familiar sound of the Central Band of the RAF playing Hubert Bath's composition 'Out Of The Blue', the stirring theme tune to the BBC Light Programme's 'Sports Report'. It didn't matter that the delay was for a little diesel shunter, travelling solo through the murky gloom at around five miles an hour and taking an age before it finally appeared. Once the mellifluous tones of Eamonn Andrews began reading the headlines and John Webster followed with the day's results, I was reminded that football had got a hold on me and wasn't going to let me go that easily. I might have supported one of the worst teams in the world, but I knew at that moment I'd be back down The Lane again the next season, Fourth Division or not. After all, we County fans might have been delusional, but we were eternal optimists too, and next year surely couldn't be any worse than this one.

Could it?

The summer of 1959 was the driest on record and, come August, Marys and the rest would kick off in a heat wave, but my abiding memories of that particular close season had nothing at all to do with the weather or even football. That last long school holiday of the decade has a special place in my heart because it was the time when I saw my first 'streak' and the Man of Steel and the Caped Crusader, better known as Superman and Batman respectively, arrived in my own back yard. These two events were entirely unrelated except in the fact that they kindled in me an interest that has stayed with me throughout my subsequent life and remains to this very day.

Now I do not refer to the unabashed need for exhibitionism of undersized men and oversized women when I use the word 'streak', but rather the affectionate term given to the world's fastest ever steam engines, the first of which I saw or, probably and more accurately, heard for the very first time on a day's train spotting excursion to Grantham. To find out how I arrived there the clock has to be turned back to our family holiday a few weeks earlier in Devon and Cornwall.

It was the usual crowd of us, Mum, Dad, me, brother Stephen, my Nan and Grandad Barnes, and my uncle Derrick, who provided the transport in the shape of a recently acquired Ford Zodiac. It was a very tight squeeze, but thankfully it had bench seats both front and back. Our first port of call was Barnstaple on the North Devon coast, and I can remember nothing of this pit-stop other than our B&B accommodation backed right onto either the railway station or, as was more likely, Barnstaple Junction yards and shed, where locomotives were housed in between outings. If I stood on the toilet seat of the communal WC across the corridor from our room, I had a clear view of all the activity below. It was so exciting that I had to keep relieving myself. Luckily I didn't have far to go.

In fact, the delights of loco spotting were only now revealing themselves to me. Derrick, on the other hand, had a great knowledge of railways but I'm not sure even he was aware that this part of the country was host to both the Western and Southern Regions of the British Rail network, or that for instance these were served by two stations in Barnstaple itself, Town and Junction respectively. What this meant was that not only would I see plenty of trains named after Castles, Halls, Manors and Granges that once belonged to the GWR (Great Western Railway; or, as known by railway buffs, 'God's Wonderful Railway') but I would also catch my first sight of the splendidly named 'Battle of Britain' class run by the Southern Region. How could any young kid not be captivated by engines called 'Spitfire', 'Fighter Command', and '601 Squadron'?

Naturally, there was a price to be paid for all this excitement. I don't think the rest of the family, Derrick excepted, shared my love of the railways, so I was dragged along to all the picture postcard villages around, and there were many, especially on the coast. Unfortunately my family, like so many others at the seaside in the nineteen fifties, fell prey to the curse of the tourist flag, that little three inch by two inch pennant made of rubberised plastic and which with a bit of spit found itself plastered on the inside of the rear car window. It seemed that wherever we went we would have to buy one of these naff mementos at each stop off to remind ourselves exactly where we'd been on what was proving to be a whistle stop vacation. Westward Ho!, my favourite only because I absolutely loved the name, Clovelly, Tintagel, Looe, Polperro and many more besides were all ticked off one by one. The view through the rear windscreen of the Zodiac was becoming more and more restricted as each day passed.

Derrick's newly purchased pride and joy was certainly being put through its paces. We were hitting all the tourist spots because our trip to the West Country was what was then commonly referred to as a 'touring holiday'. It may quite as well have been called a 'Magical Mystery Tour' because apart from the opening night in Barnstaple, I don't think anyone had any idea where we'd be pitching up the next evening. Given the beautiful weather the 'full up' signs were an almost permanent feature everywhere we went, especially as most days we didn't land at our destination until late afternoon, early evening. We had to resort to making the various tourist information centres our first port of call, sometimes with less than auspicious results. On one occasion we ended up in a council house in St Austell. Nothing wrong with that, of course; our hosts were a nice young couple, the house was very neat and tidy, and the food was more than serviceable. It was just that, well, it was hardly any different from our own neat and tidy council house at Hawthorn Crescent, and this was meant to be a holiday, after all.

However, any misgivings I might have had about that night's B&B were totally forgotten less than twenty four hours later when we were sent miles out into the back of beyond by a well meaning lady at the local tourist board in search of an isolated farmhouse somewhere on Bodmin Moor. I began to have my doubts once the road became a track, narrower and bumpier by the yard, and there was no sign of human habitation anywhere to be found. Eventually we saw a light, and a very dim and flickering one at that. I'd like to say that it was welcoming, but it wasn't.

As we drew near, a female form appeared, ancient to my young eyes, as though she was expecting us. When I think about it, I couldn't say for certain how she knew this, considering that the farmhouse definitely had no electricity, and most probably no telephone either. I think we were all a bit spooked even before we'd set foot inside the property, and as it was pretty late by this time the consensus was that it was best that we'd be better turning in more or less straightaway in readiness for the travails of the following day.

We all went upstairs in a tight convoy, one torchbearer at the front, me tucked safely in the middle. I didn't want to be last at any cost. By the time we were all tucked in I'm sure we'd frightened ourselves and each other to death. Every creak and moan in the fabric of the old building was magnified to Hammer Horror proportions, and in my particular case, sharing a room with Derrick, who wasn't averse to deliberately increasing the tension with the usual relish meted out by an uncle to a nephew, I half expected to hear the handle of our bedroom door turn slowly and menacingly at any moment. As it happened, a truly scary moment did befall my mother who, entering the wrong room, was confronted by the sight of a man lying stone still in bed. She quickly made her exit, not quite sure whether the body was dead, alive, or somewhere in between.

The night passed slowly, very slowly. It was only when the sun came up the next morning and we realised that we were all still alive that I think a general air of relaxation and relief came over us. The lady of the house served the most enormous breakfast; one that unfortunately proved beyond us. As a result she was a little miffed and we were again rather relieved when the farmhouse was quickly disappearing in the rear view mirror, impaired vision or not. We never did find out who the man in the bed was, or his state of well-being, or otherwise. The landlady never once mentioned him and my mother was too respectful, or downright nervous, to ask.

Thankfully the last three days of the trip were spent in one place, a B&B in Fowey. I think everyone was delighted to finally have a semi-permanent roof over their heads, even though it had no running water upstairs and we had to make do with the old fashioned jug and bowl for washing before we turned in for the night.

When we finally said goodbye to the delights of the West Country, the landlady of the establishment was most gracious in her parting comments. She thought Stephen and I were 'two nice, well behaved boys', which of course we were; at least that particular week. A combination of the bracing sea air and hours spent trudging up and down the area's steep hills ensured that we had little energy left for mischief. Once we'd eaten dinner, it wasn't long before we were in the land of nod.

Every night, that is, bar one. The one we spent in the back of beyond, miles from civilization and a supply of electricity, wondering whether that scratching sound was merely a branch of a tree being blown against a window, or whether it was, as Derrick would have me believe, the Beast of Bodmin Moor itself, on its midnight prowl for food, clawing at our very door.

Once back home at Killisick, and with the rest of the school holiday ahead, all memories of the South West quickly faded, save for my new interest in railways, and a few days later I set off behind 'gang leader' Michael Fox for a day's train spotting over at Grantham. The reason for venturing over into Lincolnshire when there was still a station at Daybrook and two in Nottingham became clear to me as it was explained by my elders and betters that Grantham served both the Midland and Eastern Regions of the British Rail Network and was part of the East Coast Main Line where the fastest trains in the country thundered up and down on a daily basis. As mentioned earlier these classics of steam engineering, designed by Sir Nigel Gresley, were known amongst spotters as 'Streaks', no doubt as a result of their streamlined appearance and their unrivalled speed that had reached a zenith more than twenty years earlier when one of them, 'Mallard', hit a hundred and twenty six miles an hour just south of Grantham itself.

BR LOCOMOTIVE 60013 'DOMINION OF NEW ZEALAND'   (Eric Treacy)

I really didn't quite know what was in store as I disembarked along with the rest of our motley crew at the little side platform adjacent to the main station but I didn't have to wait too long before the word went round that 'one was on its way' and sure enough, about ten minutes later, pens and pencils were eagerly poised above notepads waiting for the first big arrival of the day.

If I were to say that what happened next was a bit of a blur, it would be a massive understatement. All I could recall was a finger of a mate pointing down the line to a speck in the distance which grew slowly larger as the countdown began and an instruction on the PA system advised everyone to stand well clear of the platform edge as the impending visitor was apparently not intending to stop in Grantham any time soon. There was a slight but discernible rumbling sound and the station platform began to vibrate beneath my feet, both increasing in tempo along with my heartbeat. Before I knew it the air seemed to be sucked out from around me as something, and I couldn't identify it exactly but of course it was the long awaited express, hurtled through the narrow passageway between the platforms on its way north. The noise by now was ear shattering, the fabric of the station was rattling and shaking, and that intoxicating mix of steam, soot, smoke and oil, much beloved of all train spotters but a completely new sensory experience to me, filled the air to choking point.

As to the number of the engine, well there I had to rely upon the seasoned campaigners amongst us to let me in on its specific identity. I'm not even sure I actually saw locomotive number 600xx or whatever it was, but I heard it, smelt it, and definitely felt its presence, and I did catch a glimpse of the rear of the train as I plucked up enough courage to look up the line and catch the back of the guards' wagon as it disappeared rapidly on its way to Newark and beyond. After the gentility of trackside spotting in sleepy Devon, this had proved a most exhilarating experience, one that would to my great delight be repeated twice more that day. I'm still not sure whether I made a better fist of actually seeing the next two 'Streaks' as I did the first but three of the beauties made their way into my notebook nevertheless.

Clambering aboard our stopping train back to Nottingham Midland, we compared notes to make sure we hadn't missed any numbers. Michael's notebook was the bible against which we lesser beings checked our scribblings and once I was happy with the contents of my own I settled back into my seat and watched as the countryside passed slowly by. Michael lit up a surreptitious fag, as was his wont, and disappeared in a haze of smoke behind some magazine or other. A few weeks earlier an article in the press had been published saying that filter tip cigarettes had helped manufacturers maintain sales after reports had linked smoking and lung cancer for the first time. I'm sure that he wouldn't have read it himself; I can't for one minute imagine it being the kind of material to be found in the pages of the Angling Times or Tit Bits.

I would go back to Grantham on a number of occasions in the future but for the rest of the summer had to content myself with the occasional visit down to my local station at Daybrook. The contrast between the rail traffic using this sleepy backwater and the 'Streaks' of the East Coast Main Line couldn't have been more marked. The only time that the platforms had seen much activity over the years was when various clubs and associations from the district held their annual day trips to the seaside. With my Granddad Barnes being a fully paid up member of the Arnold Liberal Club, I found myself on at least one such trip for a number of years and each one was a special treat. If the bucket and spade element has faded from my memory, there was one very important ritual that hasn't, and that was the loading up onto the carriages of copious amounts of bottled beers and soft drinks, all handled with great care and accounted for with precision by the menfolk assigned to the job. I think I'd got more chance of being left behind than one of those crates of India Pale Ale.

DAYBROOK STATION : HOME ALES TRIP 1927

On one particular Saturday morning I decided to give the ABC Minors a miss in favour of two or three hours train spotting at Daybrook but with the weather remaining beautiful I had all on to stay awake as the wait between the intermittent services dragged interminably on. The number of engines that trundled through whilst I was there only just reached double figures and even then that paltry total had been boosted thanks to a couple of them making an appearance in both directions. When I finally gave it up as a bad job I had the misfortune of catching the very bus back home that was already stuffed with a bunch of kids from Killisick; the ones who'd been to see the latest escapade of Flash Gordon and the rest down at the

Metropole. Without Michael's protective company I knew that I was in for some serious verbal abuse. A report had recently been published saying that television was killing cinema but just then I felt like a certain delinquent section of cinema goers were about to kill me. In fact I wish that 'anorak', the current derogatory term for a train-spotter, had been in use back then because it would have been mild in comparison to some of the insults flying in my direction.

As it turned out something rather more pleasant was already heading my way that particular summer in the form of America's two longest serving superheroes, Superman and Batman. These two iconic comic book characters had been around since the late nineteen thirties in the USA but had only made brief appearances in reprint material in the UK; now that was all about to change. There had been a national print strike from mid June to mid August and I'd been starved of my regular diet of Roy of the Rovers so the arrival at the newsagents of these colourful imports couldn't have come at a better time. Their full colour format throughout was totally different to their British counterparts and the characters contained in the stories were like nothing I'd seen between the covers of Lion and Tiger and the rest. Costumed crime-fighters fought a constant stream of outrageous villains and I soon became familiar with the dastardly Lex Luthor and Brainiac, The Joker and The Penguin as they tried to bring about the demise of the good guys.

Another difference between these DC comics and their British rivals was the letters section, usually a page or two given over to correspondence from fans writing in to point out mistakes, or 'goofs' as they referred to them over there, from previous issues or to suggest story-lines for the future. One such fervent contributor was a young Paul Gambaccini, better known now as an author and radio and television presenter specialising in music. Like me he's never lost his interest in the genre and for a brief period in the 1990s he co-owned a comic shop in London with another well-known radio and television personality Jonathan Ross. With the issues containing the first appearances of Superman and Batman setting a prospective purchaser back in excess of six figures, it would need a salary the size of that being paid by the BBC, allegedly, to Mr 'Woss' to even contemplate building a definitive collection today.

Like the rest of my mates who'd also become enthralled by these strange new comics on the racks my spending power was obviously rather more constrained than the BBC's budget, and at ninepence a time I could only buy three a week out of my half a crown pocket money. That didn't leave much for the real essentials of life, those items necessary for the daily survival of most every youngster; sweets. If I could only manage to fend off the attractions of Lois Lane and Batwoman there were many other temptations that could be had legally for a few old pennies. The list is probably endless, depending on age and taste, but from a purely personal standpoint, here goes: Sun-Pat raisins, flying saucers, black jacks, fruit salads, sherbet and kayli, shrimps (not the maritime version), barley sugar sticks, jelly babies, liquorice wood (which we called 'chewing sticks' and only bought when the pocket money had almost run out and we were desperate), and my two all-time favourites, sweet cigarettes and Palm toffee bars.

The latter were exotic slabs of different flavoured toffee with grooves etched into the surface, dividing it into smaller pieces that you could, with a bit of practice, neatly break off with the judicious use of a piece of cutlery and the edge of a table or similar. Banana was my absolute favourite, but I loved it and them even more when they had softened up. This could be achieved by leaving it lying around for a while, but normally the urge to break it up there and then was too hard to ignore. The best way to get your hands on a more malleable bar was by the adoption of a little bit of pre-purchase selection. Now I'm not saying that shopkeepers were any better or worse fifty years ago than they are today but to my certain knowledge there were no sell-by dates on the sweets I used to buy, so Palm toffee bars of varying vintages could be found alongside each other on most counters. A discreet feel along the display was all that was normally needed to pick out the most desirable. If it bent, that was the one. Happily for other prospective buyers the bars did come in a wrapper.

When it came to applying the 'bendability' rule to packets of sweet cigarettes however, I have to admit that my nerve didn't quite extend to taking the fags out and checking them individually. That's not to say that I hadn't come up with a pretty decent test though, which amounted to shaking the product, rather than distorting its shape. If the cigarettes rattled around inside the box, chances were they were still rather firm. A lower, more muffled, sound usually meant they were on the turn, and a rather more attractive proposition as a result.

This most idyllic of summer holidays ended with a weekend on the East Coast at Mablethorpe, a small resort north of Skegness not only favoured by the unwashed masses of the East Midlands but also visited by literary giants Alfred Lord Tennyson in the 19th century and by D. H. Lawrence in the early 20th. I loved it because it had a railway station, a glorious expanse of beach where we could play football all day and, equally as important as I was becoming increasingly interested in popular music, a coffee bar halfway between the two where we went for a nightcap as part of our late evening constitutional. Apart from developing a taste for a mug of the most delicious Horlicks, made using frothed-up milk from a gleaming silver contraption on the counter, I became inexorably drawn towards another of the establishment's shiny machines; the gaudily lit juke box over in the corner. 'Living Doll' had given Cliff Richard his first number one in July and was still receiving plenty of airplay but it was a song that just failed to make the top spot around the same time that was proving to be the most popular in the café. It was a catchy number called 'Lipstick on Your Collar', sung by Italian-American Concetta Franconero, rather better known as Connie Francis.

On the way back to our chalet my mother and I launched into a rousing imitation of the girl group intro to the song that went 'Yeah yeah, yeah yeah, yeah-yeah...', stumbled our way through the story telling verses about the cheating boyfriend, and let five year old Stephen finish off with the closing line '...told a tale on you'. We murdered the song and probably caused chaos in the shipping lanes of the North Sea but I don't suppose Connie was too bothered about the competition. She was, after all, already well on the way to becoming the most successful international female vocalist of the nineteen fifties and sixties.

The family vacations might have been over for another year but once back home in Arnold there was ample compensation in the form of the imminent arrival of the new football season. On a personal level I'd have to put up with life in the basement division with the Magpies, but hope springs eternal and I was as enthusiastic as ever as the season kicked off at Meadow Lane in glorious weather in front of a shirt-sleeved crowd just shy of ten thousand hopeless devotees. At least this time disappointment wasn't the reward for their support as Notts overcame an early deficit to end up winners by the odd goal in three. Over the river at Trent Bridge Middlesex took advantage of the scorching weather, a featherbed wicket, and a parched outfield to lay waste to the Notts' bowling and rattle up two hundred runs in only two hundred and seventeen balls, a pretty quick effort for the times and easily the season's best. Away from the banks of the Trent the rest of the East Midlands' professional sides had an awful time. Each playing away, the combined might of Forest, Leicester, Derby, Lincoln, Mansfield, and Chesterfield couldn't muster a single point between them, and a few miles down the road from the latter's Crooked Spire, Marys themselves came up against a pretty daunting obstacle in the shape of the newly formed Alfreton Town.

During the close season the Derbyshire side had been created from a merger of two teams, Alfreton United and Alfreton Miners Welfare, and nine of the players facing the Saints on the opening day of the new campaign were professionals. By contrast Marys had been pursuing their policy of signing former League players on permit forms and Syd Gray and Charlie Moore had persuaded three more to join the club's roster. They were Aubrey Southwell, Roland 'Tot' Leverton, and Peter Williams.

Aubrey, now thirty eight years of age, had been a rock steady fixture at full back for the Magpies, racking up well over three hundred league appearances whilst inside forward 'Tot', five years his junior, had seen service with both Forest and Notts, as well as Walsall, in a full-time professional career approaching two hundred games. Peter, a winger and the youngest of the trio at a mere twenty seven, had been on a part-time contract with both Derby and Chesterfield, but his desire to pursue his off-field career had limited him to fifteen first-team appearances.

PW : I'd signed amateur forms in 1950 for Notts County and played in their youth and reserve teams but in May that year I was called up into the RAF to do my National Service. I played for South Normanton during this time in the Central Alliance and it was there that Derby

County spotted me. As soon as I finished my National Service in 1952 I signed professional terms for Derby, fifteen pounds a week, two pounds a point. I played a couple of games in the First Division, including one against Manchester United, but mainly for the second eleven. I was part-time and constantly being asked to go full-time but I never seriously considered switching because I wanted to continue my studies in accountancy. I was there for two seasons, then went to Chesterfield where I played in the Third Division before joining my ex-Derby team-mate Ray Middleton and the Hazledine brothers over at Boston United.

In 1958 I joined Kings Lynn and while I was there I suffered a serious chip fracture to my ankle. The injury was caused by Johnny Downie, an ex-Man Utd player. I was getting past the full back and he waited for me and, although you can never be absolutely sure, it seemed like he just deliberately kicked the bottom of my boot and fractured my ankle. He was a lovely player but had slowed up and used to compensate for his lack of pace with a few heavy tackles. I didn't play for six months and the injury effectively terminated my career at Kings Lynn. Syd Gray and Charlie Moore came to see me. I was working at the Home Brewery then and still recuperating from my injury but as soon as I was able to I started training with Marys and signed for the club in 1959.

PETER WILLIAMS IN HIS DERBY DAYS

(Peter Williams Collection)

Little did they know as Peter and the other two of the Saints' new signings made their debut in the Alfreton game in front of a bumper crowd of over three thousand spectators that it would turn out to be a baptism of fire. The home side, showing scant regard for Marys' reputation or status as the previous season's runners-up, raced into an early two-nil lead only for the Saints to pull one back through Keith Moore. When, soon after, Alfreton had a player taken to hospital with a badly cut head it looked as though fate was lending a helping hand in enabling the maroon and golds to weather the storm but buoyed on by the tremendous crowd the newcomers held on for over half an hour whilst a man short. When the casualty eventually rejoined the fray Marys fell apart and ended up being thrashed by six goals to two. It hadn't been the start to the season that everyone had anticipated and for poor Aubrey Southwell the game turned out to be both his first and his last in a Saints' shirt. Albert Moore, brother of Charlie and by now a fellow committeeman, and goalie Len Rockley recall the occasion.

AM : He had a terrible game. He was well past his best and some of the comments from the other committeemen weren't very complimentary.

LR : None of us played well but Aubrey had a shocker and came in for terrible abuse even from some of Marys' committeemen standing on the touchline.

AM : It was obvious that we wouldn't be keeping him. All we needed was someone with a bit of tact to tell him.

If the full back's stay was extremely short-lived, 'Tot' Leverton's fledgling career at Gedling Road would also be stopped in its tracks but for entirely different reasons. The inside-forward was still a very useful player but, now that his full-time career was over, was finding it difficult to accommodate playing with the commitments of his day job.

AM : Something to do with his work, I think. He was having to work weekends.

Disappointingly his stint would last only five matches but in that spell he'd be the catalyst for a major change in the club's ideology. Albert Moore explains.

AM : We were getting overloaded with permit players and you could only play so many in each match, you couldn't play them all. So I said well, if you go the other way [turn professional] you've got yourself covered, there's no argument and you're not looking over your shoulder. 'Tot' was the kingpin but it didn't suit everybody on the committee because you've got to get more money in then.

So, Roland 'Tot' Leverton became the first player ever to sign a professional contract for Arnold St Marys and even though his name didn't appear on the team sheet beyond the first week in September the die had been cast. The Saints were no longer an amateur outfit and another link with the past had been severed.

Unfortunately the upgrade in the club's status didn't bring about an immediate change in their fortune. Seven days after the opening day setback, the last Saturday in August saw Marys back in Derbyshire, this time at Alfreton's near neighbours, champions Belper Town, in front of another big crowd of twelve hundred and fifty. Unusually the game was played at night but the delayed kick-off didn't stop the Saints from tearing straight into the home side, with their trademark fast attacking style causing the opposition all sorts of problems. With Dennis Parr marshalling the visitors' quick tackling defence Belper were looking distinctly uneasy but around the quarter of an hour mark and completely against the run of play the title holders took the lead after right-back Barry Molyneux had conceded a penalty. Marys surged back with right-winger Mick Cripwell particularly prominent and almost grabbed an equaliser when Peter Williams crashed a shot against the crossbar. Belper held their slim lead to the interval and on the resumption the Saints again hurled everything into attack. The champions seemed certain to capitulate but it took until the sixty-fifth minute before 'Tot' Leverton smartly hooked in an equaliser off a post. It looked now as if Marys could go on and win the game but a somewhat fortuitous second goal for the hosts appeared to take the wind from the Saints' sails and their previously solid rearguard was breached twice more, with one of them again coming from the penalty spot. When Mick Cripwell reduced the deficit two minutes from time it was no more than a consolation. As the final whistle blew the maroon and golds must have been wondering how they let the game slip from their grasp; even the local newspaper admitted that Belper were lucky to come out on top and that the two penalties had proved crucial.

No points, ten goals conceded, and next to bottom in the table hadn't quite been the start that Marys' players and officials had been hoping for and the fixture list over the next ten days didn't look too inviting either; three matches, all on the road, culminating in the replayed Notts Senior Cup Final at Meadow Lane. In contrast to the previous season when the teamsheet hardly ever differed from match to match, changes were required to try and halt the slump and veteran Ron Hinson was brought back at right half with the returning John Pike taking over at inside-left. The impact was immediate with a four-two victory being recorded in midweek up at Ollerton Colliery followed by a win the following Saturday by the same score against newcomers Gresley Rovers. At least the Saints headed for their cup final clash with Retford Town better in form and spirit than would have been the case a week earlier.

The replay had originally been set to take place before the start of the season but had had to be put back until the first Monday in September and not surprisingly both sides showed a number of changes from the first game back in May. Retford's team included three new faces but Marys had no less than five players appearing this time around who didn't play at Sutton; Ron Hinson and four close season signings, three of whom, Peter Williams, 'Tot' Leverton, and John Pike, have already been mentioned. The fourth addition to the Saints' squad was left-back Norman Burton who had returned to the club following a year's spell with Gedling Colliery and had replaced the unfortunate Aubrey Southwell after the Alfreton debacle. Ironically Norman had actually played for Gedling in the two Senior Cup Semi-Final matches against Marys and under normal circumstances would have been ineligible to take any further part in the competition. Fortunately for once the Notts FA bent their own rules regarding cup-tied players.

As the two teams took to the field, the beautiful summer weather that had seen the temperature at Forest's weekend match at Blackpool reach seventy degrees in the shade was still holding up so maybe it was the heat or possibly the glaring evening sun that caused the game to get off to a most sensational start. The Yorkshire League champions launched an attack up the left straight from the kick-off. A couple of touches later and the ball was crossed deep into the Saints' penalty area. Inexplicably one of the maroon and golds' defenders, possibly blinded by the light, struck the ball with his hands and after a mere ten seconds of play the referee had no option but to award a penalty, gleefully converted by the opposition. The only upside as Marys' players trudged back to the halfway line was that there were still eighty nine and a half minutes left in the game to stage a fightback.

Unfortunately the Shamrocks pressed home their early advantage and added a second, courtesy of a thirty yard drive, on the twenty five minute mark. To the Saints' credit, however, there was no lack of belief and just before the break Ray Wilkinson equalised with a header from a beautiful cross from Peter Williams. In fact following the change round Marys really showed their paces and stormed the Retford goal, with only a couple of brilliant saves from the opposition keeper and some last ditch defending keeping the North Notts side's lead intact. Soon after it looked as though the maroon and golds' relentless attacking had paid dividends as Sid Thompson lashed in a free kick from just outside the area. Fans and players alike thought the goal was good but the referee was of a different opinion. Apparently the man in black had signalled that the free kick was of an indirect nature and as a result the scoreline remained two-one to Retford. The game turned on this incident and now it was Marys who had to weather the storm. Regrettably they didn't do the job as well as their opponents had and conceded a crucial third goal without being able to add to their own tally. In the final analysis the team had acquitted themselves admirably in their first ever Senior Cup Final. The three-one defeat was by no means a disgrace and over the two ties the Saints had more than matched their higher ranking counterparts, creating, especially in the first match, enough good chances to seal a victory. There was certainly no sign of despondency in the camp as the attention now switched back to the league campaign and the prospect of finally getting to play at Gedling Road for the first time this season.

Not far up the hill from the ground another facility capable of hosting hundreds of people was going to be used for the first time too the very next day. It was the Arnold County High School, a grammar by another name, built to accommodate the baby boomers who had now begun to reach secondary school age and the place where I expected to be in a year's time if I passed my eleven-plus examinations. The school wasn't officially opened until around three months later when the High Commissioner of India, Mrs V L Pandit, was invited to do the ribbon-cutting honours. As it happened, this esteemed lady would be only the first of a number of high profile females who would be making an appearance in the town over the next couple of years.

The visitors to KGV on the second Saturday of September were the rather more mundane players of Ilkeston Town, and the fare served up by both teams was about as exciting as the speeches would have been to the kids at the school's inauguration. The game ended in a goalless stalemate, a rare scoreline at the time. In fact, it was the very first occasion that Marys had failed to score since their elevation to the top division of the Central Alliance and ended a tremendous sequence of sixty seven games in which they'd hit the target. Reaction to this lack of goals was surprisingly swift and quite brutal in its way with only the wingers Mick Cripwell and Peter Williams retaining their places in the attack. For the Tuesday night visit of champions Belper Town three stalwarts from the previous season's ultra successful forward line returned to the side; 'Piddy' Smith and Colin Collindridge for their first games of the campaign and Geoff Parr for only his second. The casualties were Dennis Day, Ray Wilkinson, and John Pike and in John and Ray's case it signalled the beginning of the end of their careers with the Saints; they would only make five more appearances between them and neither would play for the club beyond the end of the year.

If the pressure was on their replacements to justify their inclusion it didn't seem to affect their performances although for the first half hour it was Belper who were in the ascendancy. Despite the bus carrying a number of the visitors' players to the game colliding with a lorry *en route* and causing the kick-off to be delayed by twelve minutes, the Nailers displayed championship winning form and pegged Marys back in their own half. Their incessant attacking saw them go close on a number of occasions before they finally took the lead in slightly fortuitous circumstances. Left back Norman Burton handled the ball on the edge of the box and then had to watch helplessly as the resultant free kick ricocheted off him past Len Rockley in goal. Stung into action the Saints themselves went close when Geoff Parr flashed a shot across goal that had the keeper beaten but just missed the target and then a fine save denied 'Piddy' Smith what looked like a certain goal. Not wishing to be left out of the action Colin Collindridge managed to get himself involved in a tangle with no less than two of the opposition and earned himself a sharp rebuke from the referee for his troubles. The maroon and golds were nothing if not resilient and in the seventieth minute they finally made the breakthrough with Geoff Parr cracking the ball into an empty net following another collision involving Belper players, this time the keeper and two defenders. A minute later Dennis Parr clattered into one of the visiting forwards and whilst the guy was off the field receiving attention brother Geoff took advantage of the extra man and scored his second, and what proved to be the winner, with a flashing header from a corner kick.

If Marys had had to weather the storm in that particular game they had no such problems the following Saturday when the same eleven players travelled the short distance over to Kimberley and trounced the home side five-one with Geoff Parr again amongst the goalscorers. It was a pity then that the recent improvement in results couldn't be maintained when Stamford visited Gedling Road the following week in the first round of the league cup. The Lincolnshire side played in the Southern Section of the Central Alliance's top tier and it was the first ever meeting between the two sides. In the previous campaign the Saints' fantastic run in the competition had been achieved at the expense of teams from the southern division and they had only fallen at the semi-final stage to another of them in the form of Rushden Town. Now it was the Daniels' turn to prevent Marys from progressing any further. Despite taking an early lead through a Mick Cripwell penalty the Saints turned in a below-par performance and two goals from the visitors consigned the maroon and golds to an unexpected defeat.

On being surprisingly knocked out of the competition in the first round in 1987 Boris Becker, winner of Wimbledon for the previous two years, famously put things in perspective by saying 'I lost a tennis match, nobody died'. Unfortunately, the same day that Marys were dumped out of the league cup at the first hurdle by Stamford, two sportsmen in other parts of the country did lose their lives. Racing driver John Townend was killed at Goodwood when his Lotus-Climax struck the bank at Lavant Corner and overturned and jockey 'Manny' Mercer was fatally injured when he was unseated and thrown from his mount, Priddy Fair, at Ascot. Happily, one death in any sport is now a rarity, let alone two in one day.

As the season moved into October the Saints settled into a home and away pattern of league games and with four games scheduled against colliery sides they had ample opportunity to put the setback in the cup squarely behind them. So it proved with Langwith, Ollerton, and Shirebrook all being seen off in some style and only Creswell pushing Marys' hard as the maroon and golds edged a tight contest one-nil. One other match-up in the month promised to be a tough task too, but as this time Heanor Town were the opponents it was only to be expected. The Derbyshire side were second in the league behind Alfreton, with fourteen points out of a possible sixteen and an impressive goals differential of thirty one against eight. In fact the fixture was billed as a 'needle game' and a degree of incredulity was expressed when no official linesmen were appointed for the clash at Gedling Road. In the event each club had to nominate a guy to do the job and Heanor's twelfth man, ex-Forest star Tommy Capel and only serving that role because he was carrying a slight knock, was given the job.

The glorious summer weather had continued well into the middle of the month but it had certainly taken a turn for the worse now and heavy rain had made both the ground and the ball extremely greasy. Disappointingly for the home fans it was Heanor who mastered the difficult conditions better and went ahead as early as the fifth minute. Exchanges were even up to the break and a further fifteen minutes beyond it but just past the hour mark Sid Thompson fired in a free-kick from outside the penalty area and a minute later Peter Williams headed Marys into the lead from a right-wing cross. The expected fight back from the visitors failed to produce a further goal and the Saints took both valuable points with their two-one victory.

The five straight wins in October stretched Marys' unbeaten run to ten league games and the nineteen points they picked up in the process catapulted them back up the table where they joined the usual suspects in the hunt for the title.

	P	W	D	L	F	A	P
Alfreton Town	12	10	0	2	35	13	20
Arnold St Marys	**12**	**9**	**1**	**2**	**34**	**18**	**19**
Heanor Town	9	7	0	2	32	10	14
Belper Town	10	6	2	2	33	20	14
Matlock Town	7	5	2	0	26	9	12

Whilst the Saints had been moving back into contention in the Central Alliance, Harold Macmillan had resumed his role as Prime Minister as he led the Conservative Party in a general election for the first time. The Tories were re-elected for a third successive term with a huge majority and their success was a triumph for the unflappable Macmillan who, although patrician in style, had managed to appeal to a broad cross section of the electorate. Earlier in his tenure many observers had felt that the Prime Minister's demeanour as an Edwardian aristocrat was somewhat out of tune with the times but help in this direction, in the form of what might today be called a personality makeover, had come from an unlikely source. Victor 'Vicky' Weisz was a member of the Labour Party and the lead political cartoonist of the News Chronicle and in November 1958 the first of a series of his works depicting Macmillan as 'Supermac', a spoof on Superman, had appeared in print. The intention had been to ridicule the Prime Minister but the opposite happened and the moniker ended up being used by the general public in far more affectionate terms than the artist could ever have imagined.

In his statement thanking the nation for returning him to power he stressed the need to work towards world peace but in a dig against the opposition's pre-election tactics he also talked about the benefits of unity over division. He was, of course, referring to the Labour Party's predictable if rather wearying playing of the 'class card' but I reckon he may have been slightly optimistic when he commented: "I think the class war is now obsolete". Almost fifty years later the Conservative candidate at the Crewe and Nantwich by-election would be targeted by Labour as a 'Tory toff', an outsider from a privileged background unable to relate to ordinary voters. The campaign involved Labour activists in tail-coats and top hats shadowing the opposition nominee and distributing leaflets referring to his 'mansion' and his wealth. It later transpired that his home was only fifteen miles from his constituency whilst his Labour opponent lived in Wales in a house larger than his. I suppose all is fair in love, war, and politics but when he made his comments 'Supermac' couldn't possibly have foreseen the divisions in the country that would one day be caused, directly or indirectly, by the presence at the head of government of the new female MP for Finchley, a certain Margaret Thatcher.

Unlike the resolve of the 'Iron Lady', both the weather and Marys' form as November got underway were definitely for turning. Late summer sunshine and autumnal rain had given way to ominous mists and as the Saints took the field at Heanor in the return game between the two sides, fog shrouded the ground. There'd been nothing much to choose between the teams a fortnight previously but in the re-match the hosts, with Tommy Capel back at inside-left, had by far the majority of the play. Colin Collindridge was unfortunate to see a shot come back off the post but it was no surprise when the home side took the lead and then added two more after the break. The maroon and golds' much vaunted attack had no luck in front of goal and the three-nil defeat didn't augur too well for the following week's top of the table clash at KGV with leaders Alfreton Town.

Unlike the earlier occasion when they'd drawn a blank against Ilkeston there were no changes to the forward line this time and the committee's faith was rewarded with a much improved performance from not just the front line but the whole team as well. Dennis Day got the home side off to the best possible start with a goal after five minutes and also provided the chance for Colin Collindridge to double the lead in the last minute of the half. At two-nil Marys looked well set to avenge their opening day thrashing but the second half was a different story altogether. Alfreton's side contained no less than five players who at varying points in the future would wear the maroon and gold and it was one of them, Brian Cunningham, who was largely instrumental in helping the visitors claw their way back into the game. Brian, brother of John and Ken, one of Arnold's most prominent footballing families of the fifties, had already played for the Saints, and Rovers too, and had arrived at Alfreton following spells with Ransome and Marles and Stamford. Now he was about to remind one of his old clubs exactly what they were missing and with the help of a penalty got his name on the scoresheet twice as the Reds showed why they were sitting in top spot. Both sides scored again and each had chances to seal victory but in the end a three-all draw was a very fair conclusion to what had been an intriguing battle.

Unusually, Marys were fixtureless for the next two weeks and thus ended up adding only a single point to their season's tally during November, with a resultant slide down to fourth in the table, the same position occupied at the time in Division Four, almost unbelievably, by the permanently underperforming Magpies. I'd watched in some amazement as a discernible improvement in form and results had seen them climb steadily from their customary place in the bottom half of the table to the periphery of the promotion places. It was giddy stuff, built around an invincibility at The Lane that had seen them win seven straight home games with a goals aggregate of twenty against three. When Millwall arrived at the beginning of the month the visitors had yet to be beaten this season and had equalled Liverpool's post-war record of going their opening nineteen games without defeat. Over sixteen thousand were in attendance for the eagerly anticipated top of the table clash but with Notts treating their fans to another convincing display the Lions were tamed without too much difficulty. A late goal flattered them and they were beaten far more comprehensively than the two-one scoreline indicated. However, even as we picked our way happily through the flotsam and jetsam of the Cattle Market there was always the nagging doubt, as real in a County fan's possessions as his flask, rattle, and match day programme, that this level of success, phenomenal by recent standards, couldn't continue. It didn't. The next time we reconvened in our usual places normal service was rudely resumed. Bath City were the opposition in the second round of the FA Cup and despite all stand seats being sold out and nearly twenty six thousand of us roaring the Magpies on, the visitors weathered the storm, nicked a goal straight after half time and hung on for a well deserved victory. It was the best performance by a non-league side that day but it could hardly be classed as a giant killing. Bath would end up as Southern League champions and Notts? Well Notts were Notts, after all.

If the coaches carrying the non-leaguers and their considerable number of supporters had fancied coming to Nottingham the long way round they could have headed east along the A4 to London and then sampled the delights of the newly opened M1 as they headed north. They would have had to be wary of sightseers liberally dotted around the place because the novelty of this first extensive stretch of proper motorway hadn't yet worn off. Opened less than a month earlier its completion marked the climax of a decade of rapid growth in motoring which had seen the number of private cars and vans in Britain more than double to around the five million mark. The demand had been boosted back in August by the arrival in the country's showrooms of the 'Mini'. The revolutionary design by Alec Issigonis ensured that the new addition, initially marketed under two British Motor Corporation marques as the Austin Seven and Morris Mini-Minor, would be granted 'iconic' status in later years. In fact the very first car I ever owned was an Austin Seven 'Mini' and it remained in the family for over twenty five years. Considering that it was already seven or eight years old when I first acquired it no-one could complain about its durability. Admittedly, by the time it was sold it had required a clutch change, a new steering column, had had a complete re-spray, seen off the original engine, two sub-frames, and goodness knows how many tyres, and had needed the kiss of life at the roadside on more than one occasion.

The 'Mini' wasn't the only innovation that November. The Queen's head appeared on bank notes for the first time and two Scottish airports, Renfrew and Prestwick, became the first in the UK in offering duty-free goods for sale. The latter was in the news again only a few months later when the plane carrying Sergeant Elvis Presley, returning from his two year stint with the US Army in West Germany, touched down at Prestwick to refuel and provided the King of Rock 'n' Roll with what was allegedly his only ever visit to British soil. Towards the end of the year Elvis would have a massive number one hit with 'It's Now or Never' and for the few privileged fans who'd got wind of the King's fleeting stay, it probably was.

As the football season entered December it might not quite have been make or break time for Marys but with five league games coming up before the ringing in of the sixties it would be a crucial period nevertheless. The first of the matches had South Normanton as visitors to Gedling Road and the Saints saw them off without too much difficulty. Geoff Parr and Colin Collindridge, with a couple, were the scorers in a comprehensive three-nil victory. The following week the maroon and golds headed off to the Manor Ground at Ilkeston for what looked like a far more challenging proposition. In front of just under nine hundred spectators early exchanges were pretty even with both goals having narrow escapes but as the game went on Marys were looking decidedly sluggish. Even after the break and with the slope in their favour they couldn't find a way past the Robins' rearguard. With less than fifteen minutes left and the score still goalless the game looked to be heading the way of the previous encounter between the two sides back in September but with Len Rockley the busier of the two keepers Ilkeston always looked the more likely to nick a goal. It was, therefore, no surprise when the home side went ahead in the seventy seventh minute but it was a disappointment when they added a decisive second soon after.

If the final scoreline of two-nil flattered the opposition slightly, there was no disguising the below par performance of the Saints, and the following week they showed only a minor improvement in form when they struggled to dispose of the youngsters of Nottingham Forest's A team by the odd goal in three. The final two fixtures of the year, and the decade, were back to back Christmas fixtures against Wilmorton and Alvaston, who were having a decent season themselves and were just one place below Marys in the table with a superior points to games ratio. The games looked to be close on paper and the reality wasn't any different. The Saints edged the first match over at Derby one-nil and then gained another valuable point in the return in a one-all draw. The year end had been a bit of a struggle but seven points from December's five matches was hardly a disaster and the club were now in third spot and still well in contention for honours.

The Magpies meanwhile had also secured the same position in their own division thanks to four points from their two holiday fixtures with Rochdale. The Boxing Day encounter would probably have attracted more than the fifteen thousand spectators who assembled at The Lane had it not been for the fact that County had showed worrying signs of returning to type with four consecutive defeats. The only mitigating factor was that one of these was the game against Bath and the other three had all been on the road, so the long unbeaten home record in the league was still intact.

Because it was Christmas it was back to my Nan's in good heart for a continuation of festivities and the copious consumption of food and drink around the card table. Granddad Barnes was still boycotting any game that involved ha'pennies and a spot of pressure, preferring a snooze in the back room in front of the blazing fire made from the coal that he'd helped bring up from the pitface. For us kids it would be a watching brief accompanied by a fizzy drink and some oranges and lemons, the sugared jelly kind that we only ever saw at this time of year along with Turkish delight, dates, and sugared almonds.

The pop would invariably be a bottle of Apollo, produced down the road at the Home Brewery, and which in my formative years, and those of nearly all my mates, was more a constant companion than a casual acquaintance. I'm not quite sure why the Brewery gave its soft drinks products that title but there was no mistaking its place in the locality as it was emblazoned on buildings at the Daybrook site in letters big enough to be seen from an elevated position for miles around. And it was also to be found on the shelves of numerous shops and beer-offs in town.

Ah, a 'beer-off'. Now there's a word; or two. I don't think that I've ever heard my own kids, born in the seventies, use the term, not even once, but it was a much repeated reference point back in the fifties. Of course it was derived from the longer phrase 'beer being sold off licence', which begat the more widespread derivative 'off licence', but we always knew it as a 'beer-off'. Maybe it was a Nottingham thing.

One thing for sure was that they were about the only places open on a Sunday, other than the 'Arcadia Confectionery & Tobacco Stores', and if you were a kid desperate for a drink or a snack, they were the places for you. Usually I would roll up at our nearest one with my Dad. It was located at the junction of Ravenswood Road and Coppice Road and smelled a little bit like a tap room of any of Arnold's numerous pubs, which wasn't surprising because, unlike its modern equivalent, it sold beers and ales on draught. Many's the time I've seen someone come in with a large jug and ask for it to be filled with a couple of pints.

My preferences however were strictly non-alcoholic, but equally as addictive, and actually the choice of pop back then was quite diverse. Apart from Apollo, there was Corona and Kia-Ora, with its memorable TV advert and its punch line 'A-u-r-o-r-a!! Don't forget the Kia-Ora!', Tizer and Vimto and the usual lemonade and orangeade and, I think, cherryade. Available too was the disgusting dandelion and burdock, which I avoided like the plague, but my own two all-time favourites were pineappleade, or maybe it was called pineapple crush, and, best of all, the evocatively titled American Cream Soda.

Now this great variety of fizzy stuff needed something to wash down, and there the choice was rather more limited. Nuts apart, I think it was a toss-up between a packet of Smiths crisps and a bag of Nibb-its. There were no Quavers, Doritos, Hula Hoops and Kettle Chips and the rest back then and, as to the crisps, it wasn't a matter of having to choose between Sour Cream and Chive or Sweet Chilli, it was more a case of whether to have them salted or not. Even then the decision wasn't necessarily made in the beer-off because all the packets were the same and the crisps themselves started off as 'plain', but deep inside the bag was a large pinch of salt encased in a little blue paper twist. The crucial question, to salt or not to salt, was thus left to the individual.

Of course sometimes, given the vagaries of early production process automation, there'd be two little blue twists in the packet and on other occasions none. Often the salt would be soggy and refuse to disperse itself evenly, leaving many an unwitting customer spitting out that one crisp to which a disproportionate amount of sodium chloride had become attached. This unfortunate occurrence is not to be confused with the deliberate act of knowingly consuming the salt, blue bag and all, which any number of my contemporaries would routinely do as a dare, and I kiddeth not.

Being the nineteen fifties, there were no warnings on food packaging, no traffic lights and dietary information to inform and confuse, no list of contents in five different languages, and certainly no nonsense like the bags of pistachios and the like that carry the message: 'this product contains nuts'.

Whilst it was obvious to all and sundry what raw material Smiths' finest were made from, the exact ingredients of the Nibb-it were apparently shrouded in secrecy. Which was probably for the best considering that only a few years ago I was told by someone 'in the know' that if I'd been aware of exactly what went into them I would have stuck to eating crisps. This revelation came about because my informant either worked in the factory making them or knew someone who did, which was highly plausible since they were produced out of an old building on Morley Street.

Before that, according to my feverish research into this much revered product, the factory was located at the top of Cavendish Street at its junction with Furlong Street, and apparently it and its products were variously referred to as Cruickshanks, Crooky Crisps, or Champion Crisps. Personally, I remained faithful to plain old Smiths when it came to a crisp, but I did love my Nibb-its. Nor was it only their indefinable taste, they were fun too, especially when they stayed glued to your tongue, amazingly defying gravity as you stuck it out of your mouth in the direction of your mates.

Come to think of it, they would have remained there for ages too if they hadn't been dislodged by the usual generous swig from a communal bottle of Home Brewery's finest mineral water. Whilst we wouldn't have realised it at the time, Nibb-its and Apollo were being produced, for our benefit, mere yards from each other in delightful Daybrook. It was kids' food heaven, right on our own doorstep.

When the fifties finally said their farewell and the new decade dawned, the year wasn't even two days old when I became reacquainted with paradise in a location not normally associated with ecstatic episodes. Back down at Meadow Lane for what we all hoped would be a continuation of County's recent good home form I don't think that any of us were quite ready for what unfolded over the next ninety minutes. Crystal Palace were the visitors, cocky metropolitans who'd entertained the crowd with a novel five minute six-a-side game before the start and who were rewarded for their progressive behaviour by two old fashioned strikes from the Magpies inside the first quarter of an hour. The Londoners weren't actually that bad an outfit and pulled a goal back in what was proving to be the most enterprising of matches. Notts restored their two goal lead after twenty-one minutes, kept it until the break, and then proceeded to add a fourth, fifth, sixth, and incredibly a seventh in front of their long suffering and still not daring to believe what they were seeing fans. As the last goal went in with only a minute to go hundreds of the younger members of the crowd down on the terraces could control their enthusiasm no longer and swarmed onto the pitch. It took some time before police and the players managed to usher them back into their enclosures where they stayed for all of a minute before repeating the exercise at the final whistle. It was the Magpies' eleventh straight home win and broke the previous record which had stood since Queen Victoria was on the throne. The Football Post summed it up by declaring that 'it was a new generation cheering a new Notts County for a magnificent start to a New Year.' I couldn't help but think that the sixties already had a completely different feel to the one that preceded it, especially when the government announced curbs on the sale of pep pills. To think that less than six years previously it had been basic foodstuffs that had been on ration.

Of course Marys' nineteen fifties had, by and large, been nothing but a long success story, but the panache they normally showed had been conspicuous by its absence as the decade had drawn to a close. Happily, whilst the Magpies were laying into Palace, so the Saints were doing the same to their own visitors Gresley Rovers, admittedly after a first forty five minutes where an early goal by the home side was followed by centre-half Dennis Parr having to make two last ditch clearances off his own goal line and the Derbyshire side scorning a chance from the penalty spot. Having been let off the hook the maroon and golds capitalised on their good fortune and scored three times after the break to win four-one. When they travelled to South Normanton the following week and went nap in a five-three victory, with Mick Cripwell and Peter Williams scoring in both matches, it looked as though Marys had definitely shaken off their December sluggishness.

Truth was they needed to have done because the next two games were both against Matlock Town and a glance at the top of the league table showed how significant the outcome of the clashes would be. As can be seen the Saints' next opponents had only dropped four points all season. They'd also been successful in the FA Cup, reaching the First Round Proper for the first time in their history, and were being talked about as favourites for this season's Central Alliance title. There were a couple of caveats however. Firstly, because of their cup exploits they had fallen behind in their league fixtures, and secondly, as well as the upcoming games against Marys they still had to meet Alfreton, Belper, Heanor, and Ilkeston twice each, ten tough matches that would show whether they were, indeed, championship material.

	P	W	D	L	F	A	P
Alfreton Town	20	15	2	3	73	25	32
Arnold St Marys	**21**	**14**	**3**	**4**	**53**	**32**	**31**
Belper Town	20	13	4	3	79	39	30
Heanor Town	19	13	0	6	58	26	26
Matlock Town	14	11	2	1	45	17	24

No matter how brilliant the weather in the preceding summer, Gedling Road was usually heavy going by the depths of winter and this mid-January was no different. Even so, straight from the kick off Marys made light of the difficult conditions and had much the better of the opening skirmishes, twice bringing fine saves from the opposition goalie. After that brief flurry exchanges were even with few chances being created and it looked as though a single goal might be enough to settle the outcome. When it came, around the hour mark, it unfortunately fell to Matlock. The goal, a header, came from a corner, a tactic that had looked the most likely to yield success when a couple of similar chances created by the away side had been narrowly off target. The Saints couldn't find a way back into the game and it ended in a disappointing one-nil defeat, their first of the season at home in the league.

The following week saw Marys without a fixture and so they'd had to kick their heels for a fortnight before having the chance to avenge the defeat over at Matlock on the last Saturday of the month. The heavens had remained open and not surprisingly, given its location at the foot of some decent sized hills, Causeway Lane was waterlogged in places and only just about playable, which is more than can be said for KGV where poor old Rovers had their second consecutive match called off because of its unfit state.

With left half Sid Thompson missing for the only time this season and the Saints' side showing four changes from the first encounter it was the home side who had much the better of the early play, twice going perilously close for Marys' comfort. The visitors were struggling with both the conditions and the opposition and it was no surprise when they went behind after a quarter of an hour. To make matters worse the deficit was doubled a couple of minutes later and the maroon and golds had all on to stay in the game. Fortunately, inspired by Colin Collindridge, they fought their way back into contention and a number of dangerous raids ended with the ex-Forest man getting a goal back with a header seven minutes before the break.

With the pitch cutting up badly the score remained locked at two-one but with less than ten minutes to go, and with the Saints pressing hard for a crucial equaliser, it was Matlock who made the breakthrough. When, only three minutes later, the home side added a fourth the game was up for Marys. As the visitors' mud-laden players trooped off the field at the final whistle, the chances of them claiming the championship had been dealt a severe blow. It would need an incredibly successful run-in and a collapse by Matlock to put the maroon and golds in with a shout but, given the Derbyshire side's domination in the last two games, it was an improbable scenario.

Two days later and over on the other side of the Atlantic in the deep south of the United States another unlikely event was taking place, one that would, in the scheme of things, ultimately change the attitudes of millions. Much like they might do on any lunch break, four black students went to the Woolworths store in Greensboro, North Carolina. At a time when segregation was still the norm in many public places they would have been expected to take the place allotted for them at the stand and eat section of the lunch counter. This day however they went to the area where chairs and stools were provided for whites. It was a pivotal moment in the non-violent Civil Rights Movement and although they were still refused service they were allowed to stay and register their protest. The next day there were around thirty activists at the store and the following day some three hundred. Many people in the north weren't totally aware of the extent of segregation in their own country and sit-ins became a powerful publicity tool in the campaign to bring about a fairer society.

Another forty eight hours later in the deep south of another continent, the British Prime Minister Harold Macmillan was entreating members of the white South African parliament to embrace the wind of change sweeping through their neighbouring countries. Unfortunately the policy of promoting racial equality didn't go down too well with the Afrikaner hosts whose determination to stick to the *apartheid* laws meant that it would be around a third of a century before they were eventually dismantled. Condemnation from the wider world, typified by a big row at the Commonwealth Conference a few months later, only served to stiffen the resolve of those in power to maintain the *status quo*.

Back in Arnold, February did see a significant change in the slightly more parochial setting of an upstairs room at the Flying Horse pub where Marys' weekly committee meeting took place. Although the Saints had taken the first tentative steps towards professionalism, they still operated the club without a manager, a guy who assumed sole responsibility for matters on the field of play. First item on the agenda was that of team selection. Until then, this had been the responsibility of the committee as a whole but with no less than fourteen members the process was unwieldy and time consuming. The response to the proposal that the process be improved by reducing the numbers entitled to cast a vote didn't quite go the whole hog and end up with a slimmed down selection committee as such. In its place came a compromise of sorts; from now on only those members who'd attended the previous match would be able to influence the composition of the team in the next one. In theory of course there could still be fourteen guys deciding who'd be in goal, play at right-back and so on, and this indecision seemed to indicate that the club still hadn't yet become quite as progressive as it appeared. Albert Moore was just beginning his long stint as a key mover and shaker at the club and could see that change was necessary. However, I still think he was being a little bit harsh when he summed up the position at the time.

AM : We were a tuppenny ha'penny club you might say.

Of course none would be working harder than Albert and his brother Charlie when it came to taking Marys forward. To that end they were always looking to bring in new players and although Charlie and Syd Gray did most of the scouting, Albert was more often than not roped in to help.

AM : Charlie used to say "Go and have a look at so and so". I used to go and he'd say "What do you think?" "No bloody good" I'd tell him. He said "That's what I thought". I said "What did you send me for then?" He said "Two opinions are better than one!"

Centre forward Billy England, who'd made his debut in the game at Matlock, was the Saints' latest acquisition, but a second opinion wasn't required when it came to getting his signature on a form. He'd let everyone know what he could do when he'd scored twice for Alfreton back on the opening day of the season when Marys were on the end of that six-two drubbing.

BE : I'd joined Alfreton from Stamford after the merger. They had a new ground and a new stand and the set-up was great. There were over three thousand at the game and I'd just come back from Lloret de Mar when it was still a nice place. I had a tan and felt like a million dollars. I remember my first goal was an absolute cracker. Our right winger blasted a cross over and as I was quite quick I just managed to get a touch on the ball and it flew straight over the goalkeeper's head. Someone told me afterwards that at Arnold's committee meeting they kept going on about "this Billy England", saying that "he ran us off the park".

Billy had obviously made a good impression on 'Kegga' and the rest but they probably would also have known about his previous exploits with Stamford and before that Eastwood Town where he'd once scored an incredible ten goals in one match against Bilsthorpe Colliery. They would also probably have been aware that he was an excellent table tennis player too and had played, aged seventeen, for England against Sweden where he had come up against Bjorn Borg's father Rune. He'd also won the Daily Mirror Men's Championship in 1953, with Ann Haydon, later to become Wimbledon Lawn Tennis champion under her married name of Ann Jones, taking the women's event. Over twelve thousand players had competed over many months for the chance of a finals night appearance with the earlier rounds played on a regional basis. The quarter finals were staged at Birmingham but the climax of the competition was played out at the famous rotunda, the Royal Albert Hall, in front of six thousand spectators. The event was televised with the semi-finals taking place in the afternoon and the finals in the evening. To top off a wonderful occasion accommodation was provided at the Daily Mirror's expense at the Russell Hotel.

Whilst the Town Ground at Alfreton, no matter how modern its facilities, could hardly compare with the Royal Albert Hall, Billy settled down well in his new surroundings and soon took his goal tally into double figures. There was, however, one aspect to the running of the club that had caused him some consternation.

BE : I couldn't understand why the right-back, a great player, was dropped after two games. Then, soon after, another good player was dropped. I asked left-back Vince Howard and I found out that there were sixty committee members picking the team in the Miners' Welfare! Of course each had got his own favourites and I thought they'll come round to me eventually!

It appeared, then, that Marys weren't the only ones with a top heavy committee but having known of the Saints' interest, Billy decided to jump before he got pushed and in doing so unwittingly began an exodus of Alfreton players over to Gedling Road.

Apart from the defeat on his debut, his arrival coincided with a marked improvement in the maroon and golds' form and he notched a hat-trick and made another in only his third outing in the four-one victory over the students of Nottingham University in the Quarter Final of the Notts Senior Cup. In their only other two fixtures in February, both league games, Marys completed relatively easy wins but even so it was news from elsewhere that received as much attention as these victories. Matlock, champions elect in most people's reckoning, at least at the start of the month, had suddenly hit a really bad patch, losing four straight games of which three were in the league.

All of a sudden the race for the title had opened up and although the Saints had only three games in March they won them all, scoring twelve times without reply. In truth they were being helped by a less than taxing fixture list; following the setback at Matlock none of their opponents in the run-in figured in the top six and they had a great chance of keeping the pressure on the leading pack. They weren't behind in their matches either and with only the Notts Senior Cup as a distraction, even the Football Post had recognised the possibilities, leading its Central Alliance news and views page with the headline 'ST MARYS FANCIED OUTSIDERS FOR HONOURS'.

Whilst the Saints were still quite rightly classed as outsiders, down at Meadow Lane second placed County were one of the favourites for a promotion spot in Division Four. In a run of form that had continued unabated since before Christmas, the Magpies were unbeaten in ten games and had extended their run of consecutive home victories to fourteen. Even those loyal fans with the deepest of rose-tinted glasses knew that the bubble had to burst and at the beginning of March it did. Lowly Doncaster Rovers were the visitors and despite Notts hitting the target on three occasions, the Maggies' defence had a particularly dismal afternoon and conceded four. It was a far cry from the first meeting between the two sides this season up at the Yorkshire side's Belle Vue ground, reputed at the time to be home to the largest pitch and best playing surface in the whole of the Football League. With Donny being easily accessible I'd been taken to the game and must admit to being impressed, especially when County hammered their hosts four-nil with centre-forward Stan Newsham grabbing a hat-trick. When Notts followed up the defeat by Rovers with another at mid-table Northampton Stan lost his place in the team, this despite being Notts' leading scorer with twenty four goals. His place was taken by a tall, raw-boned eighteen year old from Derby by the name of Tony Hateley and although his arrival didn't quite coincide with a return to winning ways, he did manage the only goal on his debut, a one-all draw at home to Torquay. As befits a die-hard County fanatic just eleven years of age, I can always say I was there at the start of his career.

March hadn't been without incident off the field either, with Harold Macmillan leading the way by reaching agreement with the USA on a nuclear test ban treaty to be put to the USSR. If that announcement was received with a healthy dose of scepticism it might also have come as a bit of a surprise to hear talk of Britain and France developing a supersonic airliner together. Plans for a Thames flood barrier, on the other hand, seemed far more feasible.

A bit nearer home a well known local gentleman, Mr Harold Cave, had his fifteen minutes of fame courtesy of the ITV quiz programme 'For Love or Money'. A garage owner on the site of the current Arnold Tyres business on the Charles Street and Nottingham Road corner of the Bottom Rec, Harold was also the Secretary of the Arnold and District Old People's Welfare Centre opposite and did an inordinate amount of work on their behalf. He proved to be a popular and successful contestant, even being called back by 'popular demand' having previously been disqualified on a nit-picking technicality, and donated all his prize money and prizes that he'd won to his favourite cause. At a value of over six hundred pounds it was very well received by the town's senior citizens.

It would certainly have come in very handy at KGV where Marys, completely independent of co-tenants Rovers, were making tentative enquiries of the Arnold Urban District Council as to the possibility of them building the new stand at Gedling Road for the club. The Council Surveyor was tasked with the job of providing an estimate of the cost and in April came back with a figure of two and a half thousand pounds. It was a figure way beyond the means of either club and with the Saints' ambition not being entirely shared by their nearest neighbours there was no chance of a combined fund-raising effort either. As a kind of compromise, the Council wrote to both clubs asking whether, if the cost of the stand came out the public purse, they would be prepared to pay a charge of six pounds per match for the use of the ground and the stand. Considering that the clubs' current annual rent was twenty five pounds each, a sum that was actually down from its original twenty seven pounds ten shillings, the reply was a not unexpected 'thanks, but no thanks'.

Rovers' unwillingness to accept anything other than the *status quo* was probably a reflection of events actually on the pitch where between mid-February and mid-April they contrived to lose nine league matches in a row. I asked 'Franny' Greensmith, one of the red and whites' longest serving players, how he felt at the widening gap in the fortunes of the two clubs.

FG : Well I was coming to the end of my career anyway and it didn't bother me as much as when we were playing each other. It wasn't as if I was going to end up on the committee. When we were at the same level it was different, I was a lot more upset if they ever beat us then.

Of course, at four times in sixteen attempts, that didn't happen too often, but it was still disappointing to think that the great clashes of the past were destined to remain there. Even though Marys' Reserves were in Rovers' division now, their head to head games were no substitute for the tremendous rivalry just two years earlier.

Whilst Rovers' losing sequence was taking place the Saints' non-losing streak showed no signs of coming to an end. Although they unexpectedly dropped a point at Gedling Road against Sutton Town's second string on the first Saturday of April, prompting a headline of 'NO MORE SLIPS, ST MARYS!' in the Football Post, they more than made up for that lapse during the remainder of the run-in with a string of high scoring victories; six against Kimberley, seven against Clay Cross, and ten against Shirebrook, all scored in front of their own fans at Gedling Road. Since the defeat against Matlock Marys had racked up three threes, two fours, two fives, and now the six, seven, and ten for good measure. All the forwards were dipping their bread with Billy England getting three against Clay Cross and Mick Cripwell hitting four of the ten against Shirebrook.

The Saints' good run of form and the excellent performances of a number of the players hadn't gone unnoticed by the bigger clubs and for the local derby against Kimberley, two Football League scouts from a Midlands club were amongst the large crowd in attendance. No-one could have complained about the match, a ten-goal thriller with eight of them coming in the second forty five minutes. Marys finished up winners by six goals to four and whilst one or two of the forwards certainly did their reputations no harm the scouts were probably in no particular hurry to invite any of the two teams' defenders for a trial any time in the near future.

NOT A BARE HEAD IN SIGHT : MARYS v KIMBERLEY TOWN 23 APRIL 1960

(Courtesy Football Post)

When the Saints trounced Shirebrook in their penultimate league game of the season on the following Thursday this latest victory in their superb run had, somewhat improbably, brought them level on points in a four-way tie at the head of the table. Ohly goal average split the sides and despite having given themselves an awful lot of leeway to make up Marys still had a mathematical chance of nicking the title.

	P	W	D	L	F	A	P	GA
Alfreton Town	31	24	2	5	112	41	50	2.73
Matlock Town	31	24	2	5	92	34	50	2.71
Heanor Town	33	25	0	8	102	38	50	2.68
Arnold St Marys	**33**	**23**	**4**	**6**	**102**	**48**	**50**	**2.13**

Their slim chances took a turn for the better when Alfreton began to implode, picking up just one point out of a possible four in their next two games, but with the division's newest side scheduled to finish their season at home against Heanor, there would have to be an improbable combination of results, an avalanche of goals, to put the Saints in with a realistic chance. There was a distinct possibility that goal average could again leave Marys ending up as bridesmaids for the second season in a row so it was therefore fortunate in some ways that the long-time favourites Matlock didn't falter at the death, picking up maximum points from their last three fixtures to claim the title.

On the first Thursday in May and with KGV now turned over to Arnold Cricket Club, the Saints were shunted back up to their original home at Church Lane for their own final game of the season against Creswell Colliery. They edged a one-nil victory to finish a highly respectable third, four points behind the champions and level with Heanor, who'd despatched Alfreton by five goals to two the previous evening.

The only other development that had taken place in the closing stages of the season had been the appearance at right half for the last six matches of coach Noel Simpson. Seeing as they scored twenty six times in his first four games, his prompting from the middle of the field certainly helped his forwards find the net but he was unable to inspire them in their Notts Senior Cup Semi Final against Sutton Town's Midland League eleven. In a thoroughly disappointing performance the Saints were hammered five-nil by their neighbours up the A60 and any hopes of them lifting Nottinghamshire's premier trophy for the first time would have to be put off for another year.

MARYS v SUTTON TOWN : NOTTS SENIOR CUP SEMI FINAL 30 APRIL 1960
Back Row (l to r); B Molyneux, N Burton, L Rockley, N Simpson, D Parr, S Thompson. Front Row; M Cripwell, D Day, W England, C Collindridge, P Williams. Mascot, T Gray.

(Courtesy Football Post)

Despite this disappointment, it had been another excellent season for Marys. Professionalism had been embraced and their on-field reputation as one of the fastest and most attractive non-league teams in the area had been reinforced by many fine performances, home and away. They'd ended the season much the same as they had twelve months earlier with a long unbeaten league run, this time winning ten games out of eleven, drawing the other, and hitting forty nine goals in the process. A little more consistency in mid-season and the Saints might even have claimed the title for themselves. A little more consistency next season and they probably would.

In the Fourth Division Notts were playing out a scenario not entirely unlike that of Marys'. Except in County's case, finishing five points behind the champions Walsall came with the lovely consolation prize of promotion to the Third, and even though they were tied with Torquay United on points, goal average in this particular instance favoured them over the Devonshire side and gave them the runners-up spot. I don't think I'd missed a home game all season and I'd watched as the crowds grew from under ten thousand at the outset to nearly twenty three thousand for the top of the table clash with the Saddlers in the middle of April. It was a bit of a disappointment when only thirteen thousand returned for the final home game but Darlington weren't that attractive a proposition, at least on paper, and promotion had already been guaranteed.

To me it didn't matter, I was in footy heaven. The game turned out to be far livelier than expected, with Notts coming out marginally on top in a nine goal thriller. When the Magpies' first goal went in after just ten minutes it was their one hundredth in the league this season and was the cue for the first, but not the last, pitch invasion of the afternoon. When the hundred and third was registered it set a new record for the League's oldest club. Five years of heartache was completely forgiven and forgotten. County's achievement might not quite have ranked with their nearest neighbours' FA Cup win a year ago, but to me it was vindication of my unswerving support for one of sport's perennial under-achievers. Tony Hateley had scored eight times in ten starts and an Eastwood youngster by the name of Jeffrey Astle had recently signed professional forms. As we made our way back to our car, the Cattle Market had never smelled sweeter.

Like most of my friends at Killisick, my love of football was all consuming but right up until a few months after my fifteenth birthday, I'd never actually get to play in an organised game; not one. I'd played it in every form in every place with every different type of ball since ever I could walk, but a 'proper' match, an official game, had eluded me. The reasons for this were twofold. Firstly there was the small matter of Richard Bonington School not having a pitch of its own. I don't suppose anyone in charge there had thought about playing all of its games away or even getting permission to play on the Top Rec, only a brisk walk away down Calverton Road. Funnily enough we did have inter-class games there but even then we had to carry our own posts with us and they were really only like broom handles stuck in a round flat base. One time we drew eight-all, a low scoring game in those days, and I scored all our goals. The equaliser came with the last kick of the game. I scored directly from a corner, but the referee, sorry teacher, said he wasn't ready so I did it again. The only downside to these sessions was the fact that to get to the ground we had to file past the graveyard of St Marys Church and where on more than the odd occasion and for no apparent reason we were made to wait patiently in line for an inordinate amount of time. Or so it seemed. The second reason for me missing out on organised football came when I progressed to a rugby playing school at the start of the upcoming season, effectively condemning myself to years of the oval-ball game rather than the sport I loved.

Of course, I had played disorganised football ever since I was a toddler, especially from about the age of seven. Living close to the large recreation field on the estate, every waking hour found me playing in some sort of match. All age-groups took part, often as many as fifteen a side, and the games seemed to be almost never-ending. I actually think they might have been if the requirements of food and sleep hadn't interfered with proceedings. Of course the score-lines were always of rugby-style proportions, not that anyone could actually remember exactly what the final tally had been.

On occasions, we also travelled to away matches. Well, travelled might be putting too fine a point on it, as all it entailed was probably a half-mile trek by a motley collection of young kids to the next open space, grassed or not, where we would take on the local outfit. One day we drew two-all against a bunch of smelly bruisers on a postage stamp size bit of land. It was so low scoring because there were more than twenty of us on the equivalent of a five-a-side pitch, and the 'ball' was a small stone; all very exciting, and a very far cry from the organised academies and age-group teams that proliferate today.

Yet I often wonder who had the better deal. When I look at organised games today between kids as young as nine, I feel that much of the spontaneity and improvisation that we took for granted has all but disappeared. Some of these kids have got boots with their own names on, for goodness sake. Whatever was wrong with those Co-op specials endorsed by the great Sir Stanley Matthews? What of the colours too? Now there are ten year olds wearing red boots, blue boots, silver and white. I remember being told, when they first came into vogue, that you'd better be a hell of a player if you were going to wear white boots and the only time that we ever had parents yelling at us from the touchlines was when we were being chased up for being out way past our bedtimes; which, admittedly, was quite often.

It was almost inevitable that one of my fellow footballers would usually be Michael Fox. Of course I'd already experienced many exciting episodes with him and managed to live to tell the tale but this particular summer there was another incident where his seniority almost got us into big trouble yet again. One day Michael, his brother Peter and I had made a den in some undergrowth nearby, and being kids we decided to light a fire. To keep the fire alight we devised a little hearth with some bricks and bits and bobs, but we didn't have enough material to enclose the flames and keep them going. Michael had a clever idea. He'd seen a big drum not far away, so we dragged it into the den and it fit perfectly. The fire blazed beautifully. Sitting around chatting, there was the unmistakeable sound of rumbling. We thought that it might be coming from outside, so Peter, being the youngest, was sent off to have a look; nope, nothing there. But back in the den, there was no doubt that the sound was getting louder, and where it was once a deep slow rumble, it was now much more like a high fast grumble. I don't know when we realised what a dangerous situation we were in, but thank goodness we'd made more than one entrance to our little hideaway. Just as the drum was about to explode, we turned and ran in different directions. I was the luckiest of the three; scratches down my arms and legs, and a blackened face. Michael and Peter bore the brunt of the blast. When we rendezvoused some way from the scene, I couldn't believe what I was seeing. Their parents encouraged short hair, this being summer too, and Michael often had a flat top as well but now, whatever hair they'd had was completely singed; I didn't know whether to laugh or cry. Well I laughed because I couldn't help myself, but I knew there'd be tears before bedtime. The upshot of it was that my two friends spent a miserable summer being shut away indoors, firstly as a punishment and secondly because it took quite a while for their hair to grow back and Mrs Fox was not the kind of woman who'd send her boys out looking anything other than spick and span. Next time we met, we agreed that it probably hadn't been water, as we'd originally imagined, in that drum.

Maybe it was the times but it seemed that we were always getting into scrapes one way or another. If we weren't getting banged about by older lads in the massed football games then we'd probably manage to inflict some degree of damage on ourselves thanks to the nature of our 'toys' which, being boys, were more akin to weapons of choice. Basic artillery was the pea-shooter, then a catapult, which we knew better as a galley, topped off by the most fiendish of them all, a homemade arrow capable of being hurled prodigious distances across a playing field. They would probably be illegal now, in fact they were probably illegal back then, but we fashioned them from an eighteen inch or so length of cane, pointed at one end and flighted at the other, with metal wire wrapped around the shaft towards the sharp end to act as a weight. Then we made a notch near the flights and using this as the starting point we wrapped a decent length of string tightly around the cane leaving about a foot or so left. Gripping this firmly at the weighted end the idea was to take a few steps run up and launch the arrow much like a javelin. I'm not sure about the actual aerodynamic principles that made it work but some of the older kids could throw it half way across the lammas, which must have been about thirty or forty yards. These weren't the kind of implements that you'd show your parents so when I came home once with a big gash under my left eye courtesy of being on the receiving end of one my days as a fledgling Steve Backley were well and truly numbered.

Such injuries were the price we had to pay for a life of thrills and spills and often resulted in a trip to the Doctors. Such visits are always connected in my mind, rightly or wrongly, with being seen by a female GP by the name of Dr Jolly. The Surgery was located in a large house off Front Street, about where ASDA is situated today, and it seemed to me to be a very serious place, no messing around allowed and total silence the order of the day. Once inside Dr Jolly's room you were assailed by a certain aroma, one that I was quite sure emanated from the glass beaker on her desk. It contained a clear blue liquid in which was dipped what might have passed for a smooth version of an emery board. For anything other than treatment for a war wound I knew that it wouldn't be long before the board was in my mouth and the Doctor was asking me to say "Aah", a task I always found extremely difficult and which normally came out as "Aargh!" Actually, I never found Dr Jolly lived up to her name at all. She was an Old School Doctor, scared me half to death. She was only marginally less formidable than the Matron on the City Hospital ward where loads of us kids were awaiting our mass tonsillectomy and the thermometer she was wielding was heading for a place where the sun didn't shine. She could do no wrong with our family though and even managed to be at my brother Steve's birth, a home affair with Those That Knew What To Do upstairs and me and my Dad in the hall, him pacing up and down listening nervously for the sound of the new arrival and me fidgeting to get back outside with my mates.

Not all of our pastimes involved dangerous toys or sport because the estate was still mainly surrounded by an unspoiled countryside of farms, smallholdings, paths and lanes.

Seagraves' Farm came right up to the hedge at the bottom of our garden and another called Lorna Doone backed onto the estate's playing field no more than a couple of hundred yards away. Behind this lay Beauty's Field, named after the horse it was home to. Access to this field was gained from 'The Obbucks', a lane that ran between the two farms, and from there it wasn't long before a deep thicket, imaginatively known as 'Copper Canyon', was reached. This was probably the source of the stream that we called 'The Dyke', complete with water rats and which ran alongside the playing field and continued all the way to Arnold Park Pond about a mile and a half away.

Because of the polio scares of the fifties and the warnings we'd received about the dangers of drinking dirty water we didn't sample the pleasures of 'The Dyke' unless we fell in it, which I managed to do on more than the odd occasion. Instead we were fortunate that there were plenty of gurgling springs where we could refresh ourselves on the sloping fields leading up to the Travellers' Rest pub on Mapperley Plains. As for food, well a particular favourite was something we called a pig nut which we grubbed up out of the ground and ate raw. They were surprisingly sweet and nutty but occasionally we ruined them by heating them up over an improvised fire and then pretended that the charcoaled remains were actually quite tasty. We didn't know it at the time but their proper title is *conopodium majus* and they are a member of the carrot family, sometimes called earth nuts. They seem to have acquired the name we knew them by because pigs, like us kids, were known to be quite fond of them. Maybe they mistook them for truffles. Of course there were also plentiful supplies of hedgerow berries and lots of opportunities for scrumping, although I must admit I preferred sentry duty to actually risking life and limb trespassing up a stranger's fruit tree.

Another admission is that a lot of us collected birds' eggs as a hobby. I'm not sure whether any of us knew that this activity had been illegal since 1954 but we carried on regardless. We were all quite adept at piercing each end of the eggs with a needle and blowing through one of the holes and forcing its contents out the other without crushing the shell. The delicate objects were then carefully laid in a shoe box containing sawdust, perfect both to protect and display them at the same time.

However this summer of 1960 was a little different to all the rest up at Killisick because I'd recently finished primary school and life would no doubt be different at my new place. All in all I'd had a great time at Richard Bonington, apart from the dinners and a bit of corporal punishment. A couple of years earlier an advertisement had appeared in the local newspaper saying: 'OFFERS INVITED FOR COLLECTION OF SWILL FROM RICHARD BONINGTON SCHOOL KITCHEN'. I'm not saying that my opinion of the food was low but if the contractors had come while our meals were being prepared they would have been hard pressed to identify the stuff they were meant to be taking away from what, truly grateful, we were about to eat. As to the grievous bodily harm inflicted on all errant pupils in schools of the fifties my angelic behaviour had spared me the cane but not the lesser sanctions meted out for minor infractions. So, in ascending order of degrees of pain, I was given the slipper with about twenty others for playing football where we shouldn't have been, the strap, which he'd given the delightful name 'tickler', from Mr Fletcher for talking in his class, and finally the ruler from the headmaster Mr 'Pop' Lucas for a spelling mistake. He was making one of his regular tours of the classroom, peering over our shoulders at our work, when he noticed that I'd misspelled a word. My reward was a blow from my own ruler, not a sharp tap on the palm of the hand, but a hard rap, edgeways, on my upturned knuckles. The only consolation is that ever since that day I've never once made an error in spelling the word 'vehicle'.

Worryingly, bad behaviour beyond the school gates during the close season certainly seemed to be on the rise. Early in May a gang of around twenty youths had attempted to rescue one of their mates from the Arnold Police Station after he'd been arrested, leading to reinforcements being called to the scene and a number of arrests being made for assault and breach of the peace. It was almost inevitable that the gang were said to have been 'Teddy Boys', the only mitigating factor for the residents of the town being that a number of them came from other districts of Nottingham, attracted to Arnold as the 'Wakes' were in progress at the time.

It was ironic that The 'Wakes' were a catalyst for violence because they were originally part of the Patronal Festival of St Marys and commemorated the Nativity of the Virgin Mary. They'd been staged at various sites around the town but by the nineteen fifties their home was The Croft, a piece of open land where the current Health Centre stands. I remember it as a scaled down version of the more famous Goose Fair with rides and stalls and the usual smells and sounds associated with a fairground. In fact it was traditionally staged immediately prior to Goose Fair week and many of the operators would go onto Nottingham when the 'Wakes' finished but in 1960 the fair had obviously made an extra appearance.

Anti-authority behaviour had also begun to rear its head on the football field too. Towards the end of the previous season a player in North Notts refused to leave the pitch having been ordered off whilst in a Notts Amateur League match another wouldn't give the referee his name when cautioned. Both games had to be abandoned. Even one of Arnold's finest had been party to a show of dissent only the previous season. Rovers' winger Roy 'Fly' Carter, who had also played for Marys and Notts Regent, was now in his thirteenth season and probably ought to have known better than replying, when asked by the man in black for his name, that it was 'Father Christmas'. Admittedly the match did take place the week before the festivities but the referee didn't appreciate Roy's humour and dismissed him just the same. This game got abandoned too, but only coincidentally because of the unplayable conditions.

Happily, at the very end of the season just passed a match took place that reinforced every football fan's love of the beautiful game and has stayed in the memory not only of all those fortunate enough to be there in person but also the estimated seventy million viewers watching it on television. It was of course the European Cup Final between Real Madrid and Eintracht Frankfurt, staged at Glasgow's Hampden Park Stadium in front of 127,621 spectators, still the biggest attendance ever for a European Cup Final, with gate receipts of fifty five thousand pounds, then a British record. Real had won the trophy four years in a row, the only club to have lifted the cup since the competition's inauguration in 1955, and boasted a multi-international side containing nine players capped at the highest level. With Alfredo Di Stefano running the game from midfield and Francisco Gento and Hungarian Ferenc Puskas wreaking havoc up front the Germans, despite having taken an early lead, had little or no idea how to deal with the mesmerising quality of the Spanish side's play. Di Stefano scored twice within ten minutes of Eintracht's opener and Puskas added a third just before half-time. The second period became a procession as the Galloping Major rattled in another three goals in a fifteen minute spell and Di Stefano completed his own hat-trick. Frankfurt, who gallantly played their part in what many observers have described as the greatest game of all time, grabbed two late consolation goals as the match finished seven-three, the highest scoring European Cup Final ever.

Even a four minute black out in the television coverage, caused by a power cut, couldn't dampen the enthusiasm of everyone watching but it was the crowd inside the stadium who added even more to the occasion with their forty five minute ovation. Wanting to show their unbridled appreciation of what they'd witnessed, every spectator stayed to see the cup lifted by Real's captain Zarraga and then paraded around the ground. At the end, the Spanish players completed a lap of honour around the Hampden track to a continuous roar that has seldom, if ever, been heard at a neutral venue. To the famous Brazilian names of the 1958 World Cup like Pele, Vava, and Didi, television coverage had now added Di Stefano, Puskas and Gento. When we convened the following day for our daily footy session at Killisick, the game almost didn't get started because we couldn't decide who was going to be who.

Marys' committee were still having the same problem it seemed, because the following week at the club's Annual General Meeting player-coach Noel Simpson was elected as Selection Committee Advisor, an appointment designed to streamline the currently convoluted process of picking the team for the next game. However, no proposals were made to actually reduce the number of members entitled to vote and so the procedure going into the new season would be as follows: 'Team selection to be by private ballot of members present at the previous match. If a player is voted into two positions and fails to get a majority vote in one position, his final selection shall be reconsidered before the team is finally selected.' A cause for confusion if ever there was one and probably the reason why Noel's services were required in the first place. However, there was another topic on the close-season committee meeting agendas of far greater significance in the long run than picking a side. It was the mess that the Midland League had gotten itself into and how this was about to impact on the make-up of the Central Alliance.

In the days long before the introduction of the current 'Pyramid' system of automatic promotion up the country's local and regional leagues, the Midland League was senior to the Central Alliance and membership of it was the natural aim of the best and most progressive clubs at Marys' current level. However, it had been on the retreat since the 1957-58 season when fifteen of its twenty-four clubs handed in their resignation. Eleven of these were the reserve sides of League clubs and when a similar withdrawal badly affected the North Eastern League eight of its members, despite the additional travelling involved, elected to join the Midland League. There were still only nineteen teams at the start of 1958-59 and a year later this had dropped to seventeen. Despite dominating the top half of the table during the two years of their involvement, the North Eastern sides defected *en masse* at the end of the 1959-60 season, citing falling gates and increased travelling costs as the main reasons behind their decision. When Peterborough United, Champions for the last five years, finally achieved admission to the Football League at the expense of Gateshead, the Midland League had only eight members and at its AGM it was decided to suspend the competition for one year.

During 1959-60 the Central Alliance had been looking at de-regionalising its current North and South set-up to create a Premier Division but only nine of its clubs, including Marys, had shown any great interest in the scheme. There was much claim and counter-claim between the Central Alliance and the Midland League that each was trying to poach the other's clubs but nothing concrete was resolved and to all intents and purposes the season to come was set to have the same appearance as the one just finished. Then came the North Eastern clubs' exodus from the Midland League and the situation changed rapidly and drastically. With cap in hand, six of the eight Midland League clubs left in limbo applied for, and were given, membership of the Central Alliance, with five taking up residence in the northern section. Despite all the close season confusion, one thing had become abundantly clear. The next season now looked set to be the Saints' toughest yet in their three years in the Alliance's top tier.

Now whilst this subject might have preoccupied the minds of Marys' committeemen and many of their contemporaries in Ilkeston, Heanor, and the like, the hottest topic of conversation in the country at large was a book by a native of the Nottinghamshire-Derbyshire borders, Eastwood born David Herbert (D H) Lawrence. In 1928 he had written 'Lady Chatterley's Lover', a novel about an affair between a bored aristocratic wife and her gamekeeper, and seen it immediately banned in this country on account of its explicit sex scenes. Thirty one years later, and with public attitudes markedly different from those of the twenties, the Obscene Publications Act had been added to the statute book in order to put a brake on what the Lord Chancellor had called 'the commercialised and deliberate use of filth for filth's sake'. On August 19, Penguin Books were prosecuted under the Act over its plans to publish Lawrence's forbidden work, and a trial date set for October.

As an eleven year old when kids that age weren't quite as well informed on such matters as eleven year olds today, I'm not sure how much of the forbidden fruit of Lady Chatterley I was meant to know about. I'm sure Michael Fox would have kept me informed anyway if I'd asked but I was still probably wrapped up in enjoying my summer holiday. Our vacation this year had been spent on the North Wales coast at Penmaenmawr and was memorable mostly for the fact that to gain access to the beach we had to walk underneath an old wooden bridge that carried the busy coastal railway line. My train spotting days were still in their infancy but, with Daybrook Station having been closed to passenger traffic back in April because Mapperley Tunnel had become unsafe, a railway track that ran along the edge of the beach was much too good an opportunity to miss. Apart from the pleasure of getting the numbers of the locomotives, there was the added thrill of frightening myself to death as I stood directly underneath the bridge, which had barely enough headroom for an adult, as the latest service clattered overhead. The sheer noise and din was exhilarating, and I'd be back there at every opportunity, a perfect contrast to the more genteel pursuit of trying to help my brother complete his 'I-Spy At The Seaside' book by looking for razor shells and starfish and funny shaped seaweed, none of which I was sure could even be found in that part of the world in the first place.

What were there in great numbers were jellyfish, whole hordes of them, though I think the correct term for them in the plural is actually 'smack'. This wasn't known to me at the time, we'd only done animals and birds as part of our rudimentary understanding of collective nouns at school, and anyway, 'hordes' still sounds much more impressive than 'smack'. Then again, maybe 'armada' would have been even more appropriate given that I was told that the particular type of jellyfish threatening life and limb of anyone risking more than a toe dip in the sea was known as a 'Portuguese Man of War'. I'm not quite sure whether anyone in our family had that much of an in-depth knowledge of marine life, but I didn't need a great deal of convincing that they were right. Nor did I require any more incentive to remain on *terra firma* than I normally needed, which to be truthful wasn't very much at all to begin with. Whatever liking of H_2O I might have been born with seems to have vanished at the very moment of my Christening when the Vicar of St Marys dripped the water on me at the font. Or was that 'dropped me in the water' at the font? Apparently I wasn't well pleased either way.

The holiday was also memorable for the very Welshness of the place names around where we were staying: Llanfairfechan, Penmaenmawr, and especially Dwygyfylchi. We were wandering around the latter one evening and with a tourist's natural inquisitiveness we asked one of the local shopkeepers the correct pronunciation. Even after a respectful 'Pardon, could you repeat that?' we were still none the wiser. Thank goodness we were holidaying between the easier-on-the-tongue towns of Bangor and Conway, although we did venture over the Menai Bridge into Anglesey one afternoon to take a look at Llanfairpwllgwyngyllgogerychwyrndrobwllllantysiliogogogoch. From then on, Dwygyfylchi was a doddle.

On our return my brand new and still unused bathing trunks were put back in the drawer until next year. If they'd been a bit bigger I could have sent them over to Marys' committee room where the unusual proposal to provide visiting teams with such items in the forthcoming season had recently been given the thumbs up. With no showers yet installed at KGV, Marys, Rovers, and their opponents still had to change and wash down the road at the Arnold Baths. Use of the adjoining swimming pool was an optional extra, a perk if you were a swimmer but no more than a mere distraction from the real inconvenience of there being no dressing rooms adjacent to the pitch. I'm not sure whether anyone had actually calculated the cost of supplying eleven new pairs of Speedos every fortnight or so, or whether the intention had been to ask for them back after they were first used and then chuck them in with the rest of the kit for the lady who did the laundry, but if it was the latter, then I'd imagine there'd be quite a few players who showed as much enthusiasm for wearing them as I did my own.

As it happened, swimming trunks might have come in very handy when Marys' season kicked off at Kimberley on the last Saturday in August. All over the country thunderstorms raged and vivid lightning and torrential rain caused a number of matches to be delayed, interrupted, or, like the Manchester derby, abandoned altogether. Despite having a slope that usually aided drainage, the pitch at The Stag Ground quickly became soaked and presented difficulties for both sets of players, and only a second half goal from the visitors separated the two sides. Lining up at outside-left for the home side was the familiar figure of Geoff Parr, now in his fifteenth season and only a couple of months short of his thirty-first birthday. If it was strange to see him in anything other than the maroon and gold, it was an even bigger surprise to see him in a Kimberley shirt.

GP : They were bad sports over at Kimberley and the crowd was right on top of you. It was a tough place to go. The Langham brothers were very lippy, they were the same when they played cricket. I think I only played about three games for them.

Whatever his final tally of appearances there, two of them were certainly against his old club because the sides met again seven days later. Geoff had brought a fine save from Len Rockley in the first meeting and now he went one better, reminding everyone at Gedling Road about his goalscoring ability by putting his new side in front after thirty-five minutes. Stung into action, his old mate Colin Collindridge equalised a few minutes later and a second goal after the break clinched the points for the home team. When Marys travelled to Derby the following Saturday and beat Wilmorton and Alvaston two-nil, they'd picked up six points out of six without ever really hitting top form, had the only one hundred percent record in the division, and were handily placed in fourth spot.

Meanwhile the Magpies had gotten off to a pretty steady start of their own but whilst the Saints were making it three out of three over at Derby, it was almost a case of nosebleeds all round for the fourteen thousand of us down at Meadow Lane when Notts hit third place thanks to a five-one demolition of Barnsley. Three goals in three minutes close to half-time had taken the wind out of the visitors' sails and another two midway through the second period sealed their fate. With County's young centre-forward discovery Tony Hateley achieving the rare feat of scoring a hat-trick of headers, valid comparisons were already being made between his prowess in the air and that of the great Tommy Lawton. Not only that, fans were actually daring to think that the last promotion achieved by the club at this level, in 1949-50 with Tommy leading the line, might be capable of being emulated by the current team.

There'd be more serious tests ahead for the Magpies of course, just as there were for Marys when their fourth game saw them come up against Worksop Town in the first clash of the season with one of the refugee outfits from the Midland League. Making his first appearance for a year was 'Tot' Leverton, now set to be available on a regular basis following difficulties with his work commitments the previous season. Joining him up front in what would be the last of only two games in Saints' colours was another ex-County man, Jimmy Jackson, bringing the number of former league players in the team to five. It would have been six but Colin Collindridge was out injured, the result of an altercation the previous Saturday. He'd begun the game against Wilmorton on the left-wing but after an exchange of late tackles with the opposing full-back had had to move to inside-right. As the ex-Forester had never been known to back down in the face of aggravation, the move was designed as much to protect his opponent as to nurse his own injury but with the game developing into a series of petty infringements there was little room for a bit of peace and quiet.

If the match across at Derby had been a somewhat fractious affair then the game up at Worksop's Central Avenue ground was, according to the Football Post, a 'comparatively fairly fought tussle' despite it having 'more than its share of halts for injuries'. These weren't minor knocks either, those needing a quick sponge down the shorts to get the player back on his feet again, they were serious injuries. 'Tot' Leverton was in the wars so often that he was almost in need of a dedicated bucket and sponge man of his own, on one occasion even suffering a concussion. With Noel Simpson having to be led from the field with blood gushing from a gashed forehead that required stitching, it was hard to believe that what was taking place was actually a game of football and not a boxing match. Amazingly the ball did stay in play long enough for each side to actually score a goal and the contest finished one-all with Billy England netting for Marys. It might have even been one-nil to the Saints but goalie Len Rockley, having one of his finest games for the club, was finally beaten just before the end.

The injuries weren't the preserve of the first eleven that day either as Len's deputy Ernie Iremonger suffered a knock-out blow of his own.

EI : I got injured playing for the Reserves against Aspley Old Boys. I collided with their inside-left Mick Hornbuckle and I was out cold. I was still out of it after the match and our right-half Barry Coombe, who lived near me in Sherwood, had to walk me home. I still can't remember anything about the rest of the game to this day.

Ernie came from a famous sporting family, his great uncles being none other than the legendary Albert and James who'd dominated the local sports pages in the early part of the century. Albert was a goalkeeper too, and made over six hundred appearances for the Magpies as well as being capped twice by The Football League. He also played first-class cricket for Nottinghamshire but it was his elder brother James who was the better all-round sportsman. Primarily a full-back, he played three hundred times for Forest and was capped four times by the Football League as well as playing twice for the full England side. He too played cricket for Notts, scoring thirty-one first-class centuries as well as being named as one of Wisden's 'Cricketers of the Year' in 1903. He was widely considered to be unlucky not to have become an international in the summer game too,

There were two other youngsters in Marys' second eleven with sporting connections, not quite so illustrious as Ernie's but both connected to the club. Seventeen year old outside-right John Moore was the son of Charlie and nephew of Albert and Keith, all of whom had given sterling service to the Saints both on and off the pitch and his right-wing partner was John Anthony, sixteen year old son of former Marys' stalwart Eric.

They were all part of a young side that had also made a decent start to the season, so it was a pity that Rovers couldn't make it a hat-trick of success for the town. Unfortunately their hangover from the previous season had continued into the new one and with only two or three players left from the glory days of their recent past the crowds for their home games had dwindled fast.

ROVERS v TEVERSAL WELFARE : SEP 17 1960   (Courtesy Football Post)

They certainly weren't in any urgent need for Marys' proposed spectator stand, so when they became the first of the two clubs to accept the Arnold Council's proposal to charge six pounds per match for the improved facilities, their decision caused a certain amount of scratching of heads outside the inner sanctum of their own committee room. Marys on the other hand were going from strength to strength and saw off Nottingham Forest A convincingly on the last Saturday of September by six goals to one. Barry Mason was promoted from the Reserves and responded with a couple of goals with Peter Williams and 'Tot' Leverton also getting on the score sheet.

KGV wasn't the only location that was earmarked for development either. Elsewhere in the district plans had been approved for a new Good Shepherd Primary School on Somersby Road, Woodthorpe to cater for junior Roman Catholics who were finding the conditions in the Church Hall on Thackerays Lane a little bit cramped, and for the older students the new Arnold and Carlton College of Further Education had recently been opened on Digby Avenue, Mapperley.

ROVERS SEP 17 1960 : Back Row (l to r); P Beardsall, S Webb, E Smith, S Archer, M Jackson, D Wheat, G Clarke, H Colley. Front Row; - -, R Maddocks, R Bilbie, - -, E Williamson.

(Sam Archer Collection)

I'd just started my secondary education too, and a daunting prospect it was. I'd been fortunate enough to have won a Scholarship to the Boys High School in Nottingham but I didn't quite know what I was letting myself in for, and neither did my parents, both being from humble working class origins. On my very first day I'd caught the 52 bus at its terminus on the estate and got off at the stop not far from the city centre just past the Forest Road junction with Mansfield Road. I didn't know at the time that my route to the school along Forest Road East actually took me along the boundary of one of Nottingham's most notorious red light districts. Then again neither did another young kid who got off with me at the same stop. His name was Bill Rowlston and he'd caught the bus in Sherwood. I know this because he was dressed in the same school uniform as me and I asked him whether the best way to the school was down Forest Road as I thought. He agreed, we got talking as we were walking, and in an irony of all ironies found out that not only were we in the same class but because of the proximity of our names in the register, I was actually given the desk in front of his as our classroom was arranged in an alphabetical, up down and back up again order. That we went on to the same University and are still in touch despite him now living in South Africa is testament to the impact these chance meetings have on all of us sometime in our life.

Back in the less academic environment of the Central Alliance on the first day of October, fate was also about to play a huge part in the future career of another new boy. Jim Bullions had not long been given the manager's job over at Alfreton and one of the first decisions he made was to give a first team debut to Arthur Oldham, a promising youngster from Keyworth. It so happened that his first appearance coincided with the visit of Marys, who had a couple of new faces in their side, too. When Colin Collindridge was ruled out by injury, John Moore's own good showings in the Saints' second eleven saw him elevated to the senior side, with Peter Williams switching wings to accommodate the youngster's debut at outside-right, and with Len Rockley having also been incapacitated by a knock, the keeper's jersey went to Ernie Iremonger.

Lining up directly opposite Arthur at the kick-off was Marys' player-coach Noel Simpson, the first time either of them had ever set eyes on each other. Just four minutes after the kick-off, it was a case of the Arnold man looking on helplessly as the diminutive forward slammed home the opening goal for the home team. It was a dream start for the number ten, but twenty minutes later it was his Saints' counterpart, the much more experienced 'Tot' Leverton, who grabbed the equaliser. With centre-forward Billy England anxious to shine against his former club, Marys went close to taking the lead on numerous occasions, but the scores remained level until half time and even a further forty five minutes couldn't break the deadlock. In the circumstances the Saints were more than happy with a point, but like the previous season when Billy England's fine performance had been the talking point in Marys' committee room, it was the impact made by Arthur Oldham that had taken the eye this time.

AO : A couple of months later, Noel Simpson turned up at the family farm at Keyworth and said "Don't ever think of leaving Alfreton without letting me know first".

At the time neither of them could possibly know that they were destined to be reacquainted a couple of years down the line and end up featuring in some of Marys' greatest exploits together, but in the meantime it was back to the business of helping pick up Central Alliance points separately. Seven days after their meeting both sides recorded handsome victories with Arthur again getting on the scoresheet in Alfreton's humiliating nine-one defeat of their previously unbeaten Derbyshire neighbours Heanor Town and the Saints finishing easy four-nil winners at Clay Cross with a couple of goals from Billy England.

This latest victory had taken Marys' long unbeaten run in the league, stretching back to the beginning of February, to eighteen matches. Their record read:-

P	W	D	L	F	A	P
18	15	3	0	66	15	33

On the other hand Arnold Rovers' own indifferent form had seen them somewhat marginalised by the publicity attached to the Saints' impressive performances but on that same high scoring day they had managed to grab a headline of their own when they defeated Notts Alliance side Bilsthorpe Colliery by the improbable score of eight goals to seven in the first round of the Notts Senior Cup. For goalkeeper Sam Archer the game capped quite an eventful couple of days.

SA : My wife Lois was expecting and I took her into the hospital early on the Friday morning, around six o'clock. I went straight on to work for eight and Paul was born at lunchtime. I wasn't there because they didn't do things like that in those days. When I went in at night time to visit I took her a load of flowers. She said "You can take them back home, I'm coming out tomorrow." I thought "That's buggered up playing football". In those days you paid as much attention to the football as the kiddies. But it got sorted. Whilst I was playing football Lois and the baby came out of hospital and her father was at home to meet her. Wetting the baby's head the night before was probably the reason I let in seven.

There was another time at Gedling Road, I don't know who we were playing, when I felt absolutely terrible. The firm I worked for, Clowers in Daybrook, had been in business twenty five years and they had a do on the Friday night at Daybrook House near where the Roxy used to be and that's the only time I ever got really drunk. I staggered out and this copper said "What you doing my lad?" and I said "I'm holding this wall up at the moment". They were all right in those days so he said "Where are you going?" and he helped me on my way. We only got as far as my mother's, just around the corner on Portland Street. Of course I was footballing the next day and I never felt so bad in all my life. It's a good job I had an easy match because I couldn't have saved any goals. I've never been drunk since.

An eight-seven scoreline was unusual even in 1960, and the final tally of fifteen goals was a rare occurrence too, at least until the unlikely feat was repeated only a few weeks later when the red and whites hammered Midland Amateur Alliance outfit Becket Old Boys by eleven goals to four in the next round. Rovers' glory days might have been over but these results served as a reminder that, despite being seemingly unable to field the same team twice in a row, they were still capable of putting out a decent enough side on occasion.

Despite their excellent start to the season Marys too had changed their line-up in every single game. When Brian Cunningham, recently back at the club after his transfer from Alfreton, made his first appearance of the season against Clay Cross, he became the nineteenth player used by the Saints in only seven matches. The current convoluted process of choosing a side had obviously not helped and so at the next committee meeting a revolutionary proposal to appoint a fixed and more manageable selection committee was finally, if somewhat belatedly, approved. It was to consist of five members, Albert Moore, Ron Hinson, Walter Archer, Syd Gray, and Len Woollacott, together with the first and second team captains. If it had taken a long while in arriving, the new slimmed-down panel took no time at all in naming an unchanged side for the next game. Given that it was a Central Alliance Cup tie against their most recent opponents, it wasn't the most difficult decision they'd ever have to make. As it turned out Clay Cross were no more of a threat in the cup game than they had been the previous week in the league, and Marys saw them off comfortably by six goals to one, with Barry Mason helping himself to a hat-trick.

The hottest ticket in town that third Saturday in October had been down at the City Ground where Forest were entertaining a star-studded Tottenham Hotspur side who'd dropped just a single point in their opening twelve games of the season. A record crowd was expected for the London side's visit and I swapped allegiances for a week and went down to see what all the fuss was about. Although heavy rain kept the attendance down, the thirty seven thousand that did turn up was a season's best and if they were disappointed that the Reds were plainly second best on the day, then we were all treated to a fine display from the visitors who, as the final scoreline of four-nil might suggest, were better in all departments than the home side. It was hardly a surprise to anyone there that Spurs went on to complete the first League and Cup double of the century.

I'd be back at Meadow Lane the following week but for Marys it was a forty-odd mile trip to play Gainsborough Trinity, another of the ex-Midland League sides currently finding a home in the Central Alliance. Unsurprisingly the Saints' team had again remained unaltered, but the status of one player in particular was about to change even as the team coach made its way towards Lincolnshire.

EI : On the bus on the way to the game Charlie Moore got me to sign professional forms, three pounds a match, two in the reserves. I'd been receiving money in the second team but I think it was a bit dodgy paying players [on the side] then, I think the FA were getting a bit keen about it. I felt good about signing professional. I was proud to be playing for Arnold St Marys, I was really.

Unfortunately the Saints' latest addition to the professional ranks was unable to prevent the home team from becoming the first side this season to deny Marys at least a point. A Billy England equaliser right on half-time wasn't enough as Trinity ran out three-one winners.

As is often the case, changes are made to a team following a defeat, and at the Monday night committee meeting the latest arrival from Alfreton, John Brady, was selected in place of Barry Mason. The decision to drop Barry must have been a difficult one because he'd averaged a goal a game in his short spell in the first team but John had scored twice on his debut for the reserves and had an excellent pedigree as a goalscoring inside-forward, netting twenty eight times in thirty eight appearances with Alfreton.

AM : John was Irish and a gentleman, very quietly spoken. He came to watch us at a game and he got talking to us. I said "Are you interested in coming here then?" and when he said he was I said "Let's get cracking then".

The Irishman's selection wasn't the only talking point at the meeting either. A letter from the Arnold Council was read out regarding the provision of a hard standing area behind the goal at the playground end. On the proviso that the club paid for the concrete slabs necessary for the job, the Council magnanimously agreed to lay them. The communiqué didn't mention whether an invoice for this labour would follow later but the lack of even the most basic of spectator and player facilities at KGV, more than four years after its opening, was hardly a sign of wholehearted support from the local Council Chambers.

However, it was a series of exchanges between Counsels three days later that most captured the wider public's enthusiasm when the 'Lady Chatterley Trial' finally got under way at the Old Bailey in London. The rights and wrongs of even bringing the case in the first place had been widely debated in the run-up to the big day with Spectator columnist Bernard Levin being a particular critic of the Home Secretary in allowing it to go ahead at all. He wrote: "It is surely going to be difficult for the prosecution to find anybody taken seriously by the literary or academic worlds to swear that publication of Lady Chatterley's Lover is not in the public interest as a literary event and that its tendency would be to deprave and corrupt those who might read it." He was sure that the prosecution would lose and added: "The case promises to be one of the most splendid and uproarious shows ever put on at public expense." However, with the defence expected to call seventy expert witnesses, including E M Forster and the Bishop of Woolwich, to testify on the book's behalf, the extensive and prolonged arguments for and against would see the case being carried over into the following week.

No doubt the opening exchanges were the talk of many a football changing room that week-end but I would have been surprised if there was any consensus for the Director of Public Prosecution's view that the liberal use of four-letter words in the novel were deemed to constitute 'gratuitous filth'. Someone had been given the arduous task of counting the number of times the f-word and its derivates had appeared in the book and had come to the conclusion that it was no fewer than thirty. However, without condoning the fact that 'industrial language' was hardly a stranger to the football arena, it was hard to see what all the fuss was about. So, on the last Saturday of October and with a good chance that the odd swear word might be heard here and there in the heat of battle, Marys endeavoured to get straight back on the winning trail following their defeat at Gainsborough.

MARYS v WORKSOP : 29 OCT 1960   (Courtesy Football Post)

The game was the return fixture at Gedling Road against Worksop Town, the side that had held them to a draw just six weeks earlier, and it was expected to be another close fought encounter. In the first meeting goalie Len Rockley had been man of the match and on this occasion it was Ernie Iremonger's turn to receive all the plaudits as he made a string of important saves but the main difference between the two sides this time however was the sharpness of Marys' forwards in front of goal. Having gone ahead courtesy of a freak own goal, the Saints then showed the large crowd just why they were one of the most exciting teams in the league, adding two more before half-time and another two late in the game. The four goals were shared around equally between 'Tot' Leverton, Peter Williams, Billy England, and John Brady. Only Colin Collindridge, returning to the side after injury, was missing from the score sheet. The balance of play had been far more even than the scoreline suggested but it was an impressive result for the maroon and golds nonetheless. It certainly augured well for the following month's tough schedule but in the meantime, as October drew to a close, football temporarily took a back seat as most of the nation's attention was once again focused upon the intriguing events unfolding at the Old Bailey.

Had there been the rolling news programmes of today there is little doubt that each thrust and counter-thrust of the 'Lady C' trial would have featured prominently in their regular updates but even with a less voracious information industry than we are now accustomed to the case still made headlines across the various news media. The trial entered its third and then fourth day but even with the counsel for the defence appearing to be doing rather better than their counterparts for the prosecution, the outcome was by no means certain. Then, in football parlance, the government's own lawyers scored a massive own goal when their leading counsel Mervyn Griffith-Jones stood and addressed the jury: "Ask yourselves the question: would you approve of your young sons, young daughters – because girls can read as well as boys – reading this book? Is it a book that you would have lying around the house? Is it a book you would wish your wife or servants to read?" If Bernard Levin had backed his opinion with a wager, then he could have collected his winnings even before the learned gentleman had resumed his seat. Elitist, patronizing, sexist, and downright condescending to women, in fact females of all ages, the tone and content of the speech might have been acceptable back in 1906 but was hardly likely to be greeted with anything other than derision in 1960. On Wednesday November 2, the twelve men and women of the jury duly delivered their verdict; 'Not Guilty'. When the three and sixpenny paperback edition of the book went on sale shortly afterwards, its initial print run of two hundred thousand copies was completely sold out on the first day. The year still had a couple of months to run, but not only did it already feel like a completely different decade to that of the fifties, to many in the establishment it was beginning to feel like a different world too.

There was no changing of the guard back at Gedling Road on the first Saturday of November as Marys picked the same eleven that had been successful against Worksop. The visitors were Alfreton but there would be little for Arthur Oldham to celebrate on this particular occasion. Despite the Derbyshire side having the better start, a goal from John Brady on the quarter hour mark settled the Saints down and from then on they were never in any great danger. They dominated the second period and added four more goals without reply, two from the Irishman to give him his hat-trick, and one each from Peter Williams and Billy England. With two of their ex-players accounting for all but one of the goals there were probably one or two questions being asked amongst those members of the Alfreton selection committee in the crowd.

Elsewhere Forest had slipped to the bottom of the First Division and were now four points adrift whilst the Central Alliance had two representatives in the First Round Proper of the FA Cup. The Northern Section leaders Sutton Town went down gallantly at Hull by three goals to nil whilst Southern Section Loughborough United went one better and held Southern League King's Lynn to a draw at Brown's Lane. Although the Leicestershire side were narrowly beaten in the replay, the performance of both clubs was a credit to them and the Central Alliance as a whole.

Even with back-to-back five-nil wins Marys knew that the majority of games this season would be tough and the visit to Creswell Colliery in the second round of the League Cup the following week was no exception. Geoff Parr, especially when playing on the wing, was only one of a number of players who found the atmosphere up there a little bit hostile.

GP : I didn't like to go to Creswell. Miners straight out the welfare. Horrible they were.

Supporters Eric and Roy Thompson weren't that enamoured either.

E&RT : These places were just miners, all they'd got was the football match on a Saturday.

Harsh, maybe, but Colin Collindridge was also about to develop a dislike for that part of the world, one that would surface again later in the campaign too. With a decent following behind them the Saints had the better of the play early on and it was no surprise when John Brady scored for the third straight game midway through the opening period. All seemed to be going well until a few minutes before half-time when Colin got into a bit of an altercation with one of the opposition players and was warned as to his conduct by the referee. Unfortunately his dander was up and shortly afterwards he committed a foul of sufficient malice that he was ordered from the field of play. This proved to be a turning point in the game as the home side, taking advantage of the extra man, scored three times without reply. With the score remaining three-one with only fifteen minutes left it looked to all intents and purposes that Marys' cup run would soon be over but in a never-say-die grandstand finish two late goals earned them a replay against all the odds. It had been the typical blood and thunder battle expected up there and apart from Colin's dismissal, both wing-halves, Noel Simpson and Sid Thompson, had picked up injuries serious enough to make them miss the next match. Even though the natives were no doubt restless after such a turnaround they could at least console themselves with the thought that incapacitating three of the four ex-Forest players in the Saints' side wasn't too bad an afternoon's entertainment.

The following Saturday, with Brian Cunningham and Billy Barnes in at numbers four and six respectively, it was the turn of Gainsborough Trinity to visit Gedling Road. The Lincolnshire side were of course the only team to have defeated Marys so far this season and with a re-jigged line-up the Saints struggled right from the outset to contain the visitors. There was a degree of inevitability when Trinity took the lead after thirty-seven minutes but happily Colin Collindridge, showing no sign of being affected by his experience of the previous week, equalised three minutes later. When Gainsborough regained the lead shortly after the hour mark it was the former Forest star who again led the comeback, scoring his second goal with less than ten minutes to go.

In the circumstances it was a point gained rather than one dropped and with Sid Thompson back the following week Marys travelled up the A60 on the last Saturday of the month to meet Sutton Town in far better spirits than they would have been had Gainsborough completed the double over them. They needed to be positive because the Ashfield side had not only shown their ability with their excellent FA Cup run but were also in terrific form in the league, leading the table having dropped only two points all season.

	P	W	D	L	F	A	P
Sutton Town	13	11	2	0	51	17	24
Goole Town	12	10	1	1	53	15	21
Arnold St Marys	**11**	**7**	**3**	**1**	**30**	**9**	**17**

At kick-off the playing surface at Priestsic Road looked in excellent condition but heavy rains that had caused matches to be postponed all over the country had saturated the turf to such an extent that three ducks had taken up residence on one of the touchlines, much to the amusement of the large crowd gathered for this critical local derby. However it was no laughing matter for either team once the pitch turned into a quagmire and with play difficult through the middle and both penalty areas resembling mud baths, the standard of football wasn't anywhere near that expected of two such highly rated teams. Even so, the flanks were marginally less problematic and it was from a cross wide on the right that Sutton created the opening goal. Thankfully Marys took only five minutes to level the scores when centre half Dennis Parr bustled his way through the morass of midfield and, under challenge from a Sutton defender, somehow managed to loop the ball over the keeper's head and into the net. There may have been a degree of good fortune about the goal but it had certainly come at an opportune moment, enabling the Saints to match Sutton despite the troublesome conditions. Half-time came and went and right throughout the second period there was little to choose between the two sides but then, with merely three minutes left on the referee's watch and a draw looking almost inevitable, Billy England popped up with the winner. With Goole dropping a point in a four-all draw with Clay Cross, it had been an extremely successful day for the maroon and golds.

DENNIS PARR BEATS THE DESPAIRING DIVE OF THE OPPOSITION'S GOALKEEPER :
SUTTON v MARYS : 26 NOVEMBER 1960   (Courtesy Football Post)

Rovers too had had a good day, beating both the awful conditions to get a game played in the first place and then getting their just desserts by disposing of Linby Colliery by four goals to two. In fact they'd had a great November, winning all four of their matches and scoring no less than twenty-seven times in the process.

It was a pity then that the news from the rest of Arnold during the past couple of months had been pretty discouraging, with the 'modern' scourge of vandalism featuring prominently in the headlines. These weren't petty incidents either, and with the 'Wakes' not being in town at the time, there were no obvious trigger points for the mayhem. The first major episode, on a Friday night in the middle of October, resulted in a catalogue of damage: the window of a dry cleaner's shop on Nottingham Road was smashed; part of the brick wall fronting the public conveniences on Front Street was demolished; a wooden seat provided for the elderly on High Street was toppled over a metal fence, causing extensive damage to both seat and fence; a litter bin was kicked to pieces; gates were torn off their hinges on Arnot Hill Road and thrown into the gardens; and a telephone kiosk and a number of shop windows were smashed on Rolleston Drive. If that wasn't enough of a depressing scenario, the very next night a further section of the public convenience wall was demolished and every traffic sign on Front Street between High Street and Worrall Avenue was bent. For good measure, the goal posts at KGV were smashed as well, the latest in a series of attacks on the district's recreation fields. Just over a month later three youths, all local, smashed twenty four windows in four houses, broke glass in more telephone boxes, damaged a pillar box and stole a motor scooter and motor cycle, presumably to make their getaway. Of course they had no licence or insurance for the vehicles either.

This anti-social behaviour wasn't restricted to Arnold either. It was reported that hooliganism and vandalism in the area's cinemas had become so bad that the Derbyshire County Council were considering introducing a bye-law to make it a punishable offence to let off fireworks inside the auditorium and to indulge in the trendy pursuit of pulling a knife out of your back pocket and slashing a few seats on your way out in appreciation of the wonderful movie you'd just been watching. Come to think of it, why would they need a bye-law when surely it must already have been a criminal offence to wantonly disfigure someone else's furniture without their prior approval?

Of course the same old clichés about 'mindless' behaviour and the rest were trotted out when it was quite patently nothing of the sort. It was wilful and deliberate and very much the same as today, almost fifty years later; except in one small detail. Now one much touted 'solution' to the problem is to have 'more bobbies on the beat' and in Arnold in particular to have a police station that doesn't close in the evening, but the facts of the matter are that back in 1960 when it was half the size that it is now the town did have a police station that was manned twenty four hours a day by officers who patrolled mainly on foot. I don't recall seeing many fast response vehicles, immortalised by the TV series 'Z Cars', tearing up and down Front Street at the time. After all, that iconic programme was based around the mean streets of Liverpool and even then wouldn't be shown for another couple of years. Another old chestnut that the current army of quick-fixers offer up is a return to those good old days of National Service. They choose to forget that, even at a time when violent misbehaviour was on the increase, conscription for young males was still in operation right up until the very last day of 1960 when the last couple of thousand received their call-up cards. Unfortunately, and depressing as it might be to admit, there were no easy answers then and there are still no easy answers now.

Whilst a growing number of delinquents were doing their utmost to rearrange their local landscapes, the Labour Party was split down the middle on whether to vote for a ban on the one thing that could do the same, but better, and on a slightly larger scale; 'The Bomb'. A furious row had erupted at the Party Conference in October over the issue of nuclear disarmament. Hugh Gaitskell, Labour leader, launched a fierce attack on the 'pacifists, unilateralists, and fellow travellers' in the party saying "There are some of us who will fight, fight, and fight again to bring back sanity and honesty to the party we love". A month later, he had another scrap on his hands when Harold Wilson made an opportunistic challenge for the Labour leadership. Fortunately, he saw it off.

At the very same time that this political wrangling was taking place another internecine feud was brewing up nearer home amongst the members of the Central Alliance. It appeared that the ex-Midland League clubs were becoming mindful of reviving the competition whilst the movers and shakers at the Central Alliance were eager to press on with their long-held plans for a Premier Division. All this managed to achieve at the outset was the prospect of two under strength leagues, weakened at each other's expense. Heanor Town had tried to act as honest broker, suggesting that the ex-Midland League sides should join forces with eight top Alliance clubs under a new set up, but the two factions seemed unable to find common ground. When, at a meeting at Worksop on the last Saturday in November, the ex-Midland League refugees made a formal agreement to re-start their old competition, the battle lines had been drawn.

Marys' position in all this wasn't that cut and dried either. As one of the Alliance's leading lights they had applied in writing for membership of the new Premier Division but now that it appeared that it was going to be of diminished status they were having second thoughts. When a second meeting took place a fortnight later, both Heanor and Matlock added their names to those committed to re-forming the Midland League, leading the Football Post to ask 'Where does the Central Alliance go from here?' The defection of the Derbyshire clubs was a particular blow because they, like the Saints, had also signed up for the new Premier Division and their decision had switched the balance of power heavily in the Midland League's favour. At Marys' weekly meeting the next day, the latest developments hadn't yet filtered through but Syd Gray told the committee that he would call an emergency meeting on receiving any important information regarding the re-formation of the Midland League. There was little doubt that he was going to be kept very busy over the next few weeks.

On the field of play itself there was no sign that the Saints' players had been at all affected by the goings on behind the scenes. The only problem they had to deal with was the state of the Gedling Road pitch when Denaby United were December's first visitors. Torrential rain had made many grounds unplayable, leading to postponement and, in a number of cases, half-time abandonment. The latter was the fate awaiting all us hardy souls gathered down at

Meadow Lane, our only consolation being that Notts' opponents Halifax had slithered around rather better than the Magpies and were two-nil up when the referee called it a day; that and the chance to queue behind the Main Stand for ages, in terrible weather, to get a refund. Thankfully the pitch at KGV, even though it was a mud-bath at kick-off, didn't deteriorate sufficiently for the match to be brought to a premature conclusion and despite losing a goal in the opening minutes and another just before the final whistle Marys rattled in three of their own in a twenty minute spell in the first half to seal victory.

One man who was particularly keen to see the game go ahead and extremely delighted at the outcome was Albert Moore.

AM : When the referee arrived he said "You can't play on this". I said "We've been working on it all morning, sweeping and squeegeeing water off the pitch and if you'd seen it then you wouldn't have played it". Anyway he agreed to play the game as we'd been working since seven o'clock, half a dozen of us, same half dozen. Then, just before kick-off, another committee man, I'll not mention his name, came on the ground and stood in the corner. He looked right up the touchline and said "That line's not very straight". I said "If you don't go away you and me's going to fall out". Trouble was it never recovered; it was awful right up to the end of the season.

Another fixture that had ended early had been Rovers' away tie in the Notts Senior Cup against Notts Alliance side Ericsson Athletic. This was unusual because the works' side's ground at Beeston was one of the best kept in the county but at least the red and whites, who were trailing two-one when the game got curtailed after fifty minutes, had another chance seven days later. Unfortunately, the replay followed a similar pattern to the first encounter with Rovers again finding themselves two-one behind at the interval and despite a gallant attempt to force a replay ended up being edged out by the odd goal in five.

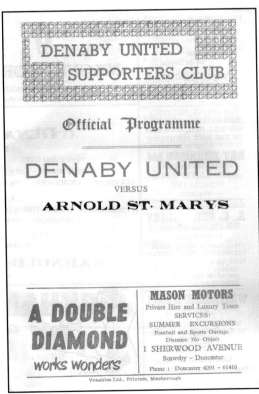

THE FAR FROM INFORMATIVE MATCH DAY PROGRAMME FOR DENABY UNITED v MARYS : 10 DEC 1960

As it happened the fixture list had also given the Saints back-to-back matches against the same opposition, a dubious blessing considering that it meant a dark December afternoon spent up in the South Yorkshire coalfields, sampling the doubtful delights of Denaby Main. Goalkeeper Ernie Iremonger wouldn't forget the game in a hurry for sure.

EI : That's where I broke my nose diving at somebody's feet. He followed through and caught me. I was still a bit dazed in the bus on the way back.

Thankfully John Brady took a particular shine to the area and hammered home an impressive four goals which, together with a Dennis Parr penalty, proved just about enough to make up for some sloppy defending that saw Denaby score three times themselves. Still, it was never an easy place to go, as bottom markers Shirebrook would find out three weeks later when, only three behind at the break, they suffered a humiliating defeat there by an astounding twenty goals to nil. Good for the home fans probably but not that great an advertisement for the league.

The following week Marys had the chance to complete another quick double when they played hosts to Sutton Town, who were still ahead of the Saints in the table and coming off the back of a seven-two victory themselves. However a win for the home side would narrow the gap between the two teams to only a single point and the maroon and golds would also have the benefit of a game in hand and with this no doubt uppermost in both sets of players' minds the game got off to a furious start. Two corners from Marys were followed by four in a four minute spell by Sutton and with both defences looking vulnerable it was the visitors who struck first after a quarter of an hour. It only took the Saints three minutes to get back on level terms through 'Tot' Leverton but the Snipes weren't to be denied and regained their lead on the half hour. This time the home side's response took a little longer in arriving but Billy England ensured the two evenly matched rivals were tied at two apiece at the halfway stage with his equaliser seven minutes before the break. The first forty five minutes had certainly been action packed and on the resumption both teams showed the same attacking instincts as they strove to take command. Poor conditions underfoot denied Colin Collindridge a glorious chance to put Marys ahead but in the sixty fifth minute Billy England found the target for the second time to put the Saints in the driving seat. Fortunately there were no slip ups in the mud and they safely saw out the closing stages to seal a great victory and a magnificent double.

Not only had they been the first side in the league to beat Sutton all season, they had repeated the feat no less than three weeks later for good measure. When they travelled to Lenton and thrashed the youngsters of Nottingham Forest A on Christmas Eve by six goals to two, courtesy of braces apiece from John Brady, Colin Collindridge, and Billy England, Marys extended their unbeaten run to nine games, including four out of four in December, and joined Goole and Sutton at the head of the table, level on points and with game in hand of them both. Only inferior goal average prevented them from taking the top spot themselves.

	P	W	D	L	F	A	P	GA
Goole Town	17	12	3	2	66	23	27	2.87
Arnold St Marys	**16**	**12**	**3**	**1**	**49**	**19**	**27**	**2.58**
Sutton Town	17	12	3	2	65	28	27	2.32

It was a pity that Marys' last match of the month had to be called off because of the unfit state of the Gedling Road pitch but the Saints had the consolation of going into the New Year having dropped the least number of points amongst all the teams in the division. Whatever changes were afoot, the club was well placed to be at the forefront of them.

In the Football League Forest had made a remarkable recovery since they began November at the foot of the First Division, racking up an eight game unbeaten run of six wins and two draws to move them back up the table. Notts were doing rather better than might have been expected considering the never ending supply of rumours regarding the club's parlous financial state, finishing the year in sixth spot, a mere three points off a promotion place, and with all to play for. A crowd of nearly twenty seven thousand for the Christmas Holiday game against Coventry should certainly have helped swell the coffers. I was certainly happy to part with my one and sixpence, or whatever it cost, especially with the Magpies running out three-nil winners.

I was of course enjoying my first Christmas holiday since I'd moved up to secondary school and, after four months spent in a distinctly different environment from anything I'd ever experienced before, I was glad of the break. Whereas Richard Bonington had been a relaxed, slightly informal, light and airy place the Boys High School was far more rigid and structured, overpowering to some extent with its grand scale and an air of bygone days. Considering that the school, founded in 1513, obviously had a bit of history behind it, I suppose I shouldn't have been surprised. We were obliged to address teachers as masters, they wore black gowns as they went about their business, and the headmaster, Mr K Imeson, donned a mortar board to great effect.

I made a conscious effort early on to stay well below the radar, especially if the Head was anywhere in the vicinity, but on one occasion I was powerless to avoid being on the receiving end of his wrath. A long straight corridor led from his office to the staff room and this particular day I found myself, much to my horror, walking a few yards behind him as he glided down the passage. When he came to the pair of doors halfway down the corridor I expected him to breeze through with his gown flowing so I wasn't quite prepared for what happened next. He pushed open one of the doors but instead of heading straight on through he half turned and caught sight of me doing my utmost to look invisible despite the obvious fact that he and I were the only ones anywhere in the vicinity. I was numb but not dumb and I realised he was holding the door open for me. I quickened my step and whizzed past him, not forgetting to offer a mumbled "Thank you, Sir" on my way through. With my heart pounding but thinking that my ordeal was over I'd gone a further couple of yards when a single word froze me to the spot. "Boy!!!!!" cried the Head, and even with my back to him I knew that the boy in question just had to be me. I turned sheepishly around and his angry gaze fixed itself firmly upon my angelic features. "Come here!" he bellowed. "You do **not** walk through a door that is being held open, you **take** it from that person. Understood?" Well I did, and I told him so, and I took the door from him and watched as he stormed down the remainder of the corridor and off round the corner at the far end. It was only when he had disappeared from sight that I realised I hadn't moved an inch and was still holding the door ajar. Just then a couple of prefects loomed large in front of me, so I started to edge away from my station expecting them to return the courtesy that I was showing them. I should have known better. They gave me a derisive sneer and swaggered on past, leaving me still doing my passable imitation of a hotel doorman. Still, both incidents had taught me as much as any lesson in class. I let go of the door and walked back the way I'd come, not wishing to bump into them or the Head any time soon.

My form master was Mr G I 'Geoff' Cushing, a decent guy even if he gave me my one and only detention whilst at the school. As I was twelve at the time and still feeling my way around the place, I never dared to ask him quite what indiscretion I'd committed to warrant such a sanction. He took us for Latin that first year, but unfortunately didn't succeed in passing on his love of the subject to me. However, one memorable lesson stays with me to this day. I'd resigned myself to another forty minutes of torture but for some reason he became sidetracked and started talking about fashion. Cue huge sigh of relief; no *porto, portas, portat* and no Julius Caesar. It quickly became obvious that he had a keen interest in the subject and I figured that we might get away with the whole lesson being Latin-free. I sat at my usual desk on the next to back row, slid back a little in my seat, and listened to Mr Cushing explaining fashion in Europe. I wasn't really listening that intently though; I mean it wasn't as if he was going to fire a question at me at any moment, so my concentration naturally wavered. As long as I didn't nod off, I'd be alright. I don't quite know exactly when it dawned on me that I knew less about fashion than I did about Latin; it must have been about ten minutes in. If any of the couture houses of the time had been mentioned, names like Dior and Gucci, I would still have been none the wiser. I didn't know who Franco was either. But Mussolini? Now I'd heard of him. I whispered to my nearest classmate, "What's Mussolini got to do with fashion?" "It's not fashion, you idiot, it's fascism!" My mother always told me to wash behind my ears, now I was thinking that I should have paid more attention to washing inside them. Suffice to say I paid slightly more attention to the subject matter from then on, and if I had been mistaken regarding content, I was spot on regarding the length of the discourse. 'Geoff' only stopped when the bell went for the end of the best Latin lesson I never had.

I might have occasionally wished I was back at Richard Bonington but the one area where my new school beat my old one hands down was in its sports facilities. Apart from an on-site gymnasium, indoor cricket nets, rifle range, two Rugby fives courts and a swimming hall about to be built, the school had the most wonderful playing fields adjacent to the Nottingham Ring Road at its junction with Hucknall Road. Covering approximately eighteen acres, there was enough space for seven rugby pitches in the winter, room for eleven age group cricket games to be played simultaneously in the summer, and six tennis courts available all year round. If the school had played football I would have been in sports heaven. As it was, and despite my best efforts to avoid the honour by being missing in action whenever anything so physically dangerous as a tackle needed making, I'd been chosen to play for the School Under-12 rugby fifteen, presumably picked at fly half for my kicking ability. Trouble was, if I overdid the footwork, the rugby master invariably castigated me verbally or better still let one of the opposition's big fat forwards flatten me a full five seconds after the ball had left my boot. If I dared protest I was duly reminded that 'this is Rugby football, not that other kind played by namby-pambies'.

I didn't take it personally. After all, you'd have been struggling to find many shrinking violets in the Central Alliance at the beginning of 1961, especially when league leaders Goole Town were the year's first visitors to Gedling Road and another hard fought contest was in prospect. The Yorkshire side had taken advantage of Marys' lack of activity on the final day of 1960 and had picked up two excellent points in a four-two defeat of Belper, putting themselves two points ahead of the Saints' at kick-off. Of course the maroon and golds did now have two games in hand and every incentive to narrow the gap yet again so it was little surprise that the action was fast and furious right from the start. Corners were forced at both ends and Ernie Iremonger was called upon to tip an effort over the bar but neither side could break the deadlock until the forty minute mark when 'Tot' Leverton headed in from a Colin Collindridge corner. The division's leading scorer, Goole centre forward Brian Howard, was well marshalled by Dennis Parr and the longer the game went on the more it looked like the points would be Marys' but then, with only a quarter of an hour left, the visitors' pressure told and they grabbed an equaliser. It was enough to secure a point and the match finished honours even at one apiece.

The Saints had again showed that they were as good as any team in the league so it was slightly disappointing the following Saturday that they only managed to register a four-two win against Shirebrook. Apart from their rugby score thrashing by Denaby the division's whipping boys had also been letting in seven and eight a game and Marys had seemed to have a golden opportunity to improve their goal average as well as picking up a couple of points. Still, they did extend their unbeaten league run to ten matches and their record in the top division since the beginning of February the previous year looked mightily impressive.

P	W	D	L	F	A	P
29	23	5	1	103	33	51

The third Saturday of January saw them take a break from league action as they hosted Creswell Colliery in the replayed Second Round League Cup tie. The match almost didn't make it, surviving a late pitch inspection before it was declared playable, and once the game was underway Dennis Parr then had the misfortune to put through his own goal. With the score still one-nil at the break Marys had all on to get back into the game and it took a Sid Thompson penalty ten minutes into the second half to bring them back level. Then, with it beginning to look like extra time might be necessary, Billy England edged them ahead after eighty minutes and Peter Williams, with a third just three minutes from the end, put the outcome beyond doubt.

It was a great result to take into the last match of the month, another tough four-pointer away to Belper. Although the Derbyshire side were lying fifth in the table they'd only dropped nine points, second only to Marys' league leading record of six, and with Noel Simpson and 'Tot' Leverton both flu victims, the Saints needed to be on their very best form. Christchurch Meadow was in its normal muddy state for this time of year but with the visitors forcing the pace play was very fast despite the conditions. Marys' forwards were in particularly sparkling form with their speedy attacks and clever interplay causing the home defenders many uncomfortable moments and Colin Collindridge was particularly unlucky when he saw a great effort strike the bar with the keeper well beaten. Then, a couple of minutes before the break and totally against the run of play, Belper won and converted a penalty. Even when a goal behind the Saints were never out the game and it looked as if a point had been salvaged when Billy England equalised with ten minutes left on the clock. Unfortunately the home side struck back almost immediately and held on in the closing stages for a crucial victory. It had been a bit of a setback but no one at the club felt the need to dwell on it for too long. Developments were taking place off the field that would ultimately have even more of a say in the future of the club than its actual performances on it.

Syd Gray hadn't had cause to call an EGM but nevertheless the thorny issue of the re-formation of the Midland League was still high on the agenda at each weekly committee meeting. Both the Central Alliance and the group of breakaway clubs had held separate get-togethers of their own early in the month and there was little sign of a *rapprochement* between the two sides. It looked as though there could be only one winner and after 'a long and interesting discussion' on 16 January Marys' committee decided by a unanimous vote that 'the club apply for membership of the Midland League'. The die was cast and when it was also announced that Alfreton Town were following suit the Football Post declared the contest between the two leagues well and truly over: 'It is no good beating about the bush. The fact must be faced that it is the Midland League which has won the right to stage senior football in the Midlands. The strength of the proposed Central Alliance Premier Division has been sadly reduced and plans to continue with it seem futile.'

Making the headlines in the national press in January was an announcement that an oral contraceptive pill was to be made available in Britain. Already launched in the USA the previous year, it would be initially prescribed to married women only, a policy that wouldn't change until 1967; highly successful right from the start, within three years the birth rate actually began to fall. This was the outcome expected but every action is at the mercy of the Law of Unforeseen Consequences and in the case of 'The Pill' the unintended effect was the ushering in of sexual freedom for women of all ages, married or otherwise, and the sexual revolution that followed.

Elsewhere a skinny young kid from Minnesota had not long arrived in New York City. He was a folk-singer, although when he was trying to find work in the Big Apple he was turned away because he sounded 'like a hillbilly'. He sang old blues numbers and tunes by Woody Guthrie but would soon develop a brilliant writing style of his own, one that would mark him out as one of the greatest talents of his time. His name was Bob Dylan and in less than a couple of years of having his finger on the pulse he would write 'The Times They Are-A Changin''.

Now I'm absolutely sure that as February dawned Syd Gray and Charlie Moore and the rest of Marys' committee had absolutely no idea who Bob Dylan was, after all, apart from family and friends, he was still completely unknown in the USA let alone the UK, but times were certainly changing with regards to Arnold's leading football club and the developments were coming thick and fast. Firstly, the Management of the Central Alliance released those clubs who'd not yet applied for membership of the Midland League from their existing obligations concerning the formation of their own Premier Division. Secondly, discussions regarding the provision of a new stand were re-started in earnest in expectation of the requirements of the Midland League regarding the ground facilities of their member clubs and finally, considering that professionalism was now the norm at the club, a special committee was appointed to decide which of the current contracted playing staff were to be retained for the following season.

In fact there seemed to be more action off the field than on it as the Saints only managed to fit in two matches, both cup ties, during the whole of the month. Gedling Road's notorious drainage system meant that yet another home game was called off following heavy rain and the last Saturday of February saw them fixtureless without any interference from the weather. They were due to play Goole but the league leaders had rearranged a delayed match with Matlock and neglected to tell anyone in Arnold about their change of plans until late in the week. By then two buses had been booked to take the players and supporters up to Yorkshire and apart from the embarrassment and cost of their subsequent cancellation, the blank day meant that the Saints had at least sixteen matches to fit in with just eleven weeks left in the season. As to the matches that went ahead the first of the two ties was the Senior Cup Quarter Final away to Ericsson Athletic, conquerors of Rovers in the previous round, but this time the Notts Alliance side found their latest opponents from Arnold a much tougher proposition. Two goals from Peter Williams, another from John Brady, and a successfully converted penalty by Sid Thompson, all before half-time, gave Marys a four goal lead. Despite a spirited fight back by the home side the Saints ran out comfortable winners by six goals to two to take their place in the Semi-Finals for the third consecutive year. The other tie, at home against Worksop in the League Cup, was a rescheduling of the postponed fixture a fortnight earlier but unfortunately Marys chose to give one of their least impressive performances of the campaign and went down by two goals to nil. Not only were they out of a competition that they could quite realistically have won, beaten by a side they'd already defeated five-nil, but they'd failed to score for the first time all season and their long unbeaten home run, stretching back now over a year, had been ended too.

SID THOMPSON SCORES FROM THE PENALTY SPOT : ERICSSON ATHLETIC v MARYS, 11 FEB 1961 (Courtesy Football Post)

Still, the prospect of challenging for a Central Alliance and Notts Senior Cup double together with a place in the soon to be reconstituted Midland League kept spirits at the club extremely high as March approached and the business end of the season was about to commence. Two of the players, Billy England and Peter Williams, were both enthusiastic about where the club was heading.

BE : I thoroughly enjoyed it. There was a terrific atmosphere at the club. We felt we could really do something.

PW : Marys were a really, really good club. They looked after their players and had good support, excellent support. There were always big attendances at away games because of their reputation. In 1960-61 we had a powerful team, a lot of experience, a lot of gelling. 'Tot' Leverton, for instance, brought a lot of 'nous' to the team, a lot of organisation. I enjoyed playing with them because they were a go-ahead club, very entrepreneurial, and they were verging on becoming fully professional. Syd and Charlie would go and see all the players they wanted and I rated their assessment, it was very good.

It was praise indeed from the Saints' winger but the committee obviously felt that they had to extend their scouting policy and as a result an advertisement appeared in the press for 'Professional footballers of Midland League standard'.

MARYS CAST THE NET FOR PLAYERS : 25 FEB 61

(Courtesy Football Post)

The Central Alliance tried one last time to organise a get together with the Midland League but their request for a meeting was turned down. The two competitions were now certain to go their separate ways but one thing was certain, some of the would-be Midland League clubs were going to be disappointed. At their latest meeting the Midland League confirmed their decision to limit the number of clubs to twenty and twenty-two had already indicated their intention of applying for membership. Eleven of these were the founder members, and as such guaranteed a place, so at least two clubs out of the remaining nine were destined to be left out. In the final shakedown, two factors would determine which of those nine would be the fortunate ones; the strength of their playing record, and the quality of their ground facilities. The first would be based on the immediate past, the current season, and the potential for improvement in the future, whilst the second criterion, equally if not more important in terms of immediate status than the first, would encompass the clubs' on-site amenities such as changing rooms, covered accommodation, refreshments and toilets. No one other than the most jaundiced observer could query Marys' playing record; their first two years in the top Division had seen them finish second and third and now, entering the home straight of the current season, they had dropped fewer points than any of their rivals for the title. Only off the field could their credentials be questioned and here, unfortunately, they had no control over the situation.

The truth was that the Saints' rapid climb to the top of the Central Alliance hadn't been matched in any way by developments at Gedling Road. In fact there had been no visible developments at all and the ground looked exactly the same as it had back in 1956 when it was first used; a football pitch in six acres of otherwise unutilised space. Admittedly, just this very month, outline plans for a new pavilion at KGV had finally seen the light of day but they had been a very long time arriving; almost five years in fact, and still with no certainty that they would ever reach fruition. Prior to this no attempt had been made to erect a permanent building of any sort, or even a temporary one for that matter, not even a public convenience. It was almost as if the Council weren't quite sure what to do with the land following Mrs Farr's gift of it some ten years earlier; or weren't prepared to spend any money on it other than mow the grass once in a while.

As to the provision of a stand at KGV, the club had had no help from the Council whatsoever. Entirely the brainchild of the Marys' committee, the plans for covered accommodation for eight hundred spectators had originally been drawn up by Mr Stanley Snell, a Redhill neighbour of Syd Gray, and submitted as long ago as November 1958. Although approval had been granted by the following March, the conditions attached to the consent were quite onerous:-

- The specification had to be approved by the Council.
- The back of the stand had to be constructed in brickwork.
- No advertisements were to be displayed anywhere on it.
- The building would belong to and be under the control of the Council who could use it or allow it to be used on such terms and conditions as they, in their absolute discretion, thought fit.
- Whenever football teams or others were allowed the use of the stand the charges to be made for admission would be subject to the approval of the Council.

The most contentious condition however was this:-

- The Council were to be under no obligation to the club(s) providing the stand to allow them the use of it or the ground.

In other words, build it at your own risk.

To a man, the members of Marys' committee were devoted to their club, but the world of planning and local politics was alien territory for the majority of them. Additionally, and with the greatest of respect to them, many of them didn't own the house they lived in or even run a car, so the prospect of them raising the capital for such a speculative venture was out of the question. So, with the more pressing matters of progress on the field as their immediate priority, developments regarding the stand proceeded very, very slowly and it was a further twelve months before the Council Surveyor provided his estimate of two and a half thousand pounds in response to an enquiry from the club as to the possibility of the Council themselves building it. Apart from the toe-dipping exercise of the Council asking both Marys and Rovers whether they would be prepared to pay an additional 'match day charge' for the facility, very little had happened in the ensuing twelve months. Now, with the Midland League certain to go ahead and with the club not wanting to be left on the outside with their nose pressed up against the windowpane, Syd Gray announced that tenders were being invited for the stand and that it was hoped that it would be ready for the start of the following season. The thorny question of its financing wasn't mentioned.

On the field of play all the club could do was continue to confound the critics who'd ever doubted their elevation to the top division of the Central Alliance in the first place and keep picking up points in their extremely realistic quest of claiming the title at only the third attempt. Even the defeat against Belper and a dearth of league games in February hadn't particularly weakened their position at the top of the table and they were still the side who'd lost least points going into this critical stage of the season.

	P	W	D	L	F	A	P	GA
Sutton Town	25	17	4	4	84	36	38	2.33
Goole Town	24	15	5	4	86	41	35	2.10
Arnold St Marys	**19**	**13**	**4**	**2**	**55**	**24**	**30**	**2.29**

First up in March were Shirebrook Miners Welfare, the poorest side in the division by some distance, having conceded a staggering one hundred and fifty six goals in only twenty three matches. For some reason Marys had struggled to see them off in January so now they had ample chance to set the position straight. Regrettably, even with home advantage, the Saints struggled to dominate their struggling opponents and could only manage to win by three goals to nil; Sid Thompson missing a penalty midway through the first half seemed to be symptomatic of Marys' performance all afternoon.

The following week the maroon and golds travelled over to South Normanton, another side who were having a difficult season and lying just two places above Shirebrook. They had, however, brought back an excellent point from their previous week's visit to Belper and, playing with the confidence they'd gained from that result, they more than matched a strangely subdued Marys. When they scored a minute before the break it was no more than their efforts deserved; little had been seen of the Saints' much vaunted forward line. Thankfully the visitors' performance in the second period was much improved and a goal apiece from Peter Williams and Colin Collindridge was enough to see them safely home.

Although these latest two matches had seen Marys well below their best, they at least had the consolation of picking up maximum points in their bid for the championship. Unfortunately, the two teams above them did the same so the *status quo* was maintained. The only other side apart from the top three who had a realistic chance of the title were the current champions, Matlock Town, who, despite languishing way down in tenth spot, had an enormous amount of games in hand on the leaders and had dropped fewer points than anyone in the division other than the Saints.

	P	W	D	L	F	A	P	GA
Sutton Town	27	19	4	4	89	37	42	2.41
Goole Town	26	17	5	4	93	43	39	2.16
Arnold St Marys	**21**	**15**	**4**	**2**	**60**	**25**	**34**	**2.40**
.....								
Matlock Town	19	12	3	4	71	39	27	1.82

Fourteen months previously the fixture list had thrown up back to back matches between Marys and Matlock and the outcome, a double for the Derbyshire side, had more or less put paid to the Saints' title hopes and provided the springboard for their opponents to go on and win the championship. Now, with the league even more finely poised than it was then, fate had decreed, against the odds, that the two sides would face a reprise of the previous year and meet home and away on the last two Saturdays of March. A couple of decent performances and Marys could look forward to the run-in with great confidence.

The first of the two clashes was over at Matlock and with attacking football made difficult by the windy conditions defences were on top until the half hour mark when the home side made the breakthrough, scoring at the third attempt after a couple of efforts had somehow been blocked by a combination of Ernie Iremonger and his defenders. The Saints, to their credit, came straight back on the offensive and a minute before the break only the woodwork prevented them gaining a deserved equaliser as Colin Collindridge's fierce drive hit the underside of the bar and was hurriedly cleared off the line with the keeper well and truly beaten. A goal then and Marys would have come out for the second period with the momentum very much in their favour but the disappointment of the near miss seemed to weigh heavily on them with the result that the home side looked far more dominant and stretched their lead with another couple of goals. At three-nil there was no way back for the maroon and golds. The only consolation as they journeyed back from the Derbyshire hills was that they wouldn't have long to wait for a chance to redeem themselves.

The first changes for five weeks were made when right-winger Mick Cripwell came in for his first game of the campaign and recent signing Fred Martin took Sid Thompson's place at left-half. Fred, now thirty-five and a work colleague of Albert and Charlie Moore at Ericssons, had been on Blackburn Rovers' books and had seen Football League action with Accrington Stanley, whilst Mick's record with the Saints was second to none. He soon showed that he was more than capable of reproducing the great scoring form he'd displayed over the previous three seasons when only a fine save from the Matlock keeper denied him a certain goal. He was also extremely unlucky again when the visitors' left-back blocked another goalbound effort right on the line. It was unfortunate too that Dennis Parr had given Matlock an early lead with an own goal after Marys had gone close in the game's opening stages. It stayed one-nil until half-time and then, on the resumption, Peter Williams, who'd moved to inside-right in place of John Brady in order to accommodate Mick's return, fired in the equaliser. It was no more than the Saints deserved and the goal opened the game right up. Both sides went close with Colin Collindridge only narrowly off target but it was the visitors who scored the next, crucial goal. With Marys finding themselves stretched in search of a second equaliser Matlock delivered the killer punch to give them an unassailable three-one lead. There was to be no way back for the Saints. The champions had not only completed another quick-fire double like they had the previous year, but they'd again dealt a severe blow to the maroon and golds' dreams of bringing the championship to Arnold for the very first time.

It hadn't been a great start to the weekend but just twenty-four hours later the mood in Marys' camp was certainly far more upbeat than it might otherwise have been following a heavy home defeat. The final meeting regarding the re-constitution of the Midland League was scheduled to take place at Worksop, now established as the geographical centre of the new competition, the next day. Despite the poor results against Matlock, the Saints' deputation of Syd Gray and Charlie Moore, armed with plans for the pavilion and the stand, started out in good spirits. One requirement for membership that had already been set was that clubs' grounds should be no more than fifty miles from Worksop and with Arnold twenty-five miles away, only four other clubs would be nearer the new HQ than Marys. With nine places still up for grabs and with only eleven applicants in the hat, it seemed inconceivable that the Saints could lose out to such clubs as the underperforming Wilmorton and Alvaston or the distant Wellingborough Town.

With pleasantries exchanged the meeting settled down to the business of the day; ratification of the constitution followed by election of members. The first blow to all eleven of the prospective applicants that weren't classed as founders came when the delegates were told that the league would limit itself to eighteen teams rather than the figure of twenty that had originally been announced to the press. Then, when it was realised that founder member Skegness Town's ground was seventy miles from Worksop, one of the league's key rules had to be 'stretched slightly' to avoid an embarrassing situation. If this stretching didn't quite reach Wellingborough, over a hundred miles away in Northamptonshire, then it provided an unexpected lifeline for three of Skegness' Lincolnshire neighbours. Bourne, Spalding, and Stamford were all beyond the fifty mile radius but actually nearer to Worksop than the seasiders and it seemed improbable that any of them could now be excluded on geographical grounds.

If Syd and Charlie had an uneasy feeling about the way the meeting had progressed so far they were about to become even less hopeful than ever. Almost as if a side's playing record was of no consequence, the founder members then determined that, following the inevitable elimination of Wellingborough under the distance rule, precedence would be given to those clubs whose grounds provided the best facilities. Wilmorton, who played on a Derby Corporation owned pitch and had no facilities for taking a gate, admitted that they weren't surprised at their subsequent failure to obtain a place. Their recent playing record hadn't been anything to shout about either. Creswell Colliery, on the other hand, despite a similarly poor showing on the field of play, were rather more vociferous when their application was turned down. One of the club's officials said "We are dreadfully disappointed. Although our dressing room accommodation may not be on the ground, it is only seventy five yards away and we have individual showers and lockers for each player."

All of which left just one more club destined to end up as losers and, with seven of the remaining eight hopefuls all with changing facilities adjacent to the playing surface and many of them having covered accommodation for spectators too, the writing was on the wall for Arnold's finest. It was a real stab in the back for Syd and Charlie, who'd both worked tirelessly in pursuit of the club's Midland League dream but as the meeting had unfolded there had been a degree of inevitability about the outcome. It was acknowledged that the club could hardly have done more out on the pitch, outperforming everyone other than Matlock in their three years in the top division, but ultimately they were let down by the fact that they played on a parks' pitch that had no facilities whatsoever and they changed even further away from their ground than the seventy five yards that had scuppered Creswell's application.

It was a very solemn and severely chastened Syd and Charlie who headed back down the A614 after the fateful meeting but by the start of the weekly committee session the following evening the mood had turned to one of anger and recrimination. Not with them of course; in fact a motion to thank them both for their wholehearted endeavours to get the club admitted to the Midland League was carried 'without dissent'. No, the bitter disappointment felt by one and all resulted in fingers of blame being pointed outside the club, primarily at a certain number of the league's founder members who it was felt had gone back on their previous indications of support and then towards the Arnold Council for its inability or unwillingness to provide facilities worthy of not only the Saints, and Rovers for that matter, but of the whole public facility six acre site at KGV.

Before the meeting at Worksop Marys' committee had done all in its power to show the new league that it ticked all the right boxes. It had confirmed that it was in a sound financial position, had begun looking around for better players for the following campaign, and had also indicated that they would be willing, should it be desired by the other members, to drop the 'St Marys' from the club's name. What wasn't made public was the less than encouraging comment that 'We don't want church sides in the Midland League', attributed to one of the Derbyshire town sides, that had precipitated the committee's offer. It was hardly an open arms invitation to join the club.

There wasn't going to be a warm welcome either for the Arnold Council who, when the tone of the Monday night meeting gradually went from merely angry to downright incensed, must have had its collective ears burned by the 'heated discussion' taking place. As a result it was decided to invite representatives of the Council to the following week's meeting in order that the lack of facilities at KGV could be discussed frankly. In the meantime Syd put on a brave face in his role as Secretary and club spokesman and told the Football Post diplomatically that "Although we are bitterly disappointed we will try again next year."

It remained to be seen just how the players themselves would react to the unexpectedly bad news but on the very first day of the new month, Easter Saturday, no side could have offered them a better test of their resolve than the equally disappointed Creswell Colliery. There'd been plenty of bite and not a little excitement too when the two sides had met earlier in the league cup and the latest episode at Gedling Road promised more of the same. With inside-right Barry Clarke making only his second appearance of the season and number ten Ron Haynes his first, the forward line had an unusual look to it but with the experienced 'Tot' Leverton and Colin Collindridge to the fore it was Marys who took the lead when Ron scored after thirty five minutes. Although the visitors pulled back onto level terms two goals from the ever reliable Mick Cripwell in the fifty third and fifty eighth minutes put the Saints well into the driving seat. However, Creswell had shown plenty of fighting in the first two matches and they did so again. Unfortunately the maroon and golds' defence buckled under the pressure and conceded three goals to give the Derbyshire side an improbable victory by four goals to three. If the wheels weren't coming off Marys' wagon completely then they were certainly beginning to wobble a bit.

MARYS v GOOLE TOWN 8 APRIL 1961 : Back Row (l to r); N Simpson, N Gough, D Parr, E Iremonger, B Molyneix, F Martin. Front Row; M Cripwell, C Collindridge, B England, E Wright, G Parr. Mascot T Gray.

(Geoff Parr Collection)

On the Easter Monday the Saints redeemed themselves somewhat with a five-nil thrashing of Wilmorton and Alvaston, again at KGV, with Billy England helping himself to four goals, two in each half, and Noel Simpson weighing in with a rare strike of his own. Unfortunately the following Saturday saw the maroon and golds travel up to Goole, take part in a splendid advertisement for the Central Alliance, but return home pointless having suffered their second odd-goal-in-seven set back in a week.

Then, as if four defeats in five matches wasn't bad enough, the club received even more disappointing news when the Council informed them that the estimate for the cost of the new stand had increased alarmingly from two and a half thousand pounds to three and a half thousand. If that wasn't depressing enough on its own then there was a *caveat* too. The Council also said that no assurance could be given as to the probable date the stand would be available owing to the fact that if work on it proceeded before 1962 it might be necessary to take precautions against subsidence from coal-mining under the field by the National Coal Board, and such precautions would only add to the cost.

It certainly seemed that not only were Marys unloved, they were also downright unlucky. After all the Council were, belatedly, finally planning to erect a pavilion on the opposite side of the pitch, merely fifty yards away from the intended site of the stand, which itself would run alongside the Friar Tuck car park and be no more than ten or fifteen yards away from the pub itself. There were apparently no subsidence problems hampering the pavilion's construction, nor had there seemed to be many such concerns when Home Ales' latest hostelry was completed only a couple of years earlier. Then there were the houses within a stone's throw on Hallams Lane, Gedling Road, and Central Avenue, the latter of which were being built at that very time; none of them looked in much danger of disappearing into a hole any time soon. Trust the Saints to locate the only coal seam in the vicinity over which to erect their lightweight steel, corrugated panel, open fronted, and open ended, spectator enclosure.

Once the implications of this latest setback had been realised, ie that the club wasn't going anywhere for at least a couple of years, a run-in that would have been testing enough anyway assumed an even greater degree of difficulty. Home and away clashes with Ilkeston and Heanor brought just one point and the league season ended with three straight defeats. A Central Alliance campaign that had promised so much drifted into anti-climax and a fifth place finish, brightened only by the appearance of young inside-forward cum wing-half John Anthony, promoted to the senior side after a string of excellent performances for the second team.

It would have taken a very miserable person indeed to deny Marys the chance of any glory at all in such a shatteringly disappointing end to the season but a historic success did come their way in the one other competition they were still contesting, the Notts Senior Cup. Having seen off Ericssons in the Quarter Final back in February, the Saints had been drawn against Division Two leaders Ransome and Marles in the Semis. Played at Meadow Lane the match was much closer than the teams' differing status might have indicated and the Newark side more than matched their senior opponents for the majority of the game. It took a goal from the evergreen Colin Collindridge to see the maroon and golds safely through to the Final after Billy England had opened the scoring and a young centre forward called Joe Boucher had got his name on the scoresheet for Ransomes.

The Final was also played at Meadow Lane and once again it was the Yorkshire League's Retford Town who were standing in the way of Marys' hopes of winning the Senior Cup for the very first time. If the Saints had any greater incentive than that to win the trophy then they could also remind themselves that their opponents had been the only non-Central Alliance club to be given a place in the new Midland League. The maroon and golds had gone very close to beating Retford in the first game of the Final two years earlier but had finally succumbed to them in a held over replay by three goals to one. On this occasion they again took the lead, courtesy of a fine header from Peter Williams, but unlike 1959 they didn't allow Retford back into the game, denying them the equaliser that they were desperate to secure. With Arnold supporters forming the majority of the crowd of two and a half thousand Marys held on for a famous victory.

MARYS v RETFORD TOWN : NOTTS SENIOR CUP FINAL : 6 MAY 1961 Back Row (l to r); B Molyneux, N Gough, E Iremonger, N Simpson, D Parr, J Anthony. Front Row; J Moore, R Leverton, B Coombe, C Collindridge, P Williams. Mascot T Gray. (Courtesy Football Post)

A few weeks earlier I'd been down at Meadow Lane to see the Magpies beat Shrewsbury in a typical end of season stroll; Notts couldn't go up and their visitors couldn't go down. Actually I was delighted that County were 'languishing' just outside the promotion places but I had to admit that the most excitement the seven thousand fans received all afternoon was hearing the news come through from Wembley that England were taking the Auld Enemy, Scotland, apart. The old guy in the scorebox was doing his best to keep pace with the torrent of goals being wired through to him but he was fighting a losing battle. For some reason my Dad and I hadn't come in the car so after the game we were walking back through the Meadows when we called into a shop owned by a friend of his and listened to Sports Report. One scoreline dominated the headlines, England NINE, Scotland three, and the poor incumbent between the sticks for the visitors, Frank Haffey, became the first of a very long list of custodians from North of the Border to be lumbered with the mocking moniker of 'Scottish Goalkeeper'.

However, for Marys, a season that had promised so much for so long, that had then looked like ending in disaster both on and off the field, had finally delivered a happy ending. They might have unhelpful landlords, there might even be a few coal miners hacking away at the black stuff deep down beneath their pitch, and they might be a couple of years away yet from the promised land of the Midland League, but whilst they bided their time Syd and Charlie and the rest could at least look at their reflections in the gleaming Senior Cup trophy and tell themselves they'd done as much as they could for their club.

There was one other guy who, despite his own advancing years, had also given everything he'd got in Marys' cause over the past season. He was Colin Collindridge, forty now but still showing the same feistiness and passion for the game that he'd displayed throughout his career. It was in the very last league game of the season that he'd shown that he was still up for the battle and I'll leave it to the reminiscences of Albert Moore and Roy and Eric Thompson to provide the detail.

AM : We went to Creswell, last match of the season.

The place where Colin was sent off earlier in the year for a straight foul on a member of the opposition he'd taken a particular dislike to.

AM : It was a battle royal this match, everybody was kicking and shoving and there was a bloke with a dog on the line and his wife and it might have been his son and he was on at Collo all through the match; "I'll let my dog go on you!"

E&RT : This winger came flying down and [Barry] Molyneux hit him, wrapped that bloke round the fence around the pitch. This winger's dad was there and he'd got a ruddy great dog with him.

AM : When we were coming off the ground at the end of the game me and our Charlie walked off with Colin. You had to go outside the ground to get to the changing rooms and we were walking in front of this bloke with this dog and he was off again. All of a sudden Collo turned round and grabbed him by the balls and said "Now let your bloody dog go".

E&RT : Collindridge got hold of him by his taters and put his foot in his chest and told a woman close by to get him to pull the dog back.

AM : He frightened this bloke to death. The other two who were with him took the dog away because Collo wasn't going to let go until the dog had gone. He must have been in agony. We used to have a bit of fun about it after because every time we saw a dog messing about on our ground we used to say "Send for Collo!"

"Send for Collo!" indeed. For the man with a voice now so high that only his dog could hear him it should have been more like "Send for the Nurse!"

I'd managed to survive my first year at secondary school, just, and was looking forward to the summer holiday with even more enthusiasm than usual. We were going to give Scotland a try but first we spent a long weekend on the flatter, less taxing terrain of the East Coast. It was the same bunch that had pitched up two years earlier in Devon and the previous summer in North Wales, which meant seven of us requiring accommodation with only five berths in our year-old touring caravan. The previous year my Nan and Granddad were dispatched to other lodgings but this time it was my Uncle Derrick and me who were excommunicated, and we weren't even to have the luxury of a roof over our heads either. No, from now on overspill numbers would be accommodated in a separate tent, recently purchased and not yet used, pitched adjacent to the van, and we had drawn the short straws.

Actually, I found it all quite exciting. I'd tucked myself into my sleeping bag while Derrick made sure everything was safe and secure and looked forward to my very first night under canvas. All was well until I was woken by the wind which had begun to get up and buffet the tent quite alarmingly. Unfortunately, it was merely the precursor of the howling storm that was to follow, and it wasn't long before torrential rain lashed down and the wind reached hurricane force.

My uncle's beauty sleep had been broken too and we lay there talking about the chances of the tent being either flooded by an overflowing dyke or, even worse, it being lifted off the ground with us still in it. My young mind was racing with the possibilities of these two fates. As I've mentioned, anything to do with water was definitely inclined to fill me with dread, but I didn't fancy the idea of free-form flying much either.

However, if I thought it couldn't get much worse, it suddenly did. Derrick asked me if I could hear a scratching sound outside the tent. I told him to stop larking around, that he wouldn't get me on that one again, but then my heart stopped as I could hear it too, intermittent but persistent. The wind was roaring and the rain was driving relentlessly down, and the scratching became more insistent. And I knew there wasn't a tree within a hundred yards.

I encouraged Des to go and have a look but he seemed disinclined to venture out from deep within his sleeping bag. It must have been like this for an hour or so until the wind began to drop slightly and the earlier ferocity of the rain abated somewhat. Almost as if choreographed, the scratching had ceased too. I think we must have decided that it was safe to go back to sleep because, the next thing I knew, night had turned into day and we were asking each other whether we had actually imagined the events of the early hours.

Derrick got up and unzipped the entrance to the sleeping compartment but immediately stepped back with a jolt. "Crikey!" he exclaimed, "it's a flipping dog." And sure enough it was, a big, black, menacing beast of a thing panting and slavering and scaring us half to death. Well that's a slight exaggeration. It was black, but that's about it. It looked half starved and certainly more scared than we had been, and as soon as Des popped his head back through the entrance the poor thing turned tail and was off through the same small gap that it had created earlier. All that scratching had been the poor mutt pawing at the outer zip of the tent sufficiently for it to open up and let it squeeze into the welcoming shelter beyond. We felt rather guilty by now, but I consoled myself with this thought. It might have been a skinny little runt but it had been clever enough to find a way to avoid staying out in the worst of that night's tremendous storm; clever enough then, I reckoned, to carry on finding the odd bone or two to keep itself from starving.

The rest of the mini-break was blessed with decent weather and once the site had dried out it was a perfect place for family games of football, cricket, French cricket, rounders, in fact anything other than tennis, and the reason for this was that my Granddad, as befitted a working man of his generation and a lifelong miner to boot, thought that the other summer sport was, how can I put it, not quite manly. It was okay for the distaff side, even if he hadn't bothered watching Angela Mortimer defeat Christine Truman in an all-English Ladies' Final at Wimbledon a few weeks earlier, and he might have had a grudging admiration for the Men's champion, the Aussie Rod Laver, but that was about as far as he was prepared to bend. Later on, even the great public parks product Jimmy Connors and his arch-rival John McEnroe at the height of their effin' and blindin' brilliance couldn't persuade him to alter this long held and pretty entrenched viewpoint.

I actually didn't know of my Granddad's antipathy towards the tennis club set when I first picked up a racket, and in fact I wasn't aware until some time later that there was even a vestige of a class divide regarding the sport. To me, anything that involved a ball was just too attractive a proposition to turn down, so me and my best mate from the top of Birchfield Road, Bill Nightingale, used to play as often as we could, and if he wasn't available I'd cajole some other pal or two to join me on court. We'd pack up our kit-bags, make sure we'd got a bottle of Apollo fizzy pop with us to keep us going through our upcoming exertions, and head off down into Arnold. I'm not sure of the exact date that the courts were laid at KGV but once they were that was normally our first port of call. Failing that it was a further trek to Arnold Park where there used to be some decent grass courts or onto Valley Road if all else failed. At the start we didn't have much of a clue how to play, other than by imitating what bit of Wimbledon we might have seen on TV, but we got better and better and by the time I left Richard Bonington I could at least play to a level where I wouldn't disgrace myself.

Sports at Nottingham High School followed a traditional pattern of rugby in the winter, athletics in the spring, and cricket in the summer. There were no opt-outs of the first two but quite a few kids chose a racquet over a bat when given the opportunity. I stuck with the cricket. After all, it wasn't only a football pitch that was missing at primary school, we didn't have any facilities for the summer game either, so I was quite looking forward to playing the sport on a proper, organised basis. I didn't do too badly at it either, getting picked for the school team, and as I still had the chance to play tennis outside school hours I couldn't have been happier.

On moving up to the School I had anticipated that there might be a prevailing attitude of 'us and them', especially as half were scholarship boys like me, and the other half the sons of parents wealthy enough to pay for their education. Being born into a working class family in a working class environment and having been brought up on a council estate where everyone was having to deal with the gradual but slow post-war economic progress, I'd never encountered situations where I might have been made to feel inferior to anyone, so I suppose my apprehension was natural. I needn't have worried. I was pleasantly surprised that the School was a real meritocracy. It was ironic, then, that it was on that usually most level of playing fields down at the School's beautifully appointed sports facility at Valley Road that I was first on the receiving end of a bit of overt snobbery. That it happened to be connected with tennis would obviously have come as no surprise to my Granddad.

Ever the one for a challenge, I'd put my name down for the first-year tennis tournament, a singles knockout championship. As the luck of the draw would have it I'd been plucked out of the hat to play against a member of the school team in the first round. There were only four boys who had that particular honour so I could consider myself somewhat unlucky to be facing one so early on. Still, by now I fancied my chances as a bit of a player, even though there was the small matter of not having received a single minute's coaching in all my life. Despite not having a backhand worthy of the name and, given my less than ferocious service, never likely to ever be called 'Rocket Rog', I still figured, ever the optimist, that being pretty fit and able to cover the court might give me an advantage against most of my opponents, members of the school team or not.

However, on the particular evening of this, my first ever competitive match, I was not only handicapped by a lack of coaching, but I'd also had to spend some three hours before my scheduled tie playing an obligatory game of cricket. Unsurprisingly I was slightly weary as I trudged back into the changing rooms to swap cricket flannels for tennis shorts, cricket boots for my Dunlop Green Flash plimmos, and cricket bat for a very sorry looking tennis racquet.

Well I thought it looked ok actually. So, it didn't have the luxury of a proper racquet press, popular at the time, nor even a cover like those of today, and I had wrapped some adhesive backed plastic tape around the handle to give me a better grip; so what? Maybe it was the fact that the tape was a startling dayglo yellow that invoked an outburst of loud guffawing from those seated nearest me. That severe lack of approbation only succeeded in strengthening my resolve. I felt very much like 'Tough of the Track' Alf Tupper, comic book hero of the working class underdog, or at least his younger brother, as I made the long walk over to the tennis courts muttering to myself, "I'll show 'em".

When you're that age, peer group disapproval comes keen, but the hurt only lasted as long as it took to beat my more favoured opponent at the first hurdle. There was no one left back in the changing rooms by the end of the match, so I had no immediate chance of wiping the smirks off a face or two, but I made sure I milked the occasion for all it was worth the next morning at school. It was the winner's responsibility to enter the result on the tennis noticeboard in the school's main corridor, so I made sure that one or two of my 'supporters' quite clearly saw the name 'Rann' being neatly entered into the allotted slot in the next round. I was even a bit of a star for a few days as word of my giant-killing achievement went around.

Unfortunately, and as is often the case, the 'minnow' came up against another 'big boy' at the next hurdle. It was just my luck to be drawn against another tennis club player from the school team, and to exacerbate the situation, this particular member only happened to be the son of none other than the form teacher in charge of the school's tennis programme. Almost inevitably, there was to be no repeat of my success of the previous round, and even though I lost in two straight sets, I didn't disgrace myself, winning six or seven games with my all action style. 'Style' might be a bit of a misnomer, but at least it wasn't a thrashing. I still didn't tell my Granddad that I'd been beaten by a fee-paying 'toff'.

If money could buy an education then a plentiful supply of the folding stuff certainly came in handy if a person wanted to run for the Presidency of the United States of America. Joseph P Kennedy Snr had built up a large fortune as a stock market and commodities speculator and by investing in real estate and a variety of industries. By the end of the fifties he was reckoned to be one of the twentieth richest people in the USA but even before then he'd had designs on using his wealth and extensive network of contacts to help take his first son, Joseph Jnr, to the White House. Sadly the young man died in the Second World War but despite this setback 'Joe' wasn't to be deterred. He re-channelled his ambition in the direction of his second son with so much success that, on 20 January 1961, John Fitzgerald Kennedy became his country's thirty-fifth President. At his inauguration address he talked repeatedly of his desire for 'change' and 'renewal' and famously challenged his countrymen: "And so my fellow Americans, ask not what your country can do for you, ask what you can do for your country." It was just the beginning of a remarkable era in Western politics, one where JFK and his wife Jacqueline, both younger and with a great deal more charisma than previous occupants of the White House, received as much media attention as pop singers and movie stars; all at a time when the world's two super powers were moving the nuclear arms race into uncharted and seriously dangerous territory.

A contemporary but much less threatening contest between the USA and the USSR was the quest to be the first nation to put a man into space and almost three months into the new Presidency the Soviets stole on a march on their arch rivals when Yuri Gagarin became the first man to orbit the Earth in *Vostok 1*. The race might have been won by the Americans but several delays along the way meant that Alan Shepard's flight in *Freedom 7* didn't take place until 5 May, three weeks after Gagarin's trip. Both men returned home safely to a hero's welcome.

A day before Shepard's voyage another journey was about to commence that would be of even greater significance to millions of people in the USA, one that would provide many opportunities for heroic deeds in the face of appalling hostility and hatred. With the American Civil Rights Movement gathering momentum but still not bringing about widespread change fast enough thirteen activists, white and black and known as the Freedom Riders, together with sundry supporters, left Washington DC by two buses. The plan was to travel down through the Deep South and end with a rally in New Orleans. At each stop they would challenge the region's outdated Jim Crow laws and the non-compliance with a US Supreme Court decision taken three years earlier that had prohibited segregation in all interstate public transportation facilities.

Only minor trouble was encountered in Virginia, the Carolinas, and Georgia, but when the riders arrived in Alabama violence suddenly flared. In Anniston on 14 May one of the buses was attacked and had its tyres slashed at the station. Due to the ferocity of the attack the bus moved quickly on but with its tyres deflating it had to pull over a few miles out of town. A mob which had been following in cars surrounded the stricken vehicle and a firebomb was thrown inside. As the Freedom Riders tried to escape the smoke and flames they found their exit blocked by the surging mob and it was only a combination of an exploding petrol tank and an onboard undercover agent firing a warning shot that prevented lives being lost. Twelve of the occupants were hospitalised and the bus destroyed. The same day the second bus was attacked by a mob led by Ku Klux Klan members in Birmingham, Alabama, with one of the Freedom Riders needing fifty-two stitches to a variety of head wounds.

Although these acts of hostility prevented the original itineraries from being completed the organisers realised that if the violence succeeded in stopping the rides altogether then the Movement would be set back years. On 17 May replacement Riders, students from Nashville, were found but ended up getting arrested in Birmingham. Undeterred they resumed the journey two days later but found a huge mob awaiting them when they reached Montgomery, Alabama on 20 May. Once again there was widespread violence and bloodshed, and Justice Department Official John Seigenthaler was beaten unconscious and left lying in the street. He'd been sent down to Alabama by the President's brother, US Attorney General Robert Kennedy, to try and calm the situation.

The following night more than a thousand people packed the First Baptist Church in Montgomery to hear Dr Martin Luther King call for a massive campaign to end segregation in Alabama in a speech he gave in support of the Freedom Riders. Even more whites gathered outside the church, attacking Federal Marshals who were trying to protect it and throwing stones at the congregation through the windows of the building. The mob was eventually broken up by the combined effort of the Marshals and local police reinforcements and martial law was imposed in an effort to bring some stability to the situation.

On 22 May even more Riders arrived in Montgomery for the next leg of the journey to Jackson and behind the scenes heated negotiations were taking place between the Kennedy administration and the Governors of Alabama and Mississippi. They cooked up a plan that would end the violent attacks on the Riders but would let state authorities arrest them for violating existing segregation ordinances at the bus depots, even though the legality of such arrests was questionable.

Arrest followed upon arrest and soon, with the detainees establishing a pattern by choosing to remain in jail for the maximum of forty days rather than posting bail immediately, the local cells in Jackson began to be filled to overflowing. The Kennedys called for a cooling-off period but the Movement's organisers refused and the rides continued rolling throughout the summer months. The Riders also campaigned against other forms of segregation and eventually, bowing to public opinion, the administration called upon the Interstate Commerce Commission to issue yet another desegregation order. It issued the necessary directives and by 1 November the Civil Rights Movement had won a great victory. Passengers would now be allowed to sit wherever they pleased on interstate buses and trains, signs denoting 'white' and 'coloured' were removed, previously separate drinking fountains, waiting rooms, and toilet blocks were desegregated, and lunch counters began serving people irrespective of the colour of their skin. Despite the bravery of the Freedom Riders the struggle for equal rights for American blacks was far from over and there would be more bloodshed down the line but extensive media coverage of the summer's events had at least brought the images of the conflict to the attention of the rest of the nation. The Rides might have embarrassed the administration, who had tried unsuccessfully to maintain a degree of neutrality as the drama unfolded, but with television and newsreel cameras bringing the conflict into millions of homes the country as a whole was shown a face of the South that it had never seen before. The Kennedys had been fearful of upsetting the Southern Democrats on whom they depended for support and likewise executives of the major TV networks were nervous about alienating their southern affiliates for very much the same reasons. Ultimately, the question of right and wrong became so clear cut that sitting on the fence was no longer an option.

By contrast, even as the Freedom Riders were readying themselves for the journey to certain arrest at Jackson on 25 May, JFK showed rather more enthusiasm for another project, one that would capture the American public's imagination rather than fuel its fears; that of putting a man on the moon before the decade was out. His problem this time was that support for this ambitious plan was thin on the ground and in asking Congress for $531 million dollars he had to defeat arguments from politicians both on the right, who wanted the money to be earmarked for military purposes, and on the left, who were desirous of it being used for social programmes. History shows that JFK got his way and in doing so not only accelerated the Space Race between the USA and the USSR but also ensured that the Cold War between the two warmed up a degree or two as a result.

Just under three months later, early in the morning of Sunday 13 August, the temperature rose even more sharply when the borders of communist East Germany were closed and the construction of the Berlin Wall commenced. Actually, it began life as a ninety-six mile long barbed wire fence but its erection was still a desperate move by the German Democratic Republic, to give it its proper title, to prevent East Berliners from escaping to the West of the city which, under the Potsdam Agreement reached following the end of WWII was under the joint control of the Americans, the British, and the French.

West Berlin's geographical position deep into Soviet-controlled East Germany made it a focal point for the clash of ideologies that fuelled the Cold War. However, with many people in the East far from enamoured with the dead hand of communism, a large number were choosing to flee to the West and their absence, damaging in propaganda terms as well as being a drain on the workforce, precipitated rumours about a wall. In just twenty four hours those rumours became fact as streets were torn up and barricades erected. The military were called out to man crucial points on the map and cross-city transport was suspended. At the close of the day West Berlin was completely cut off from the East.

The idea that a regime's best interests are served by incarcerating its citizens was not one shared by the writer of an article in The Observer back in May. Under the title 'The Forgotten Prisoners' Peter Benenson wrote: "Open your newspaper any day of the week and you will find a report from somewhere in the world of someone being imprisoned, tortured, or executed because his opinions or religion are unacceptable to his government. There are several million such people in prison – by no means all of them behind the Iron and Bamboo Curtains – and their numbers are growing." He then wrote of the power of public opinion and of his view that no government is immune from the pressure it can bear: "That is why we have started Appeal for Amnesty, 1961. The campaign, which opens today [May 28], is the result of an initiative by a group of lawyers, writers, and publishers in London who share the underlying conviction expressed by Voltaire: 'I detest your views but am prepared to die for your right to express them.' We have set up an office in London to collect information about the names, numbers, and conditions of what we have decided to call Prisoners of Conscience, and we define them thus: Any person who is physically restrained (by imprisonment or otherwise) from expressing (in any form of words or symbols) an opinion which he honestly holds and which does not advocate or condone personal violence."

From small acorns large oaks do grow and following a meeting soon after the article appeared, delegates from Belgium, the UK, France, Germany, Ireland, Switzerland, and the USA decided to establish a 'permanent international movement in defence of freedom of opinion and religion'. The organisation known today as Amnesty International was the result and it now has more than two million members, supporters, and subscribers in over a hundred and fifty countries and territories, in every region of the world. Amnesty's remit, though entirely honourable, couldn't by necessity operate on a grand scale, especially in its earliest days, but its members would have concurred entirely with the sentiments voiced by President Kennedy when commenting later on the Berlin Wall: "Freedom has many difficulties and democracy is not perfect, but we have never had to put a wall up to keep our people in."

The Wall stood for almost thirty years before it was eventually dismantled but in the Arnold of 1961 quite a few less well-known ones were being pulled down either by accident or design. Vandals continued to take great pleasure in turning the town's outdoor toilets into public inconveniences as well as providing a steady flow of repair work for local jobbing builders although one potential target that, remarkably, seemed to be of little interest to the delinquents was the Bonington Cinema, probably the largest building in the town centre. Having screened its last picture show some three years earlier it was still standing, unloved and unused, as a relic of a bygone era. New construction projects were taking place further up Front Street but they were piecemeal affairs and it was in the expansion of the district's residential area that most obvious progress was being made.

There was however one new building going up that summer that was of great interest to the town's sports enthusiasts and to Marys and Rovers in particular; it was the long-awaited construction of the pavilion at KGV. Almost five years after they'd first charged the two clubs rent for using the ground, the Council had at last found the will and the funds to erect the single storey facility which would at least provide rudimentary shelter, storage, and toilet amenities to the public using the recreation field. Unfortunately, and quite unbelievably, the pavilion had been designed without any showering facilities. Any thoughts that the Saints might have entertained about gaining acceptance to the Midland League at the end of the forthcoming season had just been dealt a fatal blow. The league's rules were pretty explicit regarding this matter; separate, on-ground, bathing facilities had to be provided for visiting teams. Marys couldn't meet these requirements in time for the start of the 1961-62 season about to start and now, unless there was a massive change of heart, and building plans, by the Council the club wouldn't be able to meet the ground criteria for 1962-63 either.

When the lack of showers had been brought to the attention of the committee, Syd Gray was immediately instructed to fire off a letter to the Council, presumably to enquire about the chances of the omission being remedied. At the same meeting that this decision was taken, three recently elected Arnold Councillors had been invited along to discuss the current position regarding the ground. They were Councillors Barrass, Harker, and Elliott, and all three were sympathetic to the club's plight. Albert Moore was one of fifteen Marys' committee men who attended that crucial get-together.

AM : We could see that all these teams like Alfreton and the rest were getting help from their Councils and we were getting none from ours so we had this meeting with the Councillors. They were all Labour, although it didn't really matter which party they were from. The important thing was they were on our side.

Even with these three gentlemen on board the prospects of the Council giving them any tangible help soon was pretty remote and there must have been occasions when Marys' committee had doubts that their own ambitions would ever be matched by that of the town's elected representatives.

AM : It did feel sometimes that the Council didn't really want us there but all we wanted was to provide the best football possible for the people of Arnold. We were even prepared to do all the work ourselves but there were obviously some people at the Council who weren't so keen. I think that Syd [Gray] might have ruffled a few feathers down there. He only wanted what was best for the club like all of us but he could be a bit 'bull at a gate'. He wanted things to get done straight away; that was his nature.

However, it wasn't long after the meeting with the three Councillors that Marys' committee might have been forgiven for coming to the conclusion that their lack of support from within the Council Chamber ran much deeper than a few ruffled feathers. Firstly, the Council itself was told by the National Coal Board that as there was no problem with subsidence it was safe to proceed with repairs and improvements to the Arnold Baths. Secondly, it was reported that at a meeting of the Council Estates Committee a motion had been proposed that 'in future football clubs should not be allowed to make any charge for admission to football matches on playing fields owned by the Council'.

Now I'm neither a geologist nor a conspiracy theorist but it does seem slightly odd that with the Baths being given the all-clear, and after all they were only just down Hallam's Lane at that time, the threat of subsidence seemed to be delaying only one building project in the area; Marys' proposed stand. As to the matter of admission charges it didn't take a genius to see who the target of that thinly veiled attack was. Of all the recreation grounds under Council control, KGV was the only one whose teams attracted a crowd big enough to take a gate, and even then Rovers, thanks to their diminishing status on the field of play, were down to a handful of diehard supporters. That only left the Saints and it must have been galling for their committeemen to realise that there were people in a position of power who didn't, quite clearly, share their enthusiasm in wanting their club to even exist in its present form, let alone advance.

On this occasion, thankfully, the motion wasn't carried, but the detractors had shown their hand and from now on, Marys' tenure at the ground would always have a question mark hanging over it. The meeting did resolve that all future rent payments by both clubs at KGV would include the use of dressing rooms, (meaningless at the moment because without showers the clubs would continue using the Baths), and more saliently the permission for the clubs to charge admission to the football enclosure on the understanding that no attempt was made to exclude members of the general public not wishing to enter the enclosure from entering the playing field.

Considering that there had never been any barriers, turnstiles, or other encumbrances preventing free access to the recreation ground, this latter issue seemed to be much ado about nothing. One of the hundreds of supporters happy to cough up his entrance fee each home game was Geoffrey King, and he recalls the rudimentary means by which the club took his money.

GK : They had a little wooden hut that they used to wheel out each game. Ron Hinson used to stand inside with either Albert Moore or Jack Brace, collecting the money.

Ron might have been a fine wing-half for the club back in the nineteen fifties but he was hardly 'bouncer' material. Then again he didn't need to be because invariably those people who supported the club were more than willing to contribute to club funds and happily handed over their bob a game whilst anyone wanting access to the recreation field but weren't interested in the football only had to walk up the entrance path and pass behind the hut.

The Council's decision to allow matters of admission to continue much as they had before merely signalled an uneasy truce but at least the band of disgruntled rate-payers, dog-walkers, and those poor souls who had nothing better to do than object to no more than one quarter of KGV being used once a week for a couple of hours, eight months of the year, for a decent standard of football watched by hundreds of people, some of whom might even have been dog lovers themselves and most certainly would have been rate-payers too, could sleep easily. Syd and Charlie and the rest probably decided it would be more advisable to keep one eye open.

All the off-field activities in the close season almost overshadowed developments on the playing side but there was no let up in preparations for the new season, one which saw the creation of the Central Alliance Premier Division from the wreckage of the previous year's competition. Of course it might have had the same title but it didn't have anywhere near the same status as it would have had if a large part of its membership, seventeen teams in all, hadn't defected to the Midland League. What was left was a mishmash of sides from both North and South sections of the former Division One together with four teams from Division Two and a couple of new entrants from other leagues.

When the make-up of the Premier Division was first announced it contained sixteen clubs and amazingly, considering that they had only finished half-way up Division Two the previous season, the list contained the name of none other than Rovers. With the season rapidly approaching, it appeared that there must have been a change of heart at the club because they never did make it to the top division, their place being taken even more improbably by Aspley Old Boys who'd finished even lower than the red and whites down in nineteenth place. One other late arrival was that of Boston United who'd finished bottom of the Premier Division of the Southern League and were struggling for money. Welcoming them to the Central Alliance, the League Secretary said "[They] should be happier in the Alliance if only for the fact that the Directors would know there was not so much red ink on their bank statement".

Their financial problems didn't stop them from being rated as one of the two sides most likely to mount a serious challenge for the title and it was no surprise to anyone when the name they were bracketed with was that of Marys, the previous season's highest finishers of all the Central Alliance clubs still in the league. Truth be told, finishing outside the top two places would be seen as a major step back by anyone associated with the club and even though they had had to set their sights somewhat lower when looking for new players, they were still advertising for fresh blood right up until the very first day of the season, August 19.

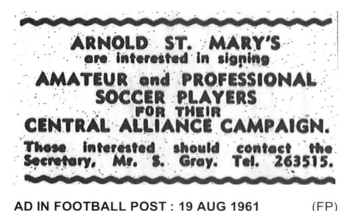

AD IN FOOTBALL POST : 19 AUG 1961   (FP)

Despite this recruitment drive and Syd Gray's pre-match protestation that a number of players were still on holiday the team for the new campaign's opening fixture included only three new faces: right-half Richard Wright, who'd previously been with Nuneaton Borough in the Southern League; inside-left Edwin Wright; and inside-right John Page who'd been a prolific goalscorer with Belper Town. They wouldn't have an easy ninety minutes in which to gel with their new team-mates either because strangely enough Marys' first opponents were none other than Boston United. To make matters even more difficult, it was scheduled to take place over at the Lincolnshire side's Shodfriars Lane ground, where a large and vociferous home crowd would only add to the problems facing the Saints.

Those difficulties were soon obvious to every one of the nineteen hundred spectators who had gathered for this early clash of the league's most highly regarded sides when the hosts roared into a two goal lead just after the twenty minute mark. Billy England had been unlucky to see a shot cleared off the line with the keeper beaten but Boston were good value for their lead and the Saints did well to keep the score at two-nil until the break. Then, as is often the case, the maroon and golds came out for the second period looking like a completely different outfit and took the game to the home side with such success that John Anthony pulled one back around the hour. This was the start of a spell of dominance by Marys that saw the Pilgrims visibly tiring and it was no surprise when the visitors equalised through Peter Williams in the seventy-seventh minute. In fact with a little more steadiness in front of goal the Saints might have brought back two points instead of just the one.

Nevertheless, Marys' tremendous fight back and excellent second half performance augured well for the season ahead, which was more than could be said for poor old Rovers whose display in both halves against Teversal was pretty abysmal. Down five-nil at half-time they recovered slightly after the break but still ended up getting whipped by eight goals to one.

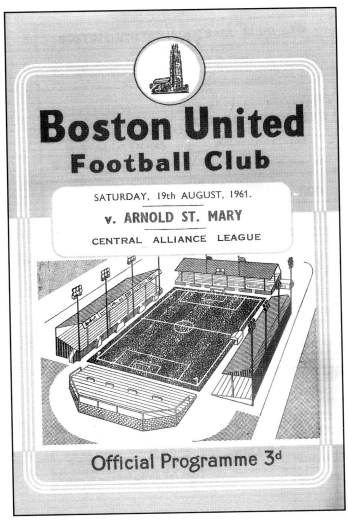

Boston United Football Club

SATURDAY, 19th AUGUST, 1961.

v. ARNOLD ST. MARY

CENTRAL ALLIANCE LEAGUE

Official Programme 3ᵈ

ELEVEN PILGRIMS v ONE SAINT ?

(Peter Williams Collection)

Inevitably there'd be alterations to the red and whites' line-up following such a disastrous start but surprisingly the Saints' eleven the following week showed a couple of changes too with ex-Notts County left-back Pat Groome, signed from Sutton Town, taking the place of Norman Gough and Colin Cann, previously at Belper, donning the number seven shirt. Their debuts would be over at South Normanton, not one of Albert Moore's favourite places to visit.

AM : The ground was good, the people weren't. They used to have a secretary who went round the ground bawling "Kick him up in the air", one of those sort. He was awful and you knew what you were going to get as soon as you got there.

Whether the welcome was hostile this particular day isn't known but Marys were certainly on the receiving end of some penetrating play by the home side that resulted in Barry Molyneux clearing off his own goal line and then the referee disallowing a goal for the Derbyshire outfit only after consultation with his linesman. Although this was the nearest South Normanton got to scoring the Saints hardly fared any better and the game ended in a goalless stalemate. It wasn't quite the result anticipated but even as the team's performance was being discussed at the following Monday's committee meeting an even greater shock awaited those members not already in the know. 'Tot' Leverton was leaving the club to sign for Cambridge United and only Marys' 'inner sanctum' knew anything about the move. Albert Moore was one of the privileged few who'd been aware of the transfer and especially to the fact that a fee of eight hundred pounds was involved, a veritable fortune in 1961 and enough to set the club up for some time to come considering that with admission just a shilling, threepence for boys and girls, and free for OAPs, the average gate receipts at the time were around twenty to twenty five pounds per match.

AM : You had to keep these things quiet. You didn't need everybody knowing what was going on.

The following Saturday, the first in September, Marys staged their first home game of the season, the return fixture with their previous week's opponents South Normanton. With 'Tot' off to pastures new his replacement in an otherwise unchanged line-up was John Watts, an eighteen year old Scot. Dominating the game from the start there was to be no repeat of the performance seven days earlier and aided by a goal in the sixty-fifth minute from Colin Cann, his first for the club, the Saints ran out comfortable winners by three goals to nil.

This first win of the season had been a timely one considering that the following week Marys made a little bit of history with their very first appearance in the FA Cup. Teams from Arnold, including an earlier version of the Saints, had actually played in the venerable competition with little success in the early part of the century but none had entered since 1926. Now it was the turn of Kegga's boys to see if they could do somewhat better than their predecessors although with bogey side Matlock Town as the visitors they obviously had their work cut out. The Derbyshire club had been the only team to truly dominate Marys in their three years in the top division of the Central Alliance, winning five of their six meetings, including all three at Gedling Road, and for the last two seasons they had almost single-handedly stopped the Saints' title ambitions in their tracks with back-to-back defeats at a crucial time.

MARYS v MATLOCK TOWN, FA CUP 9 SEP 1961 : Back Row (l to r); R Wright, B Molyneux, E Iremonger, D Parr, P Groome, J Anthony. Front Row; C Cann, J Watts, B England, J Page, P Williams.
(Courtesy Football Post)

The maroon and golds certainly didn't lack for support as the historic nature of the game and the traditional attraction of the FA Cup pulled in one of the largest crowds ever seen at KGV. Unfortunately, stage fright seemed to take hold of the home side and the visitors bossed the tie right from the kick-off, the only surprise being that it took them half an hour before they finally made the breakthrough. After that it was a bit of a procession and by the break Marys were already three-nil down. Although the Saints rallied for a brief spell in the second half and pulled a goal back through Colin Cann, Matlock added two more to their own tally to finish easy five-one winners.

The Midland League side had not only brought Marys' cup hopes to an abrupt end, they had also inflicted on the club its worst ever defeat at Gedling Road, and it was a surprise given the poor performance of all but two or three of the team that there were no changes for the next match, again at home, against old foes Aspley Old Boys. Fortunately the days when the Melbourne Road side had the Indian sign over the Saints had long gone and this week it was the turn of Marys to race into a three-nil half-time lead thanks to goals from John Watts, John Page, and Billy England. The young Scot made it four after the break but Aspley, no doubt recalling battles of old, clawed their way back into the game with three goals of their own to make the closing stages more uncomfortable for the Saints than they should have been.

At least Marys' unbeaten record in the league had been maintained and the following Saturday they had a reasonable chance of extending their run with their fourth home game on the trot against another of the previous campaign's key adversaries, Creswell Colliery. Despite his brace against Aspley John Watts found himself back in the reserves, replaced by another teenager John Moore, and Fred Martin came in at centre-half for the injured Dennis Parr. On this occasion there was no need to 'Send for Collo', currently helping out the youngsters in the reserves because, despite the visitors having had the better of the opening twenty minutes, once Billy England started the scoring midway through the half there was only one team in it and a final scoreline of five-nil, with the goals being shared around, was a fair measure of the Saints' superiority.

The final game of the month saw Marys make their second journey to Boston, this time in the first round of the Central Alliance Premier Division Cup and in the six weeks since the two sides first met the Pilgrims had firmly established their credentials at the new level they were operating. After dropping a point to the Saints on the opening day they'd rattled off four straight wins with a goals tally of eighteen against four to lead the table on goal average over Ransome and Marles with Marys tucked in a point behind in third place. The Newark side had clinched the Second Division title the previous season and early indications were that they'd be giving the two favourites a run for their money. The table before the round of League Cup ties looked like this:-

	P	W	D	L	F	A	P
Boston United	5	4	1	0	20	6	9
Ransome and Marles	5	4	1	0	15	7	9
Arnold St Marys	**5**	**3**	**2**	**0**	**14**	**5**	**8**

It definitely made better viewing than Rovers' position at the bottom of their division, formerly known as the Second and now re-branded the First. The red and whites had taken another pounding, this time from Ollerton Colliery by nine goals to nil and had only managed to pick up a single point out of a possible fourteen. Their plight wasn't helped by the fact that they'd not yet played a single Saturday game all season at Gedling Road and they'd even been drawn away to Matlock Town Reserves in the Division One Cup the same day that Marys were off to Boston. The omens weren't particularly good when they arrived late for the game against one of the division's better sides and the kick-off had to be delayed twenty-five minutes. Luckily the wait seemed to instil in the hosts a marked lack of urgency and they subsequently played the game at a canter and Rovers could count themselves somewhat lucky to come away with only a six-one defeat.

Over in Lincolnshire the kick-off was on time and the game soon developed into an absorbing contest in front of a crowd of nearly sixteen hundred. Early exchanges were even and although Boston took the lead after a quarter of an hour Billy England popped up with a header for the equaliser a couple of minutes later. From then on Marys, quicker in the tackle and more accurate in their passing than the home side, gained the upper hand and it was very much against the run of play when the Pilgrims scored from the penalty spot just before half-time. The two-one scoreline flattered the hosts and it was no surprise that on the resumption the Saints were soon back into their stride. In the seventy-fifth minute Colin Cann brought the scores level for the second time and when Peter Williams added a third with only six minutes left it looked for all the world as if the maroon and golds were home and dry. Unfortunately, right at the death, their opponents snatched the goal that denied them what would have been a thrilling victory.

Immediately after the match the Boston directors suggested that the replay might be staged mid-week under the floodlights at Shodfriars Lane but when the matter was discussed at Marys' Monday night committee meeting the idea was flatly rejected. Quite rightly 'Kegga' and Co argued that they couldn't deny their own supporters the opportunity to see a game of such importance against probably the league's most attractive opposition, even though it would have been of greater financial benefit if they'd agreed to the Pilgrims' request.

The primary reason behind Boston's thinking was that they were still severely strapped for cash, having recently had a summons for nearly one hundred and eighty pounds rates arrears adjourned for twenty eight days by the town's Magistrates Court. There was no ill feeling between them and Marys over the latter's desire to stage the replay themselves, in fact the only note of discord between the two sides had come when Billy England found himself being booked for fouling an opponent and then shaking his fist at him. Kindergarten stuff really compared with the aggression taking place elsewhere in the wider world.

Only a couple of weeks earlier more than eight hundred people were arrested in London in the largest and most violent 'Ban-the-Bomb' demonstration yet seen. Amongst those held were the actress Vanessa Redgrave, the playwright John Osborne, and the jazz singer George Melly and at one point on the very day that the USSR tested its twelfth nuclear bomb there were over fifteen thousand protestors jammed into Trafalgar Square and the surrounding streets. When the demonstrators staged a peaceful 'sit-down' as part of their civil disobedience agenda, the three thousand police in attendance struggled to make arrests and as a consequence the face-off between the two sides escalated into physical confrontation.

The following day a letter appeared in the Daily Telegraph urging people to join civil defence organisations as protection in the event of a third, and probably nuclear, world war and a few weeks later the President of the United States John F Kennedy went a stage further and advised American families to begin building bomb shelters to protect themselves from atomic fallout should World War Three become reality. It was pretty depressing stuff but at least one US citizen, the singer Bob Dylan, planned to ignore his leader's recommendation, telling everyone via his song 'Let Me Die In My Footsteps' that he "will not go down under the ground 'cause somebody tells me that death's comin' round".

If they weren't now then in another twelve months' time almost everyone above a certain age in the western world would become very aware of how close they all were to meeting their maker but the chances are that the major topic of conversation amongst Marys' players as they travelled over into Derbyshire on the first Saturday of October wasn't that of nuclear annihilation but more likely concerned the destruction of Forest by Spanish side Valencia earlier in the week.

The competition that had brought the two sides together was the Inter-Cities Fairs Cup, the forerunner of the current EUFA Cup, originally open, as its name suggests, to cities that held international trade fairs. Entrance was by invitation only and in 61-62 the Reds made their first foray into European competitive football when they joined Sheffield Wednesday and Birmingham City as England's three representatives. Of the trio Forest had by far the most difficult draw and probably exceeded all expectations by only losing two-nil in the first leg at the Stadio Mestalla. I was one of the thirty six thousand fans who'd taken their place at the City Ground for what was my, and probably their, first experience of a live match against 'continental' opposition. I'm sure that every one of us who was there has never forgotten the terrific display of the visitors and especially that of their Brazilian centre-forward Waldo Machado da Silva, or Waldo for short, who terrorised the Reds' defence all evening. It's not often that the visitors get applauded off the field at the end of the game but even Forest fans know when they've been privileged enough to witness a master class, and the Spaniards five-one drubbing of the Reds was definitely that. Waldo scored twice, laid on three more for right winger Nunez and gave centre-half Bobby McKinlay a night that he'd like to forget but probably never could. The only surprise was that the twenty-seven year old Brazilian, who had scored over three hundred times in his early career in his home country and would go on to score another hundred and fifty goals in Spain, would only wear the national shirt four times. Then again, he did have a young man called Pele blocking his path.

At least Forest would have the consolation of knowing that they went out to the eventual winners of the competition as Valencia beat all comers, including their fellow countrymen Barcelona in the final, to claim the first of their five European club trophies. In fact they gave as big a hiding to the future giants of the Spanish game as they had to the Reds, beating them by six goals to two at home and seven-three on aggregate, but it wasn't necessarily their sheer superiority that they will be remembered for, especially in Nottingham, it was the fact that they'd left the large crowd wanting more nights like they'd just witnessed, if not quite the same result.

As the Saints disembarked from the coach carrying them to their destination no one amongst them would have been contemplating being turned over in quite the manner in which Forest had but nevertheless a tough match was definitely in prospect as their opponents were Gresley Rovers, currently in fifth place and whose only defeat had come at the hands of Ransome and Marles. The home side had much the better of the first half but the score remained goalless until centre-forward Billy England capitalised on a mistake to give the Saints the lead. Rovers fought back and with two goals in fifteen minutes assumed control of the game once again. With only three minutes left another fine piece of opportunism by Marys' number nine looked to have salvaged a valuable point but with the referee about to signal the end of the match Gresley went down the other end to claim a late, late winner; the second week in a row that the Saints had been thwarted with no time left on the clock in which to mount a comeback.

There was no game the following week so the committee had plenty of time in which to analyse the defeat and choose the side for the visit to Clay Cross. Whether as a direct consequence or not, Richard Wright and Colin Cann had played their last games for the club with coach Noel Simpson taking over at right-half and a debut at inside-left being given to the club's latest signing, twenty-three year old Billy Radford, who'd previously been with Sutton Town. The number ten wasted no time in making his mark, scoring in the eighth and nineteenth minutes, and with John Page weighing in with a couple more, the outcome was never in doubt. The only negative aspect of the afternoon occurred when Noel's first appearance of the season was cut short by his ejection from the field of play for a misdemeanour deemed serious enough by the referee to warrant a sending-off but debatable enough in the player's eyes for the Saints' coach to ask for a personal hearing at the subsequent FA disciplinary meeting that dealt with his offence.

Noel's altercation apart, it had become quite noticeable that standards of behaviour in the professional game were starting to decline both on and off the pitch. The very same Saturday violence had flared at the Baseball Ground when Derby County played hosts to Liverpool in a top of the table clash in Division Two. A youth had run onto the playing area and tried to kick Ron Yeats, the visitors' centre half, and at the end of the game fighting broke out all over the pitch as hundreds of fans streamed onto the playing surface. Back in February a Forest fan had also interrupted play when he ran onto the pitch and struck out at Manchester United's Shay Brennan, and Plymouth and Gillingham both had their grounds closed for a fortnight following crowd trouble. At least Noel had the decency to leave the field of play when asked. Three weeks after his dismissal ex-Arnold Rovers' player Geoff Hazledine, now playing for Loughborough United in the Midland League, stood his ground following his own sending off for allegedly using abusive language to the referee and the game had to be abandoned. Thankfully, relationships between officials and players hadn't disintegrated completely. Towards the end of the previous campaign in a Central Alliance Cup tie between the Leicestershire side and Worksop Town three players exchanged blows but escaped with nothing more than a severe ticking off from the match official. Of course for the man in black it's always been a case of 'damned if you do, damned if you don't'.

As it happened Noel's playing services weren't required for the next game, the visit of second placed Ransome and Marles, but back in his role as coach there would be plenty of opportunity to run an eye over the opposition, Champions of Division Two the previous season and unbeaten after seven games in this one. One player in particular who had been attracting a lot of attention, not least because he'd scored in every game so far, was centre forward Joe Boucher. He'd scored against the Saints in the previous season's Notts Senior Cup and it only took him six minutes to repeat the feat this time. When the Newark side added a second four minutes later, Marys were facing an uphill battle but to their credit they fought back strongly, and a goal apiece from Billy England and John Page drew them level before the half hour mark. The scores stayed tied with both sides battling it out for that vital goal and when the Greens were reduced to ten men following an injury to one of their players the odds swung heavily in the maroon and golds' favour. However, going all out for the winner themselves they were caught out by the visitors and despite fighting hard to gain an equaliser had to concede defeat by three goals to two. It was a disappointing outcome to an otherwise entertaining match because not only did it result in the loss of Marys' unbeaten home record in the league but it also saw them slip to seventh in the table.

With a solitary win in the month October had proved to be quite unprofitable for the club, certainly on the pitch, but steps had been taken to protect their long-term interests when John Moore signed professional forms to become Marys' second contracted teenager along with John Anthony who'd put his pen to paper a couple of months earlier. Not only had their performances been good enough to elevate them to the first team, they'd also been of sufficient quality to ensure that one or two League clubs were monitoring their progress. Syd and the rest were just making sure that nobody was going to run off with their promising players without coughing up a bob or two for the privilege.

That decision was looking even more of an astute move when not long into the Saints' first fixture in November, away at Ashbourne Town, both Johns had got themselves on the score sheet to give Marys an early command of the game; John Moore's was a goal to remember too, the culmination of a solo run that had started in his own half. However, as if to show that it wasn't only the young 'uns that could produce the goods the evergreen Colin Collindridge, making his first appearance of the season a mere eleven days shy of his forty-first birthday, added another and the flood gates opened. The fact that the home side scored two of their own was largely immaterial as the Saints ran up double figures, including four for Billy England and six in the last thirty five minutes.

It had been a spectacular performance by the maroon and golds but with Boston United the following week's visitors in the replayed League Cup tie it might not have been quite the preparation needed for such a crucial match. Even though Marys were the only Central Alliance side to have stopped the Pilgrims from winning all season, and they'd done it twice on their opponents' own ground, Boston had won all ten of their other league fixtures and averaged almost four goals a game in the process. On the plus side none of these victories had been against the top sides like Ransomes and Gresley so there was a great deal of confidence in the Saints' camp as they lined up in front of another bumper Gedling Road crowd.

Straight from the kick-off Marys forced a corner on the right and although the visitors cleared the immediate danger the Saints were soon attacking down the same flank, this time testing the keeper with a deep cross. With John Moore having the early measure of his full-back the maroon and golds persevered with the tactic and with only five minutes gone the young winger crossed again and this time Billy England evaded his marker and scored with a neat header at the far post. It had been precisely the start that Marys had needed but unfortunately the home goal came under immediate pressure and in the tenth minute Boston grabbed an equaliser. Undeterred, the Saints regained the upper hand and with John Moore continually harassing the visitors' defence had by far the majority of the play and were unlucky that the scores still remained level at half-time. However the Pilgrims weren't top of the table for nothing and ten minutes after the restart they took the lead. The longer the score remained at two-one the more risks Marys took and it was no surprise that in the eightieth minute the visitors broke away to add a third and decisive goal.

BILLY ENGLAND HEADS IN AT THE FAR POST : MARYS v BOSTON UNITED 11 NOV 1961
(Courtesy Football Post)

Even though it hadn't been a league match the defeat was still disappointing and the fact that Ransomes picked up another couple of points the same day meant that Marys now trailed both the leaders by nine points. With the selection committee struggling to find a consistently successful combination it was expected that more changes would be made but when the side for the visit to Aspley the following week was announced the omission of Billy England's name on the team sheet caused more than the odd eyebrow to be raised.

BE : I'd scored four goals at Ashbourne and afterwards Noel, who was a mate of mine, came and told me that one or two committeemen had said that I wasn't trying. I asked him what he thought and he said that from his point of view I was doing fine but he was just giving me a word of warning about what was being said. I thought well if that's the case then I'd better start looking elsewhere. After the game against Boston I asked for my release but looking back I think I did the wrong thing. I jumped the gun and I shouldn't have done but I was young and aggressive and really annoyed. Apart from that I have nothing but very fond memories of my time at the club.

It's not every day that a centre-forward who'd just scored four of his teams goals needed a word of warning about his performance and it's rather unusual to let your goal-a-game leading scorer go without a fight, but that's exactly what happened. When questions as to his absence were raised amongst supporters a press statement was issued stating that Billy was taking a month off because he was moving house, which he was, but it's hard to believe that any of them truly believed it would take that long to do it.

However, life went on without him and the number nine shirt was handed to Colin Collindridge who wasted no time in celebrating his forty-first birthday three days earlier by rattling in a hat-trick. The Old Boys of Aspley had no answer to the old boy of Arnold and two more goals from Edwin Wright, making his first appearance since the opening game of the season, and one each from John Moore and John Anthony sealed a convincing seven-one victory and took Marys' tally in their last three away games to a mighty twenty-one.

They were on the road again the following week, the last Saturday in November, when they travelled the short distance to play their Nottinghamshire rivals Eastwood Town. The two sides had met back in 1958 in a thrilling Notts Senior Cup tie that went to extra time and ended five-four in Town's favour but this was the first time they'd ever met in a league competition. The Badgers were only averaging a point a game but with it being a local derby it was expected that there would be little to choose between the sides and for the first forty minutes that's how it turned out. Ernie Iremonger kept the Saints in the game with a couple of fine saves but it was the maroon and golds who made the crucial breakthrough when Edwin Wright converted a pass from Colin Collindridge five minutes before the break. In the second period both sides attacked almost by turn and it was Eastwood who scored first in the fifty-fifth minute. A quarter of an hour later the very much in-form John Moore put Marys ahead only for the home side to draw level once more soon afterwards. With the game still in the balance and little time left on the clock a slip in the opposition defence led to the ball dropping to Colin Collindridge who made no mistake from short range. The Badgers thought themselves a little unlucky to lose both points but they acknowledged that the Saints' veteran number nine had been the real difference between the two sides. Colin, nominally the centre-forward but playing a more deep lying role, was able to escape his markers and switch the point of attack at will, and even the home supporters agreed that he had been a pleasure to watch.

Another impressive performance was that of John Moore. A Lincoln City scout had been amongst the crowd and so impressed was he by what he saw that the young winger was invited for a trial at Lincoln City the following Tuesday. It went so well that immediately after the match the Imps told him that they wanted him to sign professional forms for them, subject to his release from his Marys' contract. If the Saints were struggling for a bit of consistency on the field of play then there was no faulting their financial ability off it. John was of course Albert Moore's nephew and apart from the natural pride of seeing a family member do well he was well aware of the young man's value in the transfer market. Having received eight hundred pounds from a non-league club for 'Tot' Leverton, who was thirty five at the time, the committee naturally set their sights a little higher for the sale to a League side of someone half the age.

AM : When we sold Charlie's lad to Lincoln we got money there. It set us up again.

"I reckon you got two thousand pounds for him" I said when probing Albert for details of the transaction.

AM : Yes, that's a figure that has been mentioned, you could be right there! That was another one on the secret list!

If it was good business for Marys it was a fairytale move for John who was drafted into the first team less than two weeks later and celebrated his debut by scoring with a header inside the first twenty minutes against Reading at Sincil Bank.

Whilst he was impressing the Lincoln scout at Eastwood, the Central Alliance match of the day was taking place over at Boston where the Pilgrims were entertaining Ransome and Marles. Both sides were still unbeaten in the league, having dropped just a single point each, and the outcome of their long awaited clash was expected to have a significant bearing on the destination of the title. In front of over two thousand four hundred spectators, the league's largest attendance of the season, the visitors took an early lead and dominated the game to such an extent that they were in front by three goals to one with only half an hour left to play. However, when Boston's centre-forward charged the Greens' keeper and made him drop the ball over the line the goal was allowed to stand. That incident effectively opened the floodgates. The home side ran out winners by an improbable seven goals to three and installed themselves as short-odds favourites to win the championship in the process.

As the season entered December the weather took a turn for the worse and on the first Saturday of the month Marys, on the road again and on this occasion in East Staffordshire to play Burton Albion's second string, struggled to cope with the sticky conditions and could only manage a one-all draw courtesy of a John Page penalty. The following week's game was called off and seven days later Shirebrook were the hosts for the Saints' fourth straight away fixture. Well they were meant to be the hosts but the sight of Arnold's committee men working on the pitch before the game might have given a different impression.

AM : I didn't like it at Shirebrook, they always seemed to play with a big ball, used to rattle like it had a pea in it. When we went there this time we had to clear the lines. It meant us coming home without playing otherwise. We won so it didn't make it too bad but if we'd got beat...

Indeed they did win, by three goals to one with Noel Simpson making another rare appearance, this time at inside-left, and scoring an even rarer goal to give his side the lead in the second half.

The following Saturday, two days before Christmas, Marys finally got to play at KGV for the first time in six weeks with Clay Cross providing the opposition. The Saints gave a debut to another one of their promising reserves, seventeen-year old inside forward Terry Bell, and the teenager needed less than an hour to make his mark on the match with the goal that put the maroon and golds on the way to another three-one victory.

Poor old Rovers received no seasonal goodwill at all on their second visit of the season to Matlock Town Reserves, going down this time by seven goals to nil and remaining rooted at the bottom of the division with just four points out of a possible thirty, but the best news of the day came when it was learned that Boston had lost their unbeaten league record in the most unlikely fashion, four-two against Nottingham Forest A. The young Reds were an in-and-out combination, mostly because of availability of players, and in fact had to call off the scheduled fixture against Marys earlier in the month because they couldn't raise a team; against the Pilgrims they could field future first teamers like Jim Cargill, David Pleat, and David Wilson.

For most teams in the region these were the last games of the year as the following week's fixture schedules were blitzed by snow, ice, and slush, causing the largest ever number of postponements in the Football League's history. Only the south coast and a few isolated areas above it seemed to escape the worst of the weather and Bradford City, for one, must have wondered whether their battle with the elements on their way down to Essex had been worth the effort when they ended up getting thrashed nine-one by their hosts Colchester United.

Darlington were due to play Barrow and their attempts to travel cross-country from the North East to the North West in conditions officially described as 'impossible' had to be abandoned after two and a half hours; they were only twenty five miles into their journey with eighty still to go. The team had set off early in the morning and despite warnings by the AA to turn back they had pressed on. Shovels had been packed as a precaution and they were required on several occasions when the players jumped off to clear a path for the bus or any other vehicle that was blocking their path. After being stuck several times and lost once they finally called off the attempt at Bowes, convinced by on-foot motorists heading back to the town having abandoned their vehicles further along the A66 that it was futile continuing. At least no-one could say they hadn't tried.

A couple of weeks earlier there had been a similar admiration for thwarted efforts after the popular Arnold Librarian, Ken Negus, had appeared on a television quiz show. He was one of three Nottinghamshire librarians asked to make up a team to take part in ITV's 'Pencil and Paper' programme. They travelled to the Aston, Birmingham studios for a 'live' recording which was then broadcast forty eight hours later. Unfortunately the Notts team went down by sixteen points to fourteen and when interviewed afterwards Mr Negus said that although he was making no excuses he felt that the team might have done better if they'd been more familiar with the programme's format; he himself had only seen the show once before.

Mr Negus' expertise was in books rather than TV and as far as I can remember the old Carnegie library stocked very little else at the time. It did however have a selection of daily newspapers that I used to flick through whilst idling away the odd moment but I'm not quite sure whether there was a policy to stock magazines. If there had I might have been able to see a copy of the first 'Private Eye', the satirical publication dedicated to expose inefficiency, incompetence, and most importantly corruption amongst public figures and which had first seen the light of day towards the end of the year; allegedly.

Speaking of public figures the Arnold Council's Surveyor submitted a plan and an estimate that very month for the provision of shower baths in the pavilion at KGV. The sum involved was thirteen hundred and fifty pounds, an awful lot of money, and when the proposal subsequently gained approval it was agreed that Marys be contacted as soon as possible. The purpose of that was solely to ascertain just how deep the committee were prepared to dig into the club's pockets. It's a pity that the originators of the initial pavilion plan hadn't had the foresight to include such basic facilities from the start. They might not have cost quite so much then and could even have been installed in time for Marys' latest application to join the Midland League, submitted the following month, to have a greater than the zero chance of success that it otherwise had.

A refusal of much greater significance was about to take place following an audition of a young pop group on New Year's Day 1962. Falling on a Monday, and it not yet being the public holiday that it is now, it was business as usual in the music world and four hopeful musicians from Liverpool set up their equipment in Decca Records' studios in West Hampstead in the hope of convincing producer Mike Smith that they were worthy of a recording contract. Fifteen songs and less than an hour later the producer told them that he could not see any problems and that he would let the group know of his decision as soon as possible. A few weeks later they heard that they'd been turned down on the basis that 'guitar groups are on their way out'. London based Decca opted instead for The Tremeloes, figuring that as a local group their travelling expenses would be lower. The four guys who missed out were John Lennon, Paul McCartney, George Harrison, and Pete Best, who would all, bar the last one who would lose his place as the group's drummer to Ringo Starr, go on to achieve world domination in the field of popular music under their better known name as The Beatles.

I must admit that I wasn't aware of this setback for the Fab Four at the time because no-one outside their inner circle knew too, but I had started to take an interest in pop music myself and in fact the first record I had bought was by one of the greatest 'guitar groups' of them all; The Shadows. Whilst they achieved great success in their own right they'd started life as Cliff Richard's backing group and it wasn't until the summer of 1960 that their instrumental 'Apache' hit the top of the charts. I loved the sound but couldn't afford the six bob required to buy it but I did start looking out for the top ten printed each week in our daily paper. It was early in 1961 that this casual glance developed into something stronger when a song by an unknown American climbed its way to the top spot. It was 'Poetry in Motion' and the singer's name was Johnny Tillotson. For some reason, and I'm still not sure why, I was mesmerised by the combination of his name and the song's title and wanted to find out more. My Dad told me that he used to read a music paper called 'Melody Maker' when he was younger so I dropped a comic from my weekly order at the newsagents and replaced it with this. That led me to the stuff that hadn't been reprinted in the dailies, such as the Long Player (LP) and Extended Player (EP) charts and took me one step closer to my first vinyl purchase.

EPs usually contained four tracks, two per side, and retailed somewhere around the ten bob mark. The beauty of them was the fact that they came in a glossy laminated cover, usually showing a colour photograph of the singer or group, and more often than not contained at least two, sometimes more of the act's recent hits, making them extremely good value if, like me, you couldn't afford to buy them individually. In the latter part of 1961 one release in particular dominated the EP charts and I made up my mind to save every spare bit of pocket money until I could afford to buy it. It took ages, much longer than I would have liked, but considering that it held the top spot for over half a year, an achievement that has never been bettered, it was still number one when I coppered up and headed off to the local record store.

Actually, in the autumn of 1961 Arnold didn't have a record store but it did have a shop that sold records. It was a small electrical goods shop owned by the Simpson family and specialising in anything that needed a plug. It didn't carry a large range of records but usually managed to stock the best sellers of the day on purpose-made shelving on the wall behind the counter, pigeon-holed in accordance with their position in the chart. It was a real red letter day for me when I handed over my savings, made me feel quite the grown-up. As to the actual piece of vinyl that instilled in me this feeling of being almost an adult, well it was none other than 'Shadows to the Fore', a collection of Hank Marvin and the boys' first four hits;

'FBI', 'Man of Mystery', 'The Stranger', and of course the track that started it all off, 'Apache'. It was the beginning of my love affair with records, one that has seen me purchase them in all shapes, sizes, and formats; seven inch singles and twelve inch singles, EPs and LPs, vinyl, cassette, and CDs, even floppy discs given away as membership of fan clubs and the like. It's certainly been an expensive pursuit and more often than not one that was way beyond my meagre budget, especially at the outset. There were always more discs out there than I could afford and so at Christmas 1961 I badgered my parents into buying a reel to reel tape recorder.

Apart from reading the Melody Maker and trying to pick up the wavering signal that was Radio Luxembourg, I also tuned in to the Sunday evening run-down on the charts called 'Pick of the Pops', presented by Alan 'Fluff' Freeman, and once he'd started proceedings with his customary "Greetings, pop pickers!" I clicked the button on the recorder and let it roll.

I was listening to the playback of my first attempt and everything seemed fine. Then American actor and folk singer Burl Ives came on singing 'A Little Bitty Tear' and all of a sudden the tape started to make a strange tweeting noise. I stopped the machine and checked the magnetic tape but could find nothing wrong. I ran it again and, sure enough, there it was. It sounded like the tape was breaking up or had attracted some electronic interference. I called my Dad over and he was as perplexed as I was. In desperation, we asked my Mum to listen in, never expecting that she'd be able to crack the mystery that had totally stumped two machine minded men. If it was a blow to our male pride when she announced that she knew exactly what the problem was, imagine our embarrassment when she said "It's the canary!"

There was no disputing it. Our faithful little bird, Peter by name, stuck in his cage over by the window, had somehow found Burl Ives' folksy tones very much to his liking and decided to join in. The amazing thing was he didn't bother providing an accompaniment to any other record in the top twenty, just this one. Even worse was the fact that he felt the need to twitter along to the playback as well, so we got his tweeting in stereo, twenty years before we were all tormented by 'The Birdie Song' by none other than the.....Tweets!

In his long career, Burl Ives had made a recording of 'I Know an Old Lady' in which a scatty old woman swallowed various insects and animals of increasing size until her body finally gave in. I don't think our Peter would have whistled along to that one, especially the bit where Burt told his audience that 'she swallowed a bird....'

Our singing canary was the only pet we ever had at Killisick, unless you include caterpillars and frog spawn and the ladybird that I kept in a Captain Webb matchbox feeding on a large leaf until it turned turtle. We also managed to provide accommodation for any number of short-lived goldfish too. Admittedly we lost one or two down the sink when their water was being changed, but in the main they were pretty mangy to start off with. On reflection, I shouldn't have been too surprised. These were hardly the days of Koi carp aquaria at your local garden centre, with fish costing hundreds of pounds each. Our little specimens came from much more dubious sources; either the fairgrounds of Arnold Wakes or Goose Fair itself, or more often than not from the local rag and bone man.

Funnily enough, in both scenarios, you didn't actually buy the fish. At the fair it was usually a reward for lobbing a ping pong ball into an empty goldfish bowl or some other deceptively difficult skill. The poor little goldfish would be suspended in their little water-filled plastic bags high above the stall, hoping that you'd be successful and give them a good home. If the hard part was the actual winning, then it was equally as difficult to safely manoeuvre the plastic bag and its precious cargo back safely to the house. Many's the time a distraught child could be seen standing over a burst bag, with its erstwhile contents floundering helplessly on the floor of the Forest or the Croft.

As to the rag and bone man well, the fish's journey from his cart to the house was definitely much shorter, and thus less risky, but goodness knows what conditions it had had to endure previously. Our estate's forerunner of modern day recycling referred to himself as 'rag-boh' and was so unkempt that he made television's Steptoe look smarter than a tailor's dummy.

He took mostly anything in exchange for Goldie and a few coppers; old clothes, obviously, and scrap iron too, anything with a bit of value. But it was hardly fair exchange. Our new arrival never seemed to last longer than its next proper feed. It was probably so excited to see my mother sprinkle a generous helping of 'Gussie' into the top of its bowl that it expired there and then.

On the first Saturday of 1962 and with Goose Fair a long way off goldfish might have been in short supply at the Forest but there was certainly no lack of water. The previous week's snow and ice had thawed rapidly, completely flooding the recreation ground and making all its pitches unplayable, a scenario repeated at the Victoria Embankment and all KGV playing fields in the district. County's third round FA Cup tie at home to Manchester City escaped a similar fate and I joined twenty five thousand other hopefuls to see if the Magpies could pull off a giant killing act but a combination of an extremely heavy pitch and heroics from City keeper Bert Trautmann thwarted the home side's valiant attempts to cancel out Neil Young's early strike. The game ended one-nil to the visitors.

IT'S OFF, MI DUCK : VICTORIA EMBANKMENT FLOODED : 6 JAN 1962
(Courtesy Football Post)

The whole of the Central Alliance programme was wiped out because of the weather so it wasn't until the thirteenth that Marys played their first game of the New Year, and their first in three weeks, against Kimberley Town at the Stag Ground. There was no sign of rustiness in the Saints' early play with an own goal and a strike from Colin Collindridge giving them a two-nil lead less than halfway through the first period. Sloppy defending then let the home side back in the game and at the break the scores were level two-all. It was during the second half that the effects of their lay-off began to tell on the visitors and with Kimberley having by far the better of the play, the maroon and golds were happy to hang on for the draw. It was probably a point lost rather than one gained, especially with Joe Boucher going nap in Ransomes' ten-three thrashing of Anstey Nomads. Admittedly the Leicestershire side were struggling at the foot of the table but Marys' opponents at KGV the following week, Shirebrook Miners Welfare, weren't faring that much better themselves, so hopes of a convincing victory for the Saints were pretty high.

Marys continued their policy of introducing promising youngsters into the senior side when they gave a debut to seventeen year old David Staples, a right winger who'd attracted the interest of a number of clubs. Unlike the others, however, David hadn't been a member of the second eleven.

DS : I'd been playing with Thorneywood Athletic, who were a nursery team for Forest, in the Notts Youth League. I had the odd game for Forest Colts on a Thursday and played a couple of times on the Saturday for the A team in the Central Alliance. We used to go training down at the City Ground on a Tuesday and Thursday night but for some reason Colin Baines, who ran Thorneywood, fell out with Forest and stopped the whole team from going down to train. Because I was also on Forest's books as an amateur I still trained at the City Ground but then as Colin was a big mate of Tommy Lawton, who was a scout for Wolves at the time, he told him about me and he took me to Wolves. I could have stayed at Forest but Wolves were a big team then, they were like Arsenal and Manchester United are today. I went there but I couldn't get on with the travelling. I had no car so I had to go on the bus or train and it was a three train journey, Nottingham to Derby, Derby to Birmingham, and Birmingham to Wolverhampton, so I left them and carried on playing for Thorneywood. I used to train at Robert Mellors School and one night in January Syd Gray and another couple of committee men came and said, "We've come to see if you want to sign for Marys, if you sign you're in the first team on Saturday". I mean, I was only seventeen, I wasn't starstruck but it was a big thing to be playing in Marys' first team, so I signed and played against Shirebrook in my first match.

Indeed he did, joining two other teenagers, John Anthony and Terry Bell, in the starting line-up and wasting no time at all in bringing a finger tip save from the opposition goalie and then seeing another effort flash across the face of the goal. Despite this early pressure it took Marys twenty five minutes to make the breakthrough and even then they couldn't add to their score in the first period. Fortunately the second half was a completely different picture and the Saints rattled in seven goals in the last forty minutes to run out convincing eight-one winners. With scouts from Aston Villa and Lincoln City looking on David marked his debut with a well-deserved goal of his own and all the other forwards scored too with number eleven Barry Jeffries, playing only his second game for the club, grabbing a hat-trick.

Not surprisingly David kept his place for the next week's visit to Wilmorton but the opposition on this occasion were not quite so easily overcome and Marys found themselves a goal behind at the interval. It was only a late penalty from John Page that clinched the points for the Saints, his winner following an earlier equaliser from Colin Collindridge. Still, the victory took the maroon and golds' unbeaten run in the league to nine matches and, as the table at the end of January showed, kept them firmly in touch with Ransomes and Boston at the top.

	P	W	D	L	F	A	P
Ransome and Marles	18	15	1	2	79	42	31
Boston United	17	14	2	1	62	23	30
Arnold St Marys	**17**	**11**	**4**	**2**	**61**	**23**	**26**

When a side wins it's unusual for it to be changed except for injury but the selection committee opted to omit its two youngest players for the next match away at Anstey Nomads. It was a good game to miss as the Leicestershire side, pummelled by Ransomes and Joe Boucher in particular a few weeks earlier and with only eight points from eighteen matches all season, won by two goals to nil as the Saints turned in their most inept performance of the campaign.

Either by accident or design Marys had struggled to keep the same side from one game to the next and for the following week's crucial Notts Senior Cup Quarter Final at Eastwood it was the turn of wing-half Ray Knight to become the latest seventeen year old to be given a run-out in the first team. His inclusion, following hard on the heels of that of David Staples, was big news at Killisick, especially amongst those of us who'd played, hour upon hour, on the estate's recreation field where Ray and David had honed their skills as youngsters and I had stood in awe of both of them as they went through a repertoire of eye catching drills. Albert Moore in particular was very pleased to see Ray's arrival in the first team.

AM : Ray was the apple of my eye, a marvellous player.

**A YOUNG DAVID STAPLES SHOWING HOW IT SHOULD BE DONE AT THE
KILLISICK RECREATION FIELD** (David Staples Collection)

Of course, a highly successful career in school and youth football, which he'd shared with David, was no guarantee of success later on but a Notts Senior Cup Quarter Final was a good enough place to start your senior career. Any nerves Ray might have had probably disappeared after ten minutes when Barry Jeffries gave Marys the lead. Much improved since the previous week's debacle at Anstey, the Saints' day got even better when after half an hour Eastwood were reduced to ten men following an injury to one of their players. Taking advantage of the extra man the maroon and golds added two more goals in the second half to secure a semi-final place with something to spare.

The following week Marys entertained Gresley Rovers, the side that had inflicted on them their first league defeat back in October. When Fred Martin inadvertently deflected a harmless looking shot past Ernie Iremonger after just ten minutes it looked as though the visitors might be in line for a double, especially as a strong wind kept the Saints pegged in their own half for most of the first forty-five minutes. On the resumption, however, it was a different story with Colin Collindridge in particular tearing gaps in the Gresley defence at will. Once the equaliser arrived on the hour the opposition's resistance faltered badly and two more goals quickly followed. The Derbyshire side did grab a consolation of their own but it came much too late to influence the outcome of the match and the maroon and golds took both points with a three-two victory.

For the final game of the month Marys made the short trip to Linby to play the Colliery, next to bottom in the table and having been thrashed back in January by Eastwood and South Normanton, nine- and ten-nil respectively. The only change from the previous game was the absence of John Anthony who'd been given permission to play for Lincoln City Reserves. Despite the chopping and changing to the side this campaign the tenacious young wing half had established himself as a fixture in the Saints' starting eleven and his form had been such that he'd attracted the attention of a number of league scouts. Peter Williams regularly lined up outside him on the left wing and was well placed to offer an opinion of John's ability.

PW : John was very young when he first played but he learned fast and was a hard devil. He was a hard tackler and a ball winner but he could play as well. He was a good guy to have on your side, a lot of opposition players got het up about his tackling. I'd sooner have him in my side than playing against me.

Lincoln's gain was definitely Marys' loss, at least for an afternoon, especially when the unfortunate Fred Martin saw a shot ricochet off him into the net for the second week in a row with less than ten minutes on the clock. Despite having much the better of the half the Saints were unable to grab an equaliser and with Linby riding their luck the game turned into a frustrating battle for the visitors. The second half saw a slight improvement in the maroon and golds' fortunes but it wasn't enough. They did manage to get on the scoresheet only to see the home side answer with another goal of their own and condemn them to their second embarrassing defeat of the month.

Having gone nine games without defeat to the end of the previous month, February had seen Marys gain only two points out of a possible six and look anything but a top of the table side, let alone championship contenders. Ray Knight had been the Saints' twenty-sixth player of the campaign so far and even the Football Post wondered whether the recent poor form might be attributed to having an unsettled formation. Additionally the blooding of a whole bunch of youngsters was a worthy long-term policy but wasn't necessarily a guarantee of short-term success. Thirty odd years later and having just seen a youthful Manchester United side start the season with a defeat away at Aston Villa player turned pundit Alan Hansen famously said that "You win nothing with kids". Unfortunately for him the 'kids' on this occasion were Phil and Gary Neville, Nicky Butt, Paul Scholes, and David Beckham, and they'd all end up with championship winners' medals at the end of the campaign but this golden generation apart his observation would normally be spot on and the Central Alliance was no league for an over-reliance on young players, no matter how good.

Elsewhere in the world in February another youngster was making the headlines when he claimed a world record for dancing 'The Twist', a new craze that was sweeping America. Chubby Checker's hit of the same name was one of three twist-influenced tracks in the USA Top Ten and somehow the young guy had performed the dance non-stop for an amazing thirty-three hours. The report didn't mention whether that included 'comfort' breaks but back in the UK a new product had arrived on the grocers' shelves that linked schoolboys and bodily functions and resulted in the usual toilet humour. The cause of this mirth was Batchelor's 'Surprise Peas', a freeze-dried version of the versatile vegetable being marketed as an alternative to the canned variety. In retrospect the advertising men couldn't have thought it through thoroughly enough because straight away the common question of asking what accompaniment is best for a certain type of food was twisted into the predictable playground joke:-

Q : "What goes with Surprise Peas?"

A : "Chapped legs."

Suffice to say that frozen peas soon took the place of the freeze-dried variety.

Along with seven thousand other hardy souls I encountered some pretty cold conditions of my own when on the first Saturday in March I headed off to see the Magpies entertain Barnsley. Overnight snow had blanketed a large part of the Midlands and put the match in some doubt but the goal areas and lines had been cleared and the game went ahead. County were comfortably placed in mid-table and the fixture had the air of an end of season game even with fifteen games still to go. The fact that Notts lost two-nil seemed to be of little consequence even to me. Elsewhere in the league Burnley were heading the top division ahead of Ipswich, Liverpool the second with Leyton Orient tucked in right behind them, and Portsmouth the third, a scenario that hardly seems credible today. Almost as implausibly, Wrexham thrashed Hartlepools, as they were known then, by ten goals to one. The only reason the north-easterners weren't bottom of Division Four was the fact that perennial strugglers Accrington Stanley were occupying that position at the time. For both the bottom markers however, this was all about to change as the money ran out at Stanley a week later and they were forced to withdraw from the league. Subsequently their results were expunged from the records and the 'Pool found themselves bottom of the pile, a position that, admittedly, they weren't exactly unfamiliar with.

The snow that had made many pitches difficult went one stage further at KGV and rendered it unplayable. Marys' scheduled match against Wilmorton was re-arranged for the following week but as Rovers had first call on Gedling Road the Saints had to decamp up to the Top Rec for the first time this season. Not many supporters bothered to brave the conditions and those that did might have been forgiven for wishing they hadn't bothered, a nil-nil draw being scant reward for their efforts. The only notable aspects of the game were the debut at right-half of Jack Davis, a recent acquisition from Alfreton Town and the appearance of Fred Martin at left-back; he'd now played in every defensive position in the side from number two to number six.

The following Monday, the day that Fred's old club Accrington finally pulled the plug, Marys' committee were planning for a much brighter future of their own by discussing the introduction of a matchday programme for the following season, the club's first publication of its kind since 1949-50 when they'd printed one for the first home game of each month. It was an indication that the Saints were looking ahead with rather more confidence than the team was actually exhibiting on the pitch, a fact borne out the following Saturday when they struggled to overcome their recent conquerors Anstey Nomads by the odd goal in three at Gedling Road. It hadn't helped that the maroon and golds went behind to their opponents early in the game, the fourth time they'd done so in their last seven outings, but at least the two points kept them in third place in the table as they prepared for their visit to Newark seven days later to play second placed Ransome and Marles in a crucial four-pointer.

	P	W	D	L	F	A	P
Boston United	21	17	2	2	70	32	36
Ransome and Marles	22	17	1	4	86	51	35
Arnold St Marys	**22**	**13**	**5**	**4**	**67**	**30**	**31**

Marys' bold policy of playing local youngsters of great promise continued with the introduction of sixteen year old Arnold lad Peter Burton, who'd been associated with the club since he was a boy and had been turning in excellent performances in the reserves.

PB : I'd carried the players' gear at Calverton Road and helped put the nets up on the Top Rec when I was only nine years old. When I left Robert Mellors Charlie Moore was waiting at the school gates with a signing on form and I played for the A team and then the reserves. Whenever I could I'd be down on Woodthorpe Park kicking a ball around with Terry Bell; Alan Birchenall and Micky Somers would be there as well.

Alan and Micky would both go on to play in the Football League and there was every possibility that Peter and Terry would end up joining them but for now the two friends had to settle for lining up together against Ransomes in front of a large and enthusiastic crowd over at Newark.

Whilst Marys' chances of overtaking the top two weren't that great, especially if their recent indifferent form continued, their rivals hadn't fared too well of late either, with Ransomes having lost two of their last four matches and Boston having been on the receiving end of a five-nil hammering by Eastwood just the previous week, so there was an expectation at kick-off that the Saints were at least in with a bit of a chance of success. Unfortunately it only took fifteen minutes before The Green's ace centre-forward Joe Boucher added to his impressive tally for the season with a well taken goal and he almost added a second straight after when he followed up an effort that had struck the post. Adopting a shoot on sight policy the home side peppered Ernie Iremonger's goal and it was very much against the run of play that the maroon and golds equalised on thirty five minutes, John Page latching on to a long ball out of defence to score past the advancing keeper. Undeterred, Ransomes came straight back on the attack and five minutes later their lethal number nine grabbed his second to give his side a two-one half-time lead. Immediately after the break the Newark side carried on where it had left off and with the second period barely seven minutes old the division's leading scorer struck again, beating a full-back and then the goalie before calmly slotting the ball into an empty net. It had been a masterclass in scoring and there was no coming back for the Saints. They did manage a second goal of their own but this was countered by the home side who took both points in what turned out to be a fairly comfortable four-two victory.

It had been a tough debut for young Peter but he kept his place in the side for the visit of Eastwood the following week, a game which on paper appeared a little less daunting than the clash with Ransomes. It certainly looked that way when Marys' first attack resulted in a shot being cleared off the line by the visitors' right back and even more so when, for once, the Saints opened the scoring, courtesy of a John Page penalty, after twelve minutes. The home side continued to dominate and looked as if they were in line for their third win of the season against the Badgers when out of the blue a defensive slip gave Town an undeserved equaliser. If that wasn't bad enough the maroon and golds conceded again only a minute later but in a match that was developing into an end to end battle managed to equalise straight from the re-start. The game was only twenty-two minutes old and threatening to turn into a high scoring shoot-out but somehow both defences succeeded in holding out for the remainder of the half. Sadly the first forty-five minutes turned out to be Marys' best because after the break Eastwood added three more without reply to bring the Saints' month to a miserable close.

The last two games had been a baptism of fire for Marys' latest teenage prospect but for goalie Ernie Iremonger they'd been a bit of a personal disaster. Ernie had been in good form all season and had been the automatic number one since taking over after Len Rockley's injury back at the beginning of October 1960. In fact Ernie's excellent displays had meant that Len had been unable to regain his place once fit and had moved to Alfreton. Now back from his spell at the Derbyshire club Len had been playing consistently well in the reserves and with Ernie picking the ball out of the net nine times in the last couple of matches the committee decided that it was time for a change of custodian. Ernie recalls frankly the circumstances behind his demotion.

EI : I had a complete loss of form and it was my own stupid fault. I'd started going out on a Friday night to the Festival Inn over at Trowell, staying out till twelve or one o'clock in the morning. It was stupid really. I think I started playing Sunday football as well and I shouldn't have done that either. The two didn't go together.

Despite him being a contracted professional Ernie could play on the Sabbath because the Notts Sunday League wasn't an officially sanctioned competition at the time but the fact of the matter was that even though both he and Len were pretty good keepers, as the calendar flipped over into April it didn't matter who was between the sticks; Marys' season, as far as league games were concerned, was effectively finished. In the next five matches the Saints won only the once, picked up a solitary point from three home games and in the process established the worst four game home sequence in the club's post-war history. Starting with the defeat at Newark against Ransomes towards the end of March Marys picked up a paltry four points out of a possible fourteen. Even the signing of another player from Alfreton, centre-half Derek Smith, couldn't prevent the season from ending in the anti-climax of a fifth place finish. The only truly bright spot as the campaign drew to a close was the victory over Ericsson Athletic in the Notts Senior Cup Semi-Final by a convincing three goals to nil but even that competition didn't provide the Saints with any silverware as they lost their hold on the trophy in the final, going down to Midland League Sutton Town three-one.

In the final analysis the season had been one of great disappointment. From starting out as one of the two pre-season favourites with the eventual champions Boston United, Marys never reached the levels of achievement of their previous three seasons in the top division. To finish fifth in a league much diminished by the mass withdrawal of its best teams represented a massive step backwards for a club that prided itself on being progressive. Losing to teams like Matlock, Heanor, and Belper had been no disgrace but getting beaten by Linby, Anstey, and Nottingham Forest A, three of the bottom five sides, was unacceptable.

The constant changing of the side, even when winning, certainly didn't help. Thirty-two players were tried over the course of the campaign, almost enough for three teams. Billy England had effectively been jettisoned at a time when he was in great goalscoring form and with no replacement lined up. In fact six different players ended up wearing the number nine jersey that he vacated. Of course there were one or two chinks of light amongst the gloom, in particular the introduction of a number of promising youngsters into senior football and the

111

proceeds from the sale of one of them, John Moore, to Lincoln City. That money, together with the revenue from the transfer of 'Tot' Leverton, at least ensured that the club's funds were in good order.

MARYS v SUTTON TOWN, NOTTS SENIOR CUP FINAL 5 MAY 1962 : Back Row (l to r); B Molyneux, P Groome, L Rockley, J Davis, D Smith, J Anthony. Front Row; P Burton, J Page, D Parr, P Williams, C Collindridge. Mascot T Gray.   (Courtesy Football Post)

Apart from its well-stocked coffers the club had had a poor year off the field as well. Still feeling the effects of being snubbed by the Midland League at the first time of asking the close season would see the committee going back with the begging bowl a second time, really more in hope than expectation, only to return empty handed once again. It wouldn't have helped the mood in the camp that this latest rejection took place against an expansion in the league from eighteen to twenty teams with neither of the two new entrants, Boston United and Holbeach United, falling inside the 'fifty mile radius from Worksop' rule. Nor could anyone at the club have been that impressed when a note appeared in the press at the time of their application stating that they weren't even guaranteed the use of Gedling Road in its present state, let alone be amongst the beneficiaries should the Council ever get around to allowing Marys to develop it. Of course this leak to or by the press was just mischief making of the most blatant kind and whilst there was no real reason to believe that Marys' tenure at KGV was in any immediate danger it did highlight the hazards of having the Council as landlords.

All the club could do was trust that they'd get a fair deal down at Arnold Park whilst at the same time ensuring that the standard of their own internal workings was on a par with the best that the Midland League could offer, and to this end the committee decided to bite the bullet and appoint a Manager for the first time in the club's history. On the evening of Tuesday 17 April 1962, immediately after the Saints had lost four-two to champions elect Boston United at Gedling Road, coach Noel Simpson became the first man to take up the post. Albert Moore was one of the committee members who were behind the change.

AM : We used to have a committee that was picking the team every week and it took you longer and longer to pick it. Eventually someone suggested getting a selection committee, three or four blokes, and it was still the same then, it used to take us about twenty minutes to pick the team and two hours to tell everyone why. So I said "It's time we started thinking about a manager and let him do the job. He can come and tell us why he picked it after they've played". That's why we went to Noel.

The new Manager's appointment had been unanimously agreed so it was somewhat strange that a mere three weeks later Noel had to endure the dreaded 'vote of confidence'. The team under his direct control had won four out of their six matches but had finished the season with the Senior Cup Final defeat against Sutton. The scheduled committee get-together on the Monday after the final passed off without incident but it seems that one or two members had obviously become agitated over something or other because three days later Syd Gray called an emergency meeting with the intention of having a 'strong and lengthy discussion over the policy of the club'. I guess they weren't just talking about Noel either but with the poor year they'd had and the indecision over the ground and its very impact on the future of the club it was obvious that a clear the air meeting was somewhat inevitable. Happily for the new Manager not only was the vote for him to remain in charge carried without objection but he was also 'empowered by unanimous decision to sign or reject whatever players he deemed necessary for the successful running of a probable Midland League side in the coming season'. The terms of Noel's appointment were to be a matter for discussion and negotiation between him and two nominated committee members, Bill Whittaker and Charlie Moore and all three would be collectively responsible for future negotiations regarding players' wages. The 'probable Midland League side' would of course turn out to be a Central Alliance side but at least the meeting brought some kind of closure to a campaign marked by widespread indecision.

One of the recurring problems for the committee had been exactly who to select each week and from a player's viewpoint the fact that their selection hinges on the opinion of others is one of the major drawbacks of participation in team sports. Shortly after Marys' EGM I was playing cricket for my school's Under-Thirteen XI on a very green pitch adjacent to the main square at its playing fields on Valley Road. It was the first game of the season and as befits a guy picked primarily for his bowling I was due to bat at number ten. This didn't bother me unduly because as first change bowler I expected to get a piece of the action when the other side were batting but on this day our openers rattled through the order and we ended up getting them out for a paltry twenty-one runs. It had happened so quickly that tea was deferred until after we'd batted, the expectation being that the task of making twenty-two wouldn't take that long. Unfortunately our batsmen made as big a pig's ear of it as the opposition and instead of it all being done and dusted inside two or three overs we bowlers looked on alarmingly as wickets tumbled with victory nowhere in sight. All of a sudden, or so it seemed, I started to pad up in anticipation of the fall of the eighth wicket. I was still frantically adjusting my pad straps when the umpire's finger went up once more with our score standing at a measly eighteen. Now I might have been number ten but I secretly fancied myself as at least a number seven and with that mindset I strode nonchalantly to the wicket. A quick single got me off the mark and down the other end and at the start of the next over I executed the perfect leg glance. We ran three and the game was won. I'd also top scored with four not out and milked my team-mates congratulations for all they were worth.

I looked forward all week to the next match, fully expecting to be promoted up the order. Much to my dismay, when the team sheet was posted up on the cricket notice board I'd only been named as twelfth man. Confused, I sought out the cricket Master and asked why I'd been omitted; "I thought you looked a bit apprehensive when you came to the wicket" was his explanation. This being the Nottingham High School in 1962 and me being only thirteen, any protestations on my behalf would have been pointless and probably self-defeating even if I did think then and still do now that it was the lamest possible reason for my demotion. At eighteen for eight I might have had good reason for a bit of apprehension but at that age all I was thinking about was the chance I'd been given to hit the winning runs. I wasn't selected for the third game of the season either, in fact I didn't even make twelfth man. I thought about having another word but I knew it would be futile. I would only have been told that I'd looked a little nervous carrying the drinks.

CHAPTER FIVE

1962-63

Most every close season since I could ever remember had always been a time of adventure and anticipation, especially in that part of it that had encompassed the school holidays, but in the summer of 1962 it was a time of great change as well. The place I'd called home since I was no more than two years old was now to be no more than a memory; we were leaving Killisick behind. I don't quite know how it felt for my parents, swapping a rented Council accommodation for the privilege of owning their own house, mortgage and all, for the very first time, but for me it was definitely a time of mixed emotions.

I always maintained that I could remember being pushed up Coppice Road in my pram on the way home from my grandparents' house on James Street but of course it was probably just wishful thinking on my part. Not that it didn't happen; it did, on many occasions, with a bag of coal, courtesy of my Granddad's ton a month National Coal Board allowance, slung between the pram wheels and making the incline up from Front Street even more of a struggle for my poor mother. What I could recall however was pretty much everything from school age onwards, at least the key episodes, both good, of which there were many, and bad, of which I am happy and lucky enough to admit were very few and far between.

Almost all of everything good that I experienced at Killisick was based around a distinct sense of community with the majority of our neighbours being in the same boat as us and each other. Young married couples starting families and building a future together in the far from prosperous early fifties; the Walkers and the Millwards, the Clugstons and Foxes, Staples and Nevilles, Halls and Smiths, and probably the most memorable of all, at least to me, Hughie and Cynthia. At a time in my life when every adult looked old, Hughie seemed positively ancient. That was probably because he was actually well into his forties, looked more like sixty, and chose as his preferred mode of transport a full-sized three-wheel cycle. I'm not sure how far he'd travelled when I saw him of an evening but by the time he'd negotiated the final gradient up to his house directly opposite ours his body was bent double so that his head was lower than the handlebars. It was in sharp contrast to the sight of him setting off each morning, bright and breezy and with the thin wisps of what little blond hair he still had floating horizontally behind him on the slipstream as he free-wheeled off around the bend. He certainly didn't lack for stamina and it was probably no surprise, at least to our parents, when he and Cynthia, another forty-something year old herself, joined the rest of the baby boomers with a new arrival of their own.

Now though was a time for departure; no more sledging on the lammas, probably no more all-day bike rides to Fiskerton, and definitely no more experience of the wonderful delights of the Meadowcream van as it picked its way around the estate selling the most delicious of ice creams made at its own dairy on Chapel Lane. Almost as memorable as the goodies it sold was the appearance of the van itself, a cream coloured vehicle with a large picture windscreen containing a rear facing seat next to the driver; easy for the lady who dispensed the product to pop up and down from every few hundred yards or so.

On the upside was the fact that I'd now have a greater choice of buses to choose from to get to and from school or town and no doubt there'd be new friends to make at Castleton Avenue, no more than a stone's throw or a gentle stroll around the corner from Marys' home at KGV, and which would be my home for the next eight years. Right in the middle of Arnold it was handy for pretty much everything and with no disrespect to our previous house this new one was a couple of notches above it, especially with regards to my brother's and my bedroom where a fitted carpet rather than a combination of linoleum and coconut matting was awaiting our feet as we swung them out of bed each morning. Another noticeable difference was the view from our upstairs window, which was that of an urban landscape rather than the rural one we'd been used to up at Killisick and was dominated by the Portland stone edifice that was once the Bonington cinema but was now, after a long period of inactivity, finally in the process of being demolished to make way for a new development. Ironically one of the buildings being erected in its place was a purpose built workshop for my father's car repair business which had outgrown its very first premises in some old stables on Church Drive East.

HARRY WEST LOOKING OUT OVER ARNOLD FROM THE TOP OF KINGSWELL SCHOOL c1952 – THE BONINGTON CINEMA CAN BE SEEN ON THE RIGHT OF THE PICTURE

(Martin Dermody Collection)

Our actual house move took place in June but I'd been doing my utmost during the earlier part of the year to divest myself of all my old and treasured possessions in anticipation of our relocation. Well that would have been the case had I paid that much attention to what was going on but in truth the divesting was done as a means to raise the money so that I could add to my embryonic record collection. This meant parting with all my Corgi toys in their mint condition boxes and my couple of hundred neatly kept DC Comics which I'd lovingly thumbed through but never somehow found the time to read. The cash they brought in was useful enough at the time but looking back it wasn't the best idea I'd ever had; quite a few of the comics now sell for high hundreds of pounds and many of the cars can hit three figures too.

Fact of the matter was that I was hooked on records; buying them, listening to them, reading about them, even the look and feel of them. I'd graduated from the Melody Maker to the New Musical Express (NME) because the latter's charts were more up to date and used to spend far more time devouring every word in it than I ever spent on my school work. That was probably a contributory factor in my decline during that 'difficult' second year at NHS from fourth top in my form to fourth bottom, although a broken collar bone playing Rugby for the school up at Sheffield and the onset of hay-fever in the summer, a miserable condition that has proven to be a lifelong affliction, certainly didn't help either.

Funnily enough I'd almost worn out my first purchase, the EP 'Shadows to the Fore', by the time I'd saved up enough money to buy another record early in 1962 but once I'd made the decision to have a fire sale of my collectibles I acquired them thick and fast. Still with one eye on value for money my second pick was a double A-side from the King himself, Elvis, singing two songs from his latest movie 'Blue Hawaii'; 'Rock-a-Hula Baby' and 'Can't Help Falling In Love'. I'd been to see that film and 'The Young Ones', starring Cliff Richard, at the Metropole early in the year, maybe even in consecutive weeks, and whilst the former Harry Webb didn't do anything for me, Elvis had a certain something that I found interesting enough to make me want to buy his records. Besides the kid from Tupelo my other ongoing interest was in instrumentals, of which there were many of varying degrees of quality at the time. For me the Shads were in a league of their own, which is why their number one hit 'Wonderful Land' became the next in my collection, but it was a reworking of Tchaikovsky's 'Nutcracker Suite' by a group of session musicians that became my fourth. 'Nut Rocker' was its title and the group was given the moniker of 'B Bumble and The Stingers'. It too went to number one, if only for a week, replacing the Shadows in the process, but made history nonetheless by becoming the first instrumental to take over from another at the top of the charts.

If Elvis and Hank and Jet and the other Shads exuded an air of cool it was an attribute in short supply amongst my next unlikely favourites, a Swedish group called The Spotnicks. Primarily an instrumental combo too they dressed, much as their name might imply, in space suits topped with what looked like large inverted goldfish bowls. If I was the only adolescent in the area who bought one of their records I wouldn't have been surprised but even if their look wasn't, the sound they made was pretty impressive. The track that had caught my attention was a revved up version of the old country standard 'Orange Blossom Special' and it managed to sneak into the lower reaches of the top thirty almost as we were packing our bags.

With only five records and a few leftover comics and die-cast cars to call my own it didn't take me long to say a personal farewell to the old place before heading off for the last time down Hawthorn Crescent, across the lammas and up onto the top deck of the 52 bus parked at the terminus between the estate's six shops. As soon as it kicked into life and pulled away from the pavement I permitted myself a brief look back over my shoulder. I didn't know it at the time but it would be another thirteen years before I passed that way again.

The hardest part of the move was making sure that on my return from school that evening I remembered to get off the bus at the library but with a wrecking ball doing a fine job of authorised vandalism on the old picture palace across the road I soon got the hang of it. There had continued to be a decent attempt at unlicensed destruction to the public convenience situated a liitle further up towards the town centre, so much so that its gradual demolition hardly made the news anymore but one evening a couple of months earlier some hundred street lamps in the town had been rendered useless in an orgy of glass smashing by unknown perpetrators. It was hardly *Kristallnacht* and lamp posts weren't twenty-five feet high like they are now but it seems that even then the area had as much attraction for anti-social behaviour as it ever does today.

In fairness I'd never have qualified for a goody-goody badge myself and having given both the Cubs and the Scouts a miss I was never officially obligated to carry out a good deed for the day either. However I had been taught right from wrong and one lunch time during a break from school earlier in the year a certain Tony Hateley had good cause to be grateful that I had. My old friend Michael Fox, who else, had introduced me to the joys of autograph hunting and a bunch of us had travelled down to Meadow Lane one morning to see the Magpies train. Whatever work they did in or around the pitch wasn't visible but we managed to catch a bit of a glimpse of our heroes when they all tipped out onto the cinder car park behind the Spion Kop for a kickabout. After the session was over we all waited around the players' entrance for them to emerge from the steamy changing rooms so that we could get them to sign our autograph books, or in my case a large scrapbook with a page given over to each player and liberally covered with their pasted down photos, all exactly the same, neatly cut out from the latest editions of the Football Post. Getting each of the squad to sign his name on every mugshot might seem a bit obsessive but that's exactly what we did. Happily there were no big time Charlies amongst County's finest and all our tedious requests were unfailingly accepted, even though I began to notice that most of them could sign their name without breaking stride and whilst continuing to conduct a conversation with a fellow player.

This particular day however it was my turn to do the Magpies' star player a favour. There had been the usual scramble amongst us to stick our books under the players' noses before they headed out of the ground and off down Meadow Lane and when the furore had died down I noticed a small brown envelope on the ground behind the old Main Stand. I picked it up and turned it over and in a small see-through window at the top I could clearly see the name 'T Hateley'. It was pretty thick and when I shook it I could hear coins clinking against each other. Suddenly I twigged; it was his wage packet. Without any more ado I tore off through the gates in the direction of London Road where the majority of players were strolling towards some unknown destination. Thankfully I soon spotted my man in the distance. "Mr Hateley, Mr Hateley" I called, giving a passable imitation of a younger version of Norman 'Pitkin' Wisdom in the classic comedy 'The Early Bird', and the great man turned round to see what all the fuss was about. "Mr Hateley, I think you dropped this" I gasped breathlessly as I handed over the precious package. He took one look at it, recognised what it was, and said "Thanks son" and was off. It was the talking point amongst us as we assailed the last of the stragglers, closed our books, and headed off up Arkwright Street back to town. I was feeling very pleased with myself for being so observant and diligent in repatriating the owner with his lost goods that the fact that I hadn't been given a tip for my honesty never even entered my head until someone mentioned it later. They're right, I thought, he could have at least opened up the packet and handed me the coppers inside. Then I remembered that it was a particularly fat packet, a decent wedge as they might say now, and one that was probably best not opened in front of his team mates.

I never held it against him. He was and always remained one of my favourite Magpies of all time and much later in life I had the pleasure of playing in the same side as him in a benefit match at Gedling Road. Most of the first twenty minutes or so was an attempt by all and sundry on our team to cross the ball to him a la "on me 'ead, son" but we soon gave it up as a bad job. Although the game had started with a degree of seriousness it had soon developed into a very pleasant afternoon with some fine examples of outrageous showboating from former Forest star Duncan McKenzie, then at Everton. Tony had brought along his young son Mark who'd recently completed his education at Arnold Hill School and who wasn't that many years away from being a bigger star than his dad had been, eventually winning thirty two caps for England and earning himself the nickname 'Attila' whilst starring in Italy with AC Milan. If only he'd known that back when he was still in nappies my quick thinking had ensured that his Dad actually had some housekeeping money to hand over to his Mum and keep him in Farley's Rusks for another week.

Somewhere in amongst the autograph hunting, record collecting, and house moving was another weekend trip with the family to the East Coast, the highlight of which was listening, ear clamped to a portable radio, to the commentary of England's World Cup game with Argentina in Chile whilst we were out for our traditional evening constitutional. Elvis was number one at the time with 'Good Luck Charm' but Bobby Charlton, Jimmy Greaves and the rest of the boys didn't need a four leaf clover or a rabbit's foot as they eased past the South Americans by three goals to one. This victory helped them qualify for the quarter-finals out on the coast at Vina del Mar but their trip to the seaside wasn't as pleasant as ours as they went down by the same score to Brazil. The current holders even had Pele missing with injury but they still won with something to spare and it was no surprise when they went on to retain the Jules Rimet Trophy with another three-one victory, this time against Czechoslovakia, having already disposed of the hosts at the semi-final stage by four goals to two.

Whilst the Boys from Brazil were successfully defending their title the UK's first legal casino was opened in Brighton and a Government committee urged the BBC to provide a second TV channel. The face of 'entertainment' in this country was obviously destined for change but it's hard to imagine that anyone could truly have foreseen the explosion in the industry that has resulted in thousands of gambling or gaming establishments being set up and hundreds of TV stations appear onscreen. It would be a couple of years before BBC2 actually showed its first programme but only a month after the idea was first mooted another tremendous advance in communications was made when live TV pictures were beamed across the Atlantic via the recently launched Telstar Satellite.

Just as we were about to open the airwaves to televised images from around the world new legislation aimed at making it more difficult to enter the UK became effective. The 1962 Commonwealth Immigration Act restricted the number of people allowed to migrate to the UK from its former colonies. Since most of these territories were in Africa, Asia or the West Indies, the Act was popularly interpreted as having racist overtones and hardly likely to improve the fragile community relations in those areas where there was a significant immigrant settlement. Nottingham, of course, was one of these and, whilst there hadn't been any repeat of the 1958 rioting, tensions were never far from the surface.

There was tension of another kind the day after the World Cup Final when Charlie Moore had to inform the rest of the Marys' committee that the club's latest application to join the Midland League had been rejected. It wasn't entirely unexpected but nevertheless the tone of the meeting was still pretty lively, especially when an update on the cost of the yet to be installed showers at the KGV pavilion was read out. The club had originally agreed to pay eight hundred and ten pounds as their contribution to the overall figure but that had risen to eight hundred and fifty by the time of this latest meeting. A request to increase the number of showers from eight to ten had added a further sixty seven pounds to the bill making nine hundred and seventeen in total. With the estimate for the whole job having been revised downwards to twelve hundred pounds the club were effectively being asked to pay over seventy five percent of the anticipated final cost. Not only that but nine hundred odd pounds for a few showers was a pretty hefty commitment considering that my parents had only paid two thousand eight hundred pounds for our three-bedroom detached house that very same month.

With pre-season training due to start early in July Noel Simpson had already been interviewing players with a view to signing them on the basis that the club would actually be competing at the higher level and so it might have come as a bit of a surprise to one or two of them when they heard the news that they'd be facing at least a year down in the Central Alliance. For one young man the manager had expressed an interest in, Alan Ball, it didn't matter which of the two competitions Marys would be playing in because both were a step up from the Notts Alliance where he'd been turning out in a variety of positions for Mapperley FC.

AB : I can't remember whether it was a semi-final or a quarter-final up at Gedling Colliery's ground at Plains Road but when I got there our left winger was saying that he wouldn't play against their right back Walter Kirk. The bloke who ran Mapperley turned to me and said "Alan, you'll have to play left wing" and I said "I can't play there, I've never played on the left wing in my life." He told me that I'd got to and I said "Fair enough, I'll play there then but just don't give me any fifty-fifty balls or he'll kill me." So I played left wing and had a good game and he didn't get me because I wouldn't take the ball up to him. I thought if I take the ball up to him he'll kill me so I just pushed it past him and ran, because I could leave him for speed. Walter wasn't very pleased and said "Bring the ball up to me, bring it up" and I said "No thanks, Walter." That's where I got picked up to play for Arnold. Two of the lads at work came to see me the next day and said "We've got a number for you here, you've got to ring this man" and it was Noel Simpson. They said "They want to see how you'll go with them" and all I could say was "No, I'm alright where I am." They said "You're not, you're going to sign for Arnold 'cause we watch Arnold" and then they reckoned that if I didn't join them they'd beat me up everyday at work! They were Roy Mayfield and Harry Bloomfield and they were big Arnold fans, we all worked at Simms Sons and Cooke. They kept saying "Have you rung him up?" so I did and of course that's how it started.

The first training session was nothing more than the old tried and tested road run starting out from Redhill School, working its way up to Mapperley Plains and then back down again for a well earned shower. June had been Arnold's second driest on record and grounds were pretty firm but tarmac had no give at all and was a particularly gruelling surface for the new season's opening workout.

AB : The first time I went training with them I didn't know a soul. There must have been about thirty players there and so I tagged along with a bloke called Mick Cooper and we stayed amongst the runners at the back.

From personal experience it's often harder to run with the old pros at the back than it is with the young lads up front and Alan, being the fit lad that he was, thought the same.

AB : Even though I didn't know anybody else I said to Mick "I'm running up front next time with that lot. It's too tiring back here." So I did.

Noel hadn't been the only person interested in Alan either.

AB : I had a trial for Bradford City Reserves against Hartlepool. I was outside right, another position I'd never played in before and near the end I had a chance to chip the keeper but I delayed and he dived at my feet and smothered the ball. I knew I should have chipped him but I was that shattered, my brain was. I hadn't done badly and they asked me back the following week but I said I couldn't make it. After a while I thought what an idiot I'd been. I should have gone back.

Alan would start the season in the reserves, but another young man who Noel had kept track of for the last couple of years would go straight into the first team. His name was Arthur Oldham.

AO : Noel had been pestering me to sign for him ever since I'd made my debut for Alfreton against Marys back in 1960 but I'd said to him "I'm not too sure. I'm on good money at Alfreton." Then at the end of the 1961-62 season he turned up with Charlie Moore at the family farm in Keyworth and my mother greeted them at the door. She said "What do you want?" and they said "Have you got any free range eggs?" We chatted and I agreed to sign on the same money I'd been getting at Alfreton. It was a better deal really because the traveling was far easier.

Arthur's Alfreton team mate, left back Vince Howard, was another player firmly in the club's sights.

AO : Noel was mad keen on getting both of us.

Both Vince and Arthur had been sold on the idea of joining Marys because they'd been told that they'd be playing Midland League football so it was very much to their credit that they remained committed to the cause once they'd realised that they would be in the less exalted surroundings of the Central Alliance; testament also to the persuasive powers of the manager.

The other two notable arrivals came from clubs already in the Central Alliance. The first was Mick Hornbuckle, an inside-forward from Aspley Old Boys who'd finished as their top scorer with thirty eight goals, and the second, the final piece in Noel's jigsaw, was the guy who'd given the team more trouble than any other player in the recent past; Ransome and Marles' centre forward, Joe Boucher. Not only had he tormented the Saints' defence on the three occasions he'd come up against them, he'd also plundered an incredible fifty seven goals for the Newark side the previous season with four games still left to play. Committeeman Albert Moore recalls Noel's transfer policy.

AM : Marys were built on attacking football. We hadn't got time for defensive football but Noel liked good defenders. Then again he liked good forwards even better!

Having assembled a squad that he obviously thought capable of winning the Central Alliance championship Noel spent the remainder of the pre-season improving their fitness levels before the first game on August 18. Unfortunately the headlines on that opening day of the new season were given over to an incident the previous day that had seen East German border guards shoot an attempted escaper, eighteen year old Peter Fechter, and leave him to die on the Berlin Wall; its first, but not its last, victim. West Berliners who had looked on helplessly laid flowers and wreaths and set up a memorial for the young man that still exists today.

However, whilst his sad demise was given respectful coverage in the press and people with good intentions did their best to make sure his passing wouldn't be forgotten, another death that had made the headlines earlier in the month was one that would need no memorial to remain forever in the public consciousness. On August 5 the Hollywood screen legend Marilyn Monroe was found dead at her home in Los Angeles, having apparently suffered acute barbiturate poisoning which the coroner officially recorded as 'probable suicide'. The actual circumstances of her death remain shrouded in mystery and as a result of a lack of evidence investigators weren't able to confirm whether she'd died by her own hand or was the victim of homicide.

Back in the spring she'd made her last major appearance in public, famously singing an adapted version of 'Happy Birthday' to the President of the United States, John F Kennedy, at a televised birthday party held for him at Madison Square Garden. The Jean Louis designer dress she wore for the occasion, one which was so figure hugging that it looked like she'd been stitched into it, fetched slightly over one and a quarter million dollars in 1999, a record for an item of clothing sold at auction. Just as memorable as her outfit was her entrance which, as befits a lady totally unfamiliar with the term 'punctual', was actually quite some time after the Master of Ceremonies had first announced her presence. When she eventually toddled on to the podium to deliver what appeared to be a somewhat inebriated rendition of the birthday song she was re-introduced as 'the late Marilyn Monroe'.

Looking at a clip of the broadcast today this witty description seems rather spooky, especially as there are any number of conspiracy theories linking her death with JFK and his brother Robert. There have been claims that the actress had affairs with both men and her second husband, the great baseball star Joe DiMaggio, was quoted as saying that the two were implicitly involved in her death. Other theories suggested CIA or Mafia complicity and the plot thickens when testimony from friends in her last days suggest that she hardly appeared to be on the brink of suicide.

Her brief life, lived mostly in the glare of unrelenting public scrutiny, was sadly over by the time she was thirty six. Thirty five years later another world famous blonde who was also subjected to an intolerable degree of intrusion in the name of public interest died suddenly at the same age and in the same month. She was Princess Diana and her tragic death saw an unexpected outpouring of emotional incontinence across the country as the British public 'got in touch with itself' in a manner never before seen within these shores.

Apart from their ages and month of death the two goddesses shared a number of other attributes; beauty, obviously, and, if we are to believe what we read, insecurity, fragility, and a heightened skill for manipulation. They shared one other thing in death too; the song 'Candle In The Wind'. Originally written by Bernie Taupin and Elton John as the former's tribute to the actress, the words were re-worked hastily in time for it to be performed by the singer at Diana's funeral service and a recording of it released soon after turned into the biggest selling UK single of all time. Not only that but, like it or not, images of Diana, frozen in time, still regularly make the front pages many years after her death; she still shifts newspapers and magazines. She won't ever grow old and neither will Marilyn, voted the 'Sexiest Woman of the Twentieth Century' by People magazine in 1999. For many of their fans, old and new, I suppose that's part of the attraction.

Of course down the years the general public has always been drawn to celebrities like moths to a flame and for local football fans the summer of 1962 was no exception. A few years earlier The Showbiz XI, the original celebrity football team, had been formed by British singer and actor Jess Conrad with the aim of raising money for charity. The concept was that a bunch of 'celebs' would pitch up at a local ground, normally on a Sunday, play a part serious, part knockabout game against a team from the district, with all gate receipts going to good causes. Some of the early matches were even shown on ITV. Of the games scheduled to take place as the new season was about to commence, a couple in the area caught the eye. A record crowd was expected at Skegness Town for the stars' visit with disc jockey Pete Murray, boxer Dick Richardson, and Jess himself featuring in the side and a couple of weeks later a squad including all-round entertainers and wannabe footballers Tommy Steele and Kenny Lynch was due at Grange Park, Long Eaton. Both days were unequivocal successes with the latter game being attended by an estimated five thousand spectators.

Marys weren't anticipating anywhere near that number for their opening game of the season, against Burton Albion Reserves, especially as it had to be played on the Top Rec with KGV being required for cricket, but a decent crowd still turned up to see whether Noel Simpson's new look side had what it took to stake a claim for the Central Alliance Championship. In the event they didn't have to wait too long. Arthur Oldham, playing at inside left, scored after only four minutes and the Saints' number eight, Mick Hornbuckle, added a second in the eighth. The rapid scoring didn't stop there and by half time the maroon and golds were five nil up with Arthur having bagged himself a hat-trick. By comparison the second period was a bit of an anti-climax as the home side only managed to add a couple more to their tally to finish seven-one winners. Arthur ended up with four with Mick claiming a hat-trick of his own and the only surprise of this opening fixture was that the usually prolific Joe Boucher didn't get his name on the scoresheet.

It had been just the start that the club had needed but a week later a much tougher proposition was in store as Marys traveled over into Derbyshire to play the previous season's third placed side, Gresley Rovers. Finding themselves a goal down in nine minutes the Saints knew that they'd got a job on and with the home side continuing to dominate play it was a wonder that Len Rockley's goal wasn't breached again. Somehow the visitors hung on and on the stroke of half time Arthur Oldham picked up a loose ball on the edge of the area and drilled home the equaliser. This seemed to take the sting out of the home side because on the resumption it was all Marys. Left back Vince Howard fired home on the hour and Joe Boucher opened his account for his new team fifteen minutes later to make victory certain. Rovers made a late rally and pulled a goal back two minutes from time but it proved too late to stave off defeat.

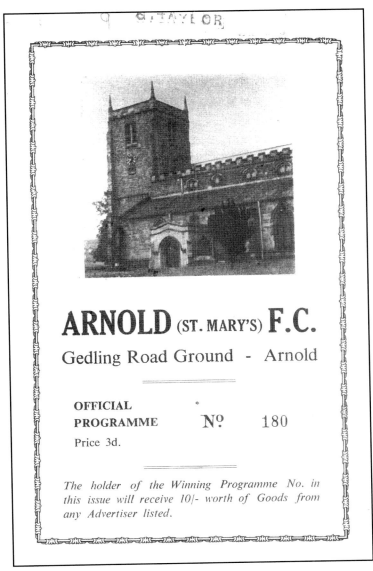

FRONT COVER OF MARYS v ASPLEY OLD BOYS PROGRAMME 1 SEP 1962 (G Taylor Collection)

Seven days later on the opening day of September Marys were back at Gedling Road for the first time this season for the visit of traditional rivals Aspley Old Boys. The showers hadn't been installed yet but there was one innovation for the players and fans alike; it was the match day programme, reintroduced after an absence of thirteen years. Unlike the publication of 1949-50 which was issued solely for the first home game of each month this latest one was intended to be available throughout the whole of the campaign. In his first notes of the season the Manager extended a warm welcome to everyone and expressed the hope that they'd see 'much entertaining football' and suggested that the Old Boys, 'worthy opponents', were certain to provide an enjoyable afternoon. Well they did precisely that, but not in the manner that Noel probably anticipated. As they had done against Burton, Marys swept into an early lead, this time through Joe Boucher, and added to their tally at regular intervals throughout the first half to turn round with the scoreline exactly as it was in the first game of the season; five-nil. The only difference on this particular occasion was that their opponents showed little or no defiance and the Saints went straight for the jugular. Aspley were 'entertaining' all right, but only in the manner that the Christians were when they found themselves pitted against the lions in Roman times. At Gedling Road there was no blood spilt but it was a slaughter nonetheless with the Old Boys' keeper having to pick the ball out of his net a further eleven times. The visitors did manage a consolation goal but the sixteen-one annihilation was the worst defeat in their history as well as being Marys' best ever victory in the Central Alliance. It also equalled the post-war club record set back in the old Spartan League days. Joe Boucher, who'd only hit the target once in the opening two matches, helped himself to rich pickings with seven goals whilst Arthur Oldham repeated his sharp shooting feat against Burton with another four to take both men onto eight in only three games.

A maximum six points from the opening fixtures would have been the aim of everyone involved with the club but the scoring of twenty six goals in the process was probably beyond even the most optimistic of expectations and whilst there were no doubt tougher times ahead it had been a great way to build confidence in anticipation of the visit of Midland League Champions Matlock Town the following week in the first qualifying round of the FA Cup. The Derbyshire club had been Marys' opponents at this stage of the competition the previous season and had utterly dominated the contest, winning by five goals to one. In seven head to head clashes between the two teams Town had come out on top no less than six times but there was a distinct feeling that the current Saints' side was better placed to give their bogey team a game than in any of their previous meetings.

Enticed by a combination of the headline victory of the previous week and the magic of the FA Cup the biggest crowd for some while descended on Gedling Road. As Notts were playing away it included me too, drawn like the rest but with the added incentive of such a match being played right on my own doorstep. A thousand programmes with a maroon-coloured cover had been specially printed for the occasion and some were no doubt still being thumbed through when Marys got off to the best possible start with a goal inside five minutes from Mick Hornbuckle. There would be no goal glut this week however and with the visitors giving as good as they got it was no surprise when they equalised right on half time. It was a crucial time to concede the lead and could have proved costly but the Saints shrugged off the setback and just seven minutes after the break seventeen year old Peter Burton cracked the ball into the net to restore Marys' lead. There were one or two league scouts in attendance including Derby County legend Sammy Crooks and they must have been highly impressed with the contribution of the maroon and golds' young outside right, especially when he doubled his tally to put the home side firmly in the driving seat. As might be expected from one of the Midland League's leading lights Matlock threw everything they could at the Saints' rearguard and added a second goal of their own but with a very partisan crowd willing them towards victory Marys hung on to their one goal lead to secure their first ever win in the oldest competition in world football.

The following week the Saints traveled to meet another Derbyshire side over at Ashbourne in the Central Alliance Premier Division Cup and despite a final scoreline of five-four in the visitors' favour the win was accomplished with a little less difficulty than it might have appeared. Three-one up at the break and then five-two ahead towards the final whistle, it was only a slackening off in approach that let the home side score a couple of consolation efforts late on.

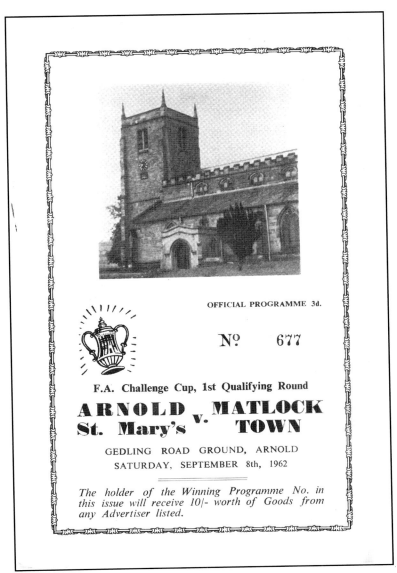

OFFICIAL PROGRAMME 3d.

Nº 677

F.A. Challenge Cup, 1st Qualifying Round

ARNOLD v. MATLOCK
St. Mary's TOWN

GEDLING ROAD GROUND, ARNOLD
SATURDAY, SEPTEMBER 8th, 1962

The holder of the Winning Programme No. in this issue will receive 10/- worth of Goods from any Advertiser listed.

FRONT COVER OF MARYS v MATLOCK TOWN FA CUP PROGRAMME 8 SEP 1962

Seven days later a repeat of such generosity would more than likely be punished even more severely because Marys were on their travels across the Derbyshire border once again to meet Alfreton Town in the second qualifying round of the FA Cup and this time their hosts, another old Midland League adversary, were expected to provide far stronger opposition. For four of the Saints' side it would be a reunion of sorts as goalie Len Rockley, left back Vince Howard, right half Jack Davis, and inside left Arthur Oldham had all been on Town's books the previous season.

In front of a large crowd of almost two thousand four hundred, many of whom had traveled over from Arnold, Alfreton, reputedly put together at great expense, built up a series of attacks and the visitors' goal led a charmed life right up until the eighth minute when a quick counter attack caught the home side on the hop and Joe Boucher converted a pass from Mick Hornbuckle. Completely against the run of play it may have been but inspired by their early lead Marys piled on tremendous pressure against a shaky Town defence and had the ball in the net twice more, only for both efforts to be ruled out for offside. Three minutes before the break it was third time lucky and there was no chance that this goal would be chalked off by a linesman's flag. Arthur Oldham, relishing his return to his old club, picked the ball up just over the halfway line, slalomed past three defenders and blasted a left foot shot past the helpless goalie. Six minutes after half time with the Alfreton defence at sixes and sevens the diminutive inside forward added a third and soon after nearly claimed his hat-trick when he went on another thirty yard dash, beating player after player only to be thwarted by the keeper at the very end. For Arthur the match had turned into a personal triumph, a showcase to remind his old club just what they were missing, and when he set up Peter Williams for Marys' fourth and final goal in the seventieth minute it put the seal on a great afternoon for him and everyone at the club.

AO : Alfreton had signed top players, league guys like goalkeeper Bob Wyllie from Mansfield Town who'd been given a club house. Manager Jim Bullions wanted a big side but I went back and just had a dream game that day. I was on a high, I couldn't do anything wrong. Everything I tried came off. There was an Arsenal scout there and he got talking to Pat Groome, asking about me and how old I was. Pat told him "Twenty-two" and the scout said "That's a shame, he's too old for us."

Too old for the Gunners but perfect for a place in Noel Simpson's plans to build a formidable side at Arnold, Arthur was already an integral part of a team that had remained unchanged all season, won six matches out of six, and were grabbing the headlines in a similar manner to two or three seasons back. The Midland League column in the following Saturday's Football Post was noticeable for the fact that it contained not a single mention of Alfreton's humbling by a club deemed inferior by the competition's management committee. Thankfully the Central Alliance round-up more than compensated for this glaring omission, leading off with the fairly predictable headline of 'SAINTS GO MARCHING ON TO CUP FAME' and following this with a glowing appraisal of the team's start to the campaign captioned 'Simpson building club into a powerful force'. It went on to conclude 'Surely now the Midland League cannot fail to ignore the claims of St Marys to a place in the competition which was refused them this season. With successive victories in the games with this league's clubs their success cannot be marked down as a fluke. Their performances make the decision not to have them in the Midland League look rather unfortunate'.

The rebuffing of Marys by the Midland League was no more than a local spat compared with the non-admittance by the University of Mississippi of a black student by the name of James Meredith. On the Thursday before the Saints' success at Alfreton he had attempted to register at the University, known as 'Ole Miss', at its Oxford, Mi campus, only to be personally refused entry by the Governor of the State, Ross Barnett. Attempts at breaking down segregation by the Civil Rights Movement and the Federal Government had met with widespread resistance in a number of the Southern States and Barnett, a particularly virulent advocate of maintaining the *status quo*, was on record as saying that no school in the state would be integrated while ever he was Governor. Meredith, who'd won a lawsuit allowing him admission to the University, tried again five days later at its Jackson campus, only to find his way barred once more by the Governor.

Communications and negotiations took place constantly between the Governor and The President, John F Kennedy, but little progress was made in brokering a deal to break the deadlock. By the weekend the atmosphere in Oxford was becoming very tense with people pouring into the town to defend Ole Miss and the Southern way of life. The start of the squirrel hunting season was imminent and the increased number of guns in pick up trucks had the authorities admitting that the situation was very dangerous.

Ironically the Oxford campus itself was deserted as many of the University's students had flocked to Jackson on the Saturday to see their football team, 'The Rebels', play against Kentucky. Once again the ubiquitous Mr Barnett made an appearance, this time to give a half-time address to all those assembled, and as he came into view the crowd went wild, waving Confederate flags in an open show of defiance before waiting for the Governor's words of wisdom. "I love Mississippi! I love her people; our customs! I love and I respect our heritage!" were the words he actually spoke, all received with rapturous applause by his adoring public.

If anyone had expected him to try and pour oil on troubled waters they had been mistaken. All he had effectively done was worsen a fragile situation, one largely of his own making and prolonged by his determined intransigence, and on the Sunday JFK announced that James Meredith would indeed be registered on the Monday and that he was planning to make a speech to the State that night. Following his appearance on air at 8pm, the Ole Miss campus turned into a battlefield with the rioters initially targeting the media and news cameramen. Federal troops and US Marshalls joined the fray and violent clashes led to the deaths of two people, a French journalist and an Oxford worker, as well as injuries to almost fifty soldiers and gunshot wounds to thirty five Marshalls.

With order restored by the following morning and an air of uneasy calm around the campus, Meredith was finally allowed to register. Barnett was nowhere in sight. It had been another bloody episode in the annals of the Civil Rights Movement, one recorded by Bob Dylan in his song about the black student's plight, 'Oxford Town', in which he sings "He come to the door, he couldn't get in, all because of the colour of his skin." Despite one more obstacle to segregation having been overcome, the events at Ole Miss had once again shown to the citizens of the USA a rather disturbing picture of life in its southernmost states.

Getting into school wasn't a problem that any of us third years had on our return after the summer holidays although there were one or two days when I thought of how I might get out of it. Studying was becoming serious, especially now we were in long trousers. Yes, strange as it may seem today, the rules of the Boys High back in the early sixties included a clothing regime of short trousers in years one and two unless there were mitigating factors. I say factors but the fact was there may have only been one; height. Tall boys were allowed to wear long trousers in year two, presumably when an early growth spurt took them to a height where shorts might have made them look a bit like Plug, one of the Bash Street Kids out of the Beano. A classmate was one of the first to be granted the concession and he did hover quite a few inches above the rest of us, but I think the decision was actually made on the grounds of compassion because not only was he lanky, he was ginger as well. With these attributes the last thing the poor boy needed was to be lumbered with a pair of short pants.

Thankfully I was the perfect height for secondary school; average and therefore subject to no ridicule. Unfortunately, compared with the emerging brain boxes in my form I was pretty average at every subject too. Every one except Latin, that is, where I was just plain abysmal. Making sense of the grammar in Caesar's *Gallic Wars* was bad enough but I even failed an audition as a timekeeper when the Latin master tried explaining to us the meter that needed to be used when speaking some piece or other. I was meant to tap out the rhythm but my fingers were all in a knot before we'd even got to the third line. I could keep time to any of the pop songs of the day but when it came to the mysteries of an iambic pentameter I was well and truly stumped. In fact it was my new found fascination with the hit parade and everything to do with it that was having a deleterious effect on my schoolwork generally and developments in October would only make it worse. It's a pity that they didn't teach Media Studies / Popular Music back in 1962. If they had I'd have at least been number one at something.

Marys' excellent start to the season would have seen them way ahead at the top of the pile too had their six games been for league points but their successful cup exploits and a blank date on the final Saturday of September had seen them play only three matches in the Central Alliance whilst other sides had already racked up as many as eight. This situation wasn't about to get any easier because their first game in October was another cup tie, this time in the third qualifying round of the FA Cup at Cheshire League side Buxton, and with the prospect of a match up against the big boys of the Football League drawing ever closer there was so much interest in the town that six coaches were laid on to carry players and supporters to the match. Regrettably two of them broke down and, most embarrassingly of all, one was the coach carrying the team who, as a consequence, had to stand and wait patiently by the side of the road to be picked up by the first of the supporters' vehicles that had started off half an hour after the players.

It wasn't the most ideal preparation for an important cup clash against a strong side like Buxton, liberally sprinkled with ex-League players such as hard-as-nails full back Norman Curtis, formerly with Sheffield Wednesday, and goalscoring winger Alf Ringstead, who'd made his name with the Steel City's other club, United, and who'd been capped twenty times by the Republic of Ireland, and it showed as the Saints found themselves with their backs against the wall right from the kick-off. John Anthony cleared up a couple of attacks as Marys gamely battled to establish a foothold but two quick goals, one from the Irish number seven and a second from his counterpart on the left wing, put the home side firmly in the driving seat. Even when Mick Hornbuckle clawed one back for the maroon and golds it was Buxton who were still making all the running and minutes before the break they restored their two goal lead and from then on the Saints were chasing shadows. They did manage a couple of late consolation goals from Peter Burton and Joe Boucher but by then the score was six-one and the tie well and truly lost. Still, it was hardly a disgrace, especially given what followed when Buxton hammered Midland League Gainsborough Trinity in the fourth and final qualifying round and then took Fourth Division Barrow to a replay in the First Round Proper.

Seven days later it was roles reversed as Marys travelled to Beeston to meet Ericsson Athletic in the league, moved easily into a three-nil half time lead and then added a fourth for good measure straight after the break only for their opponents to stage a late fightback. Thanks to some sloppy defending the scoreline ended seven-three to the Saints with Joe Boucher and Arthur Oldham grabbing a hat-trick apiece. The following Saturday, in the second round of the Central Alliance Premier Division Cup, Marys' rearguard was again found wanting and conceded two first half goals away at the less than mighty Clay Cross who were languishing third from bottom of the table before kick-off. Thankfully Joe Boucher was again in sparkling form and countered with a couple of goals of his own before completing his second hat-trick in a week early in the second half to give his team the lead. It appeared that the maroon and golds had finally got the upper hand for the first time in the game but unfortunately two more defensive lapses followed and the Derbyshire side, encouraged by their biggest crowd of the season, took full advantage on both occasions. Not only did they restore their lead, they had no trouble in maintaining it to the final whistle, running out winners by four goals to three.

Having conceded thirteen goals in three games manager Noel Simpson, who'd picked the same eleven for all nine of the previous matches, wielded the axe and goalie Len Rockley, right half Jack Davis, and centre half Dennis Parr were all omitted for the last game of the month against Ransome and Marles. The Newark side, having lost leading scorer Joe Boucher to the Saints, weren't the force they'd been the previous season but Marys, on the road for a sixth consecutive time, had a hard time breaking down the Greens' resolute defence in windy conditions that weren't at all favourable to constructive forward play. The maroon and golds' own rearguard was a lot tighter too, with replacements Ernie Iremonger, Tony Watson, and Derek Smith all helping to keep a clean sheet for only the second time this campaign as the game ended almost inevitably in a goalless draw.

Knocked out of two cup competitions and with only one victory to their name, October 1962 had certainly proved to be a less than memorable month for the Saints. By contrast however, a seismic event was taking place elsewhere in the world that would probably never be forgotten by anyone around at the time. It was the Cuban Missile Crisis, a confrontation that would bring the two super-powers, the USA and the USSR, to the brink of nuclear war, and had even a fourteen year old like me worrying whether the end of the world as I knew it was really nigh.

The crisis began on Tuesday 16, when the President of the USA John F Kennedy was informed over his breakfast that U2 spy planes had sighted Soviet nuclear missile sites in Cuba, an island ruled by the communist Fidel Castro only ninety miles off the Florida coast. JFK was told that the missiles could be ready for deployment in just fourteen days and despite being urged by some members of the Executive Committee of the National Security Council (ExComm) to authorise the bombing of the sites he instead ordered more reconnaissance to buy himself time to find a diplomatic solution. The next day another missile site was detected, one that had the capability of reaching cities such as Chicago, Washington, and New York, and the pressure on the President intensified. On the Thursday the Russians denied the presence of any Soviet weaponry on the island and twenty four hours later JFK met with his Defence Secretary and his Joint Chiefs of Staff to discuss the various military options open to them.

By now the press were beginning to get wind that something was seriously amiss and by the end of the weekend, during which time additional missiles had been detected, JFK decided that the best course of action would be a naval blockade of Cuba. Strictly speaking this would have been an act of war so the operation was given the official classification of 'quarantine'. The US Navy was put on full alert and the world's first nuclear-powered aircraft carrier, the USS Enterprise, led off the operation. With Soviet ships known to be heading towards the Caribbean it was a high risk strategy on the part of the USA and the absolute seriousness of the situation meant that the secrecy of the conflict couldn't be maintained. On the evening of Monday 22, the President addressed the nation. He began by summarising the events of the previous week and then informed his countrymen of the response scheduled to take place with immediate effect:

First: To halt this offensive build-up, a strict quarantine on all offensive military equipment under shipment to Cuba is being initiated. All ships of any kind bound for Cuba from whatever nation and port will, if found to contain cargoes of offensive weapons, be turned back. This quarantine will be extended, if needed, to other types of cargo and carriers. We are not at this time, however, denying the necessities of life as the Soviets attempted to do in their Berlin blockade of 1948.

Second: I have directed the continued and increased close surveillance of Cuba and its military build-up. The foreign ministers of the Organisation of American States (OAS), in their communique of October 6, rejected secrecy on such matters in this hemisphere. Should these offensive military preparations continue, thus increasing the threat to the hemisphere, further action will be justified. I have directed the Armed Forces to prepare for any eventualities; and I trust that in the interest of both the Cuban people and the Soviet technicians at the sites, the hazards to all concerned of continuing the threat will be recognized.

Third: It shall be the policy of this nation to regard any nuclear missile launched from Cuba against any nation in the Western Hemisphere as an attack on the United States, requiring a full retaliatory response upon the Soviet Union.

Fourth: As a necessary military precaution, I have reinforced our base at Guantanamo, evacuated today the dependents of our personnel there, and ordered additional military units to be on a standby alert status.

Fifth: We are calling tonight for an immediate meeting of the Organ of Consultation under the OAS, to consider this threat to hemispheric security and to invoke articles 6 and 8 of the Rio Treaty in support of all necessary action. The United Nations Charter allows for regional security arrangements -- and the nations of this hemisphere decided long ago against the military presence of outside powers. Our other allies around the world have also been alerted.

Sixth: Under the Charter of the United Nations, we are asking tonight that an emergency meeting of the Security Council be convoked without delay to take action against this latest Soviet threat to world peace. Our resolution will call for the prompt dismantling and withdrawal of all offensive weapons in Cuba, under the supervision of UN observers, before the quarantine can be lifted.

Seventh and finally: I call upon Chairman Khrushchev to halt and eliminate this clandestine, reckless, and provocative threat to world peace and to stable relations between our two nations. I call upon him further to abandon this course of world domination, and to join in an historic effort to end the perilous arms race and to transform the history of man. He has an opportunity now to move the world back from the abyss of destruction -- by returning to his government's own words that it had no need to station missiles outside its own territory, and withdrawing these weapons from Cuba, by refraining from any action which will widen or deepen the present crisis, and then by participating in a search for peaceful and permanent solutions.

My fellow citizens: let no one doubt that this is a difficult and dangerous effort on which we have set out. No one can foresee precisely what course it will take or what costs or casualties will be incurred; many months in which both our patience and our will will be tested, months in which many threats and denunciations will keep us aware of our dangers. But the greatest danger of all would be to do nothing.

Our goal is not the victory of might, but the vindication of right; not peace at the expense of freedom, but both peace **and** freedom, here in this hemisphere, and we hope, around the world. God willing, that goal will be achieved.

Thank you and good night.

US TV commentators called it 'the most dangerous situation since the end of World War II', adding that 'the next forty eight hours will be decisive'. Anyone hearing the speech or seeing a transcript of it would have been left in no doubt as to the gravity of what was happening, especially where JFK threatens 'a full retaliatory response upon the Soviet Union' whilst effectively acknowledging that the world is peering into 'the abyss of destruction'.

From now on every move, or at least those moves that weren't considered either a threat to national security or liable to induce panic amongst the general public, would be played out in front of an anxious worldwide audience of millions. Americans cleared food and emergency supplies off supermarket shelves, long queues were reported at petrol stations, and there was a run on tyres. Students received phone calls from worried parents urging them to come home to be with their families, just in case, and in the forthcoming days ten million people would leave the USA's cities hoping to find safety far away from nuclear targets. Churches opened all day for prayer and TV sets and radios were kept on constantly in case of breaking news.

There was no Soviet response to President Kennedy's speech for thirteen hours until a note was received by ExComm accusing the USA of piracy. With new surveillance photographs of Cuba showing that missiles were ready for launch, JFK's brother Robert received an informal communication from the USSR Ambassador that the captains of the Russian ships closing in on the line of quarantine had orders to continue their course. To make matters worse Khrushchev was alleged to have said 'If the United States tries to stop Soviet ships my submarines will sink them. I will not be the first to fire a nuclear weapon but if the US insists on war we will all meet together in hell.' It may have only been posturing on the part of the Russian Premier but no-one could be totally sure. What JFK did know was that by setting a deadline of 10am for the following morning he was taking the huge risk of worsening an already fragile situation.

On the Wednesday morning, as anticipated, the Soviet ships reached the quarantine line but received radio orders from Moscow to hold their positions. For two days the world looked on impotently. I'd not long celebrated my fourteenth birthday but I was convinced that I wouldn't be seeing my fifteenth and most everyone I knew seemed just as worried. Life didn't stop, of course, but the world did seem to be holding its collective breath. For two days behind the scenes negotiations, as well as a number of fruitless exchanges at the United Nations, took place, but there seemed to be no way beyond the impasse. The USA raised the activation level of its Armed Forces to DEFCON (Defence Readiness Condition) 2, the highest ever in the country's history and only one step below the expectation of actual imminent attack. Defence Secretary Robert McNamara, fearing that Khrushchev might react with a nuclear spasm, cautioned against humiliating the Soviets, but JFK ratcheted up the tension by issuing an ultimatum that the missiles on Cuba must be removed before the weekend.

On the morning of Friday 26 a Soviet oil tanker entered the quarantined zone but having satisfied themselves that it was *bona fide* the Americans allowed it through. Later that day it appeared that a significant breakthrough had been made when a rambling letter from Khrushchev was received saying that the Soviets would remove their missiles if the USA gave guarantees that it would not invade Cuba. Secretly JFK met with the Russian Ambassador and indicated that the *quid pro quo* of removal of UN nuclear weapons from Turkey was negotiable.

With the world still awaiting a peaceful resolution to the stand-off, a second letter was sent by the Soviets the following day, the Saturday, stating that the missile removal from Turkey must be included in the terms of settlement. Kennedy was reluctant to give this concession, knowing that it might make him look weak in the eyes of the Soviets, so he decided to ignore the second letter and formally accept the terms of the original. It worked and his gamble had paid off. At 9am local time on Sunday 28, Khrushchev announced on Radio Moscow that the missiles would be dismantled. No mention was made of the weapons in Turkey.

The rest of the weekend seemed a whole lot better, at least in the western hemisphere. In a phrase attributed to JFK but probably coined by Secretary of State Dean Rusk, the two sides had gone 'Eyeball to eyeball, but the other guy blinked first'. As JFK had promised, the missiles were removed from Turkey, albeit some four months later and well after the furore had died down; crucially, no advantage was seen to have been conceded to the Soviets. As a result Kennedy inevitably came out of the crisis rather better than his opposite number Nikita Khrushchev who, diminished by the episode, would relinquish his position in less than two years. JFK unfortunately would last only half as long, but for entirely different reasons.

It had been a scary couple of weeks, certainly the last five or six days that were played out in full glare of a fearful world audience. I turned to my record collection for a bit of reassuring normality and the track that I kept playing over and over was 'Telstar', an instrumental naturally, by the Tornados, Billy Fury's backing group. It had hit number one on October 4, had stayed there throughout the crisis and would eventually emulate the feat in the USA as well, becoming the first record ever by a British group to reach the coveted top spot.

It remains one of my all time favourite singles but it appears that a young man across the Atlantic in that October of 1962 was listening to it with an entirely different range of emotions. His name, or internet moniker, is 'Dantiger' and he hails from Long Beach, California. He became a US Marine, a member of the self-styled 'toughest fighting force in the world', although I daresay the SAS might like to take issue with that assertion. This soldier had a gentler side however, as he admitted to millions of surfers on the world wide web: "I remember the Cuban Missile Crisis was at its peak and I had a bad feeling when I would listen to this song [Telstar]. I was in High School and my girlfriend Susie thought we were doomed and cried one time and I still recall kissing her tears and they were salty but sweet. She died in a car crash two years later while I was about to leave for Viet Nam. It was my time to cry. Yes, Marines can have their hearts broken". Mine was almost broken reading his poignant recollection of his very personal take on the link between the record and the Crisis. Then I realised that the two of us, thousands of miles apart both then and now, were connected by a song named after a telecommunications satellite; which seems rather apt.

Apart from the spectre of nuclear annihilation that had hovered over the world in the latter part of the month, October was otherwise full of fun, especially in the entertainment world. James Bond, played by Scottish actor Sean Connery, made his cinema debut on the thirtieth when 'Dr No' became the first of Ian Fleming's novels about the exploits of Secret Agent 007 to be adapted for the big screen whilst dancehalls around the district were hosting a number of competitions to see who could best perform the 'Twist', the craze that had been sweeping the country all year following the success of Chubby Checker's recording of 'Let's Twist Again' which had reached number two in the charts but managed to hang around in the hit parade for well over six months.

Not quite so well known as the gentleman whose name was a variation on Fats Domino but whipping up a storm around town nevertheless was Arnold's own beat group, five young guys calling themselves 'The Beatmen'. With the world still waiting breathlessly for Khrushchev's announcement that would bring an end to the Missile Crisis the boys were the main attraction at the Blue Ball Hotel, Risley, where they had agreed to play at the annual dance of local football club Long Eaton Grange. Their first appearance had been at the Rendezvous Club in Mapperley and they'd gone on to play at the Festival Hall, Trowell, The Locarno in Nottingham, and many other venues around the Midlands whilst increasing their bookings, on average, to four engagements a week, and at the same time enhancing their already growing reputation.

A contemporary of the band, Stuart Frew, looks back to those early days on his website: 'I recall them all living in a little terrace house near a school I went to in Arnold and also seeing them appear at the Saturday morning 'ABC Minors' at the Metropole in Sherwood!' Now if I'm not mistaken the 'little terrace house' was on James Street, almost opposite my grandparents' where I was born, and the school was the first one I attended, High Street Infants. I'm sure of this because two of the group, bass player Paul Mountain and rhythm guitarist Cliff Haynes, lived on 'Mi Nan's street'. Cliff had a brother called Larry, a big pal of my Uncle Derrick from boyhood, and earlier in the year Larry and his girlfriend Doreen had arranged a blind date for Derrick with Doreen's workmate and good friend Beryl. The venue for the date was Loughborough, the event a dance, and top of the bill were none other than The Beatmen.

ARNOLD'S OWN BEAT GROUP, THE BEATMEN, c1962 : Phil Severn, Bill Brazier, Paul Mountain, Cliff Haynes, Barrie Heald.
(Trevor Peck Collection)

The group's repertoire at the time was varied, designed to cover a broad range of tastes, but I like to think that it included a version of Sam Cooke's 'Cupid', a big hit from the previous year, because as Beryl is now my Aunt, I know for sure that the God of Love's arrow most certainly found its target that evening.

The group hadn't yet managed to win a recording contract but up in Liverpool another promising combo had not long been picked up by Parlophone Records, part of the huge EMI Group, having previously been turned down by Decca. On October 5 their first record for the label hit the shops and the music world was about to undergo a revolution. It wasn't obvious at the time because like many major upheavals the beginning was somewhat muted. The record was released to mixed reviews, sold fantastically well and in enough numbers on Merseyside to see it enter the lower reaches of the charts, but never quite made the breakthrough nationally. Still, it did climb to seventeenth, which was hardly a disaster. The song was, of course, 'Love Me Do', and the group a previously little known foursome called

'The Beatles'. They might have still been scratching around for fame just then but twelve months down the line there would hardly be anyone in the UK unfamiliar with the names of John, Paul, George, and Ringo.

After all the tension of October it was to be hoped that November would be a little less stressful but when the first Saturday of the new month coincided with the First Round of the FA Cup, it was heart in mouth time again as Notts hosted Peterborough in front of a crowd of over twenty thousand with me in my normal spot, praying as usual at this time of the year for a victory to kick start a glorious cup run for the Magpies. Of course it wasn't to be. The Posh were three up at half-time and with Forest also playing at home many fans were already toying with the idea of leaving early 'to beat the traffic' whilst still emptying the contents of their vacuum flasks. The only saving grace from my point of view was that it didn't get any worse. The score remained unchanged at three-nil right to the bitter end, by which time only a scattered handful of diehards, me included, were still in the ground. Mercifully the ref blew right on time and we all trudged off into the gloom of an early winter evening.

MARYS v GRESLEY ROVERS 3 NOV 1962 : Back Row (l to r); W Archer, B Molyneux, V Howard, E Iremonger, J Davis, D Smith, J Anthony, J Browning. Front Row; P Williams, M Hornbuckle, J Boucher, A Oldham, A Ball. Mascot, T Gray.   (Alan Ball Collection)

Marys had had a much better afternoon and for one player in particular it was a day not to be forgotten. Following the goalless draw against Ransomes, Noel Simpson made a change to the forward line for the team's first home game in almost two months against Gresley Rovers, giving young Peter Burton a break, switching Peter Williams from the other flank to take his place, and promoting Alan Ball from the reserves for his debut at outside left. Ironically the change nearly didn't happen.

AB : I'd been playing in the reserve team and they'd put me at outside left, which is where they saw me play, but I hardly got a pass and I became disillusioned. Apart from that one game against Gedling Colliery I'd been playing inside forward or wing half for Mapperley and that's where I would have preferred to play.

It didn't get any better and I said to myself "This is no good". Mapperley kept saying to me "Come back, come back to us" so I made up my mind to leave but I wanted to tell Noel first. So on the Tuesday night at training at Redhill School I said "Noel, I want a word with you" and he said "Oh, I want a word with you". He asked me what I wanted to speak to him about and I said "You go first", thinking that I'll tell him my news afterwards. He said "I've had good reports about you in the reserves and you're in the first team Saturday." I said "All right then" and he asked me what it was that I wanted him for and all I could say was "Nah, it was nothing".

I played against Gresley on the left wing and they had a right back called 'Butcher' White. I thought "Well I'll not see much of the ball" but wham, straight from the kick-off the ball came out to me and I never looked back.

Indeed he didn't, becoming a fixture in a position he didn't like but in which he proved to be so successful that Noel Simpson could see no reason to play him elsewhere. The fact that, as he readily acknowledges, he was surrounded by a formidable array of talent certainly helped him cement his place in the side.

AB : At first I felt like the new kid on the block, well I was. I think I was one of the youngest in the side and I looked up to everybody else. John Anthony might have been a year younger than me but he'd been in the team for three years. I'd come from a family where things had always been hard. My dad went out to work at six in the morning and wouldn't get back till seven at night and I was always brought up to respect my elders. I had two older brothers who I used to play football with and they didn't go easy on me, saying that I needed toughening up. But, when I got into the first team, on my side of the pitch was John, Vince Howard, and Arthur Oldham. Everyone down that side reckoned the left was best. John was hard, he'd run through a brick wall and if anyone had a go at you he would sort them out and when Vince tackled he got them as well. Arthur just never stopped running and I dropped in just right.

He certainly did because the first forty five minutes against second placed Gresley, who the previous week had relieved Eastwood Town of their one hundred percent record, saw Marys' attack tear apart one of the best defences in the Central Alliance. The Derbyshire side had conceded only seven goals in eight games prior to kick-off but forty five minutes later the Saints had gone nap and when the half-time whistle blew the maroon and golds were five-one up. Joe Boucher had terrified the visitors' rearguard, scoring his third hat-trick in four matches before the half hour mark and then Alan had repaid the manager's faith in him by scoring twice in three minutes. John Anthony added the sixth after the break and the Saints played out time with little threat from the opposition. It had been a good afternoon by any standards and it was about to get that bit better. The days of the players having to trudge off down Hallam's Lane after the match to get washed and changed were finally over as the Gresley game marked the official opening of the showers at KGV. The honours were performed by Councillor J Miller, Chairman of the Arnold Urban District Council Estates Committee, and this is what he had to say: "The Council are pleased to add yet another amenity to the ground and to fulfil a long awaited desire of the Football Club". Long awaited it had certainly been but thanks to the massive input of Marys' committee, both in providing over seventy five percent of the funding and even assisting physically with the actual installation, the task had finally been completed. It was only to be hoped that the Council wouldn't take as many years to give the green light for the next stage of development; a new stand.

As it happened a combination of Mother Nature and an uneven fixture schedule would ensure that Marys would only get to use the showers just once in the next four months and another hazard, that of having to share KGV with Rovers, meant that their next home match the following week had to be rescheduled for the Top Rec. In sharp contrast to the labyrinthine dealings with the Council regarding Gedling Road the Committee had had no such problems in installing showers in the caretaker's old house at the Calverton Road School that doubled as the changing facilities for games played at Church Lane. With the co-operation of the Vicar of St Marys, the Rev N Todd, and Mr Hammond, member of the Trustees' Board, the club had acquired a ten year lease on the building and wasted no time at all in carrying out renovations, installing showers, and creating a recreation space for social activities for both the club and the church. Many Committee members had again given up their spare time in a hands-on effort to get the job completed for the start of the season and as an example of what can be achieved when all the interested parties are singing off the same hymn sheet (pun definitely intended) it could hardly have been bettered.

OPENING OF THE SHOWERS AT KGV 3 NOV 1962 : (L to r) S Gray, N Simpson, Cllr J
Miller, C Moore, W Parr.
(Courtesy Football Post)

The Saints' visitors on that second Saturday of November were Anstey Nomads, next to
bottom in the table and not expected to give Marys much of a problem. They didn't. The
maroon and golds hit double figures for the second time this season, winning twelve-three.
Everyone in the forward line got on the scoresheet with Joe Boucher notching five, Alan Ball,
Arthur Oldham, and John Page, deputising for the injured Mick Hornbuckle, getting a couple,
and Peter Williams chipping in with one of his own to make up the dozen. It took the Saints'
goal tally in the league past the fifty mark in a mere seven games, with forty-one of them
coming in just four home matches.

For Marys' fans it didn't matter where they played, goals seemed to be guaranteed whenever
they took the field, and those supporters who travelled to Leicestershire for the return game
with the Nomads a fortnight later were given another treat as seven more rained past the
home side's unfortunate keeper. The only surprise was that Joe Boucher didn't bag a hat-
trick, having to settle for a couple as the goals were once again shared around. The Saints
had been without a fixture the previous week so even though their three games in November
had yielded maximum points and an incredible twenty five goals they still found themselves
no higher than fourth in the table.

	P	W	D	L	F	A	P
Kimberley Town	10	9	0	1	37	16	18
Gresley Rovers	12	8	2	2	35	18	18
Creswell Colliery	13	7	2	4	23	21	16
Arnold St Marys	**8**	**7**	**1**	**0**	**58**	**12**	**15**
Eastwood Town	8	7	0	1	24	10	14

Still, there was a fair way yet to go, much like there had been for long-time Rovers' fan
Frances Whitt following a day's shopping in Nottingham back in the middle of the month. She
had been waiting with her young daughter for her bus at the terminus on Long Row, Market
Square, right outside Lyons' Tea Rooms, but when it arrived she made a fateful decision not
to board it.

FW : It was November 14 and I'd been Christmas shopping with my three year old daughter Denise. We'd been in town and we'd done quite a lot of shopping but when it came to catching the number sixty-nine bus home I had a horrible feeling; a feeling of dread. I'd always had a fear of Gregory Boulevard, always, because I'd been in a car once there and the door had shot open and I always had that horrible dread feeling that it would happen again. For some reason on this particular day I didn't want to catch the bus in the Market Square and have to go past the Boulevard so I pushed Denise all the way from town, past Gregory Boulevard, and caught the next sixty-nine that came along at the stop outside where Clarendon College is. For some reason I still couldn't settle so when we arrived at the old Arnold Swimming Baths on Arnot Hill Road I got off with Denise because for some reason I wanted to see my Mum and Dad who lived nearby on St Albans Road. I went straight in and said "Hey up, I'm here. See you later" and walked straight back down and caught the next sixty-nine that came along. Why I went to see them I'll never know.

From the Baths to Frances' house wasn't far and would normally take no more than three or four minutes by bus but this particular evening events were about to take a distinct turn for the worse and turn her thoughts of dread into a real cause for fear. The bus picked out its normal route along Hallam's Lane, past KGV, and then off up Gedling Road, past the Friar Tuck Public House and Kingswell School, before turning left onto Rolleston Drive. It was a journey Frances had made many times before; another couple of stops and she'd be almost outside her house. Except on this particular night the bus didn't make it. Less than a hundred yards past the junction a large pile of grit had been heaped on the nearside kerb.

FW : There was a great big pile of gravel in the road with no warning lights around it. It was six o'clock and dark. The entrance to the bus was at the back then and I sat back of the driver's cab and Denise sat across from me. All of a sudden we struck the gravel.

After hitting the obstacle the bus tilted over, careered through a hedge, and crashed onto its side only a few feet away from the front wall of number thirteen where the lady of the house had been preparing tea.

FW : When the bus tipped over I hit the glass at the back of the driver's cab and then shot right through the front window. My face was all cut and we rolled down into the front of the houses and luckily there was a very bonny lady next to us on the bus and she'd cushioned my daughter. We were very lucky. I came off worse but at the time I just grabbed Denise to me and held on. I didn't think of anything at the time, I suppose it was just instinct that made me cling on to her.

Ambulances were quickly onto the scene and took Frances and eleven other injured passengers to the General Hospital in Nottingham. Many, like her, had had lucky escapes and none were apparently seriously injured, even the driver, but Frances was more concerned than the others, and with good reason. She was eight months pregnant.

FW : I was very, very big, massive, and I was worried about the baby, but it was a waste of time going to hospital. They never examined me, never bothered that I was pregnant. They just said "You've got facial injuries and a broken nose" and that was it.

Unfortunately, even though Frances was allowed home later that night she still had the trauma of having to catch a bus the very next morning as the hospital wanted to give her another check-up.

FW : I still don't like going on buses or coaches after all these years but I had to go on one the next day. I had to because we hadn't got a car and we just could not afford a taxi.

In today's culture of rampant compensation there would be every chance that as a heavily pregnant and unwitting casualty of an accident Frances would have been assailed by offers to handle her claim as soon as the news of the accident was out, but in 1962 the reality was very different.

FW : My coat and everything I'd got on was badly damaged, the Christmas presents were all broken, even Denise's push chair. Someone, I'm not quite sure who it was, handled the insurance claim with the Corporation and I got the sum of sixteen pounds. Then they had the cheek to take ten per cent off me for handling the claim! I ended up with fourteen pounds eight shillings!

However, that wasn't the end of the unfortunate episode.

FW : When the baby was born he was blistered to hell. They had to bath him in tincture of violets. Denise kept saying she didn't want a blue baby, just an ordinary one. The hospital didn't know what caused it. They thought it might have been the force of the water but it was probably the trauma of the accident. Denise stuttered very badly for a while afterwards too. It was fright, really.

So, with the sixteen pounds, net of its ten percent fee, not even covering the replacement cost of the damaged clothing, Christmas presents, and child's push chair, what value did the insurers put on the personal injury aspect of the claim; the lacerated face, broken nose, blistered baby, stuttering infant, and a lifelong fear of travelling on public transport? The answer was nothing; not a penny. Amazingly Frances remains stoical about the whole traumatic incident.

FW : That's how it was. You just had to get on with it. That's what you were expected to do.

The only light-hearted moment came when Frances was taken to the General Hospital after the accident.

FW : I sat in the hospital and this poor old man came in and I kept looking at him. All of a sudden I realised it was my Dad. We don't know how he'd got down to the General, he might even have run down, but he must have been in a bit of a panic because he was still in his pyjamas and slippers and had come without his teeth which he'd left back at home. Oh he did look a sight!

If Frances didn't have enough on her plate with her pregnancy and the aftermath of the accident she also had the misfortune to be following Rovers each week at a time when neither they nor their reserve side could buy a win. Probably the red and whites' most ardent fan, it must have been pretty demoralising for her to see Rovers at the bottom of Division 1B of the Central Alliance but with the second team starting November with horrendous back to back defeats thirteen-one and seventeen-one there was obviously very little chance of its players challenging for a place in the first eleven.

The days of the old rivalry between Rovers and Marys were unfortunately now deep in the past, no more than a pleasant but fading memory, but at least the Saints were giving the town's football lovers something to be enthusiastic about. Their first three games of December were won comfortably, if rather less spectacularly than the previous month, but one of them, the three-one victory in the return fixture over at Burton Albion Reserves, was reckoned by manager Noel Simpson to have been the team's best performance of the season so far. The reason behind his assessment was that Albion's first team, who played in the Southern League, were fixtureless that particular Saturday and their manager Peter Taylor, who would become famous as assistant to Brian Clough a few years later, decided to strengthen the second team by including no fewer than nine players with first team experience.

Marys' only blemish during the month came with the pre-Christmas visit to Clay Cross, the only Central Alliance side to have beaten them all season. That setback had come in the League Cup but this time around the Derbyshire side repeated the feat to become the first team to lower the Saints' colours in the league, winning three-two after the maroon and golds had held a two-one half-time lead. The Saints were rather unfortunate in that the game escaped the widespread fog that had swept across the country, resulting in a dozen Football League games having to be postponed, a number of others being abandoned once underway, and the decimation of the fixture schedule at local level.

However, the weather was about to take a further turn for the worse just as Santa was due to make his annual appearance. A belt of rain over northern Scotland on Christmas Eve turned to snow as it moved south, giving Glasgow its first white Christmas since 1938. The snow reached southern England on Boxing Day and became almost stationary. However it didn't stop me and six and a half thousand other mad Magpies' fans from braving the elements to see Notts beat Northampton two-one with goals from Tony Hateley and Jeff Astle but the crowd would obviously have been much greater if it hadn't been for the appalling weather. Up the A60 where Mansfield Town were having one of their better seasons the Stags' game was also on but only lasted thirty six minutes. Field Mill's faithful were being rewarded with a twin strike partnership of their own in Ken Wagstaff and Roy Chapman, who would end the campaign with the remarkable tally of forty-one and thirty-seven goals respectively, but on this particular day the warmth of the fireside hearth proved too tempting for many of them and the much reduced turnout was the club's second lowest crowd of the season when it might otherwise have been its best.

Elsewhere in the Football League two other centre-forwards were both having days they would never forget. Bert Lister hammered in six goals as Oldham Athletic beat Southport eleven-nil but it was a rather more famous number nine who grabbed the headlines when a collision with the Bury goalkeeper on a frost-bound Roker Park pitch effectively ended his career at the early age of twenty-seven. It was of course Sunderland's Brian Clough, whose prolific goalscoring would see him finish with two hundred and fifty one league goals in only two hundred and seventy three matches. The injury he had picked up was a tear to his cruciate ligament, serious still today but not necessarily the career-ending condition it once was. Fortunately for the football fans of the East Midlands, especially those in Nottingham and Derby, his forced retirement meant that he would turn his hand to management rather sooner than he might have anticipated.

In his trademark green jumper Old Big 'Ed would blow a gale through English football but that prospect was still a couple of years away. Much more imminent was the storm heading south even as he was in his hospital bed recuperating. At the weekend, with a couple of inches of snow having already fallen in the Channel Islands and a foot of the stuff blanketing much of southern England, a raging blizzard hit Wales and the south-west causing drifts up to twenty feet deep. Villages were cut off, some for several days, and power and telephone lines were brought down. Roads and railways were blocked and transport brought to a standstill. Stocks of food ran low and with farmers unable to reach their livestock thousands of animals starved to death.

The arctic conditions also forced the cancellation of sporting events, with football particularly badly hit. The combined effects of frost, ice, and snow resulted in the Football League suffering the worst day for postponements in its history, with thirty five of its forty six games being called off. Forest's home game against West Ham United was one of the few to escape but the pitch was still bone hard and covered in snow. Unsure of what studs to wear a few of the Hammers' players were still checking out the surface half an hour before kick-off, many of them wearing overcoats because of the freezing temperatures. Even when the game began quite a few of the visitors had chosen to wear gloves, a rare sight back then but one which would only serve to give credence to the 'southern softies' tag. As it turned out the claret and blues had the last laugh, coming back from three-one down to win by the odd goal in seven. Marys were due to travel to Creswell and a win would have taken them to the top of the able for the first time all season but that fixture also fell foul of the inclement conditions, leaving the Saints in third place.

	P	W	D	L	F	A	P
Gresley Rovers	14	10	2	2	42	20	22
Kimberley Town	15	10	2	3	49	25	22
Arnold St Marys	**12**	**10**	**1**	**1**	**68**	**16**	**21**
Eastwood Town	12	10	0	2	39	17	20

With the club well positioned to challenge for the championship, Marys' committee had taken the opportunity during the month to launch a charm offensive with a circular to all Midland

League clubs updating them of the progress that had been made in improving the facilities at Gedling Road. The league's meeting to discuss applications for membership wasn't due to take place for another six months but Syd Gray and company thought it was best to start campaigning as early as possible and consequently Bill Whittaker had been nominated as the committeeman most likely to be successful in carrying out the necessary canvassing to enable the club's dream to be brought to fruition.

Away from the football world but still in the district there'd been another concerted effort to solicit votes that same month when a referendum was held in Arnold, Carlton, and elsewhere in support of a proposal to extend the Nottingham City boundary to incorporate the satellite towns surrounding it. This attempt at expansion had been tried back in 1919 and now, forty three years later, it was being tried again. Fortunately, the good citizens of Arnold saw fit to maintain their independence, with ninety-two percent giving the proposition the thumbs down.

As the old year came to a close and the new one slowly dawned the question of whether you lived in the City or the County didn't seem to be of that great a concern. The most pressing problem for most everyone across the whole country was finding a way to cope with the atrocious weather and the hardships it had brought along in its wake. It may have been sledging heaven for kids, and I must admit that even at fourteen I went along with my brother Steve, purely as an observer of course, as he hurtled down the steep slopes of the nearby Kingswell School playing field, but the severity of the cold and snow would offer a challenge of a different kind for just about everyone else.

When it wasn't snowing, which wasn't often, the country simply appeared to freeze solid. January daytime temperatures barely crept above freezing and night frosts produced a temperature of minus sixteen degrees centigrade in places as far apart as Gatwick and Eskdalemuir. Freezing fog became a frequent hazard but the severity of the cold wasn't restricted to the land. The sea froze over up to half a mile from the shore at Herne Bay, the Thames was iced over from bank to bank in places, and ice floes appeared on the river at Tower Bridge as well as in the Bristol Channel, disrupting a ferry service in the process.

For the good citizens of Arnold a diversion from the difficulties they were experiencing came from an unusual source when in the middle of the month Fine Fare opened the first supermarket in the town. Situated on that stretch of Front Street which is now pedestrian only, it announced its presence with a fanfare of publicity, part of which was an invitation to 'Come and meet that glamorous star of television, Katie Boyle'. Miss Boyle was indeed glamorous, born in the same year as Marilyn Monroe, and if she didn't quite have the sexual allure of the former Norma Jeane, she exuded a certain high class beauty befitting the daughter of an Italian marquis and one-time fashion model for 'Vogue'. She had brains too, hosting Eurovision Song Contests whilst showcasing her talent as a multi-linguist. Taking a temporary break from the snow slopes of Kingswell I was almost inclined to bunk off school to catch of a glimpse of this lovely lady but smitten as I was the risk wasn't worth taking, not even for the added attraction of being able to purchase a plump, oven-ready roasting chicken for four shillings, less than half its normal price of nine bob.

Now for anyone familiar with the standard layout of a supermarket these days, with fruit and vegetables as you go in and that most staple of all diets, bread, at the very farthest corner to ensure that you pass the other counters that you had no intention of buying anything from but end up doing so just the same, the layout at Fine Fare forty five years ago seems quite archaic. I'll let the store's publicity blurb elaborate.

> "A Fine Fare Supermarket is no ordinary Supermarket. It is a super foodstore with a difference. Everything in the store is designed with one object; to make shopping easier and more pleasant, and to afford every comfort to the customer."

So far, so good, although it does sound a little like a modern 'mission statement'.

"The departments are laid out in main meal order, starting as you enter the shop with soups and finishing up near the exits with the sweets. Intelligent emphasis is put on colour schemes, making selection easier, as tins in particular are laid out in contrasting colours to enable the customer to spot exactly what **she** is looking for.

The emphasis on the 'she' is mine but, then again, this opening took place before the sexual revolution, aka male emasculation, arrived that saw couples of all ages clogging up the aisles of every shopping emporium in the country, maybe even the world, whilst discussing such inanities as "What would you like for your tea? Fancy a bit of ham?" and so on. I know this because through dint of family circumstance I am a reluctant customer of said emporia and having to dodge between a flotilla of overstacked trolleys is not exactly my idea of fun. However I digress. Let the marketing men of Fine Fare explain the real difference between then and now.

"The fresh fruit and vegetable department allows every **housewife** to inspect and scrutinise the produce on display and satisfy **herself** that it is crisp and fresh. It is so important for **her** to see what she is buying…"

No ambiguity there about the woman's role in society, obviously, although the fact that Miss Boyle, patently not a 'housewife' in the everyday sense of the word, was opening the store seemed to be lost on the company's copywriters.

There was one other distinctive feature that seems to have been dropped from today's supermarket 'shopping experience' and that was the use of music to accompany the shopper as they wandered up and down the aisles.

"A unique feature of the store is the soothing background music played for the added comfort of customers. Background music is one of the newest customer amenities to be provided by the more imaginative shopkeeper. It must be listened to with the inner ear, almost subconsciously, as distinct from the strident foreground music of juke boxes and radios."

Not having witnessed the event personally, I trust that Katie got out of town none the worse for her own 'shopping experience'. I'm sure she did because I can still remember her looking absolutely divine as she oversaw some younger but nowhere near as captivating models daubing soap suds over their faces in an advertisement for 'Camay'. If her stopover in Arnold had scarred her, she certainly didn't show it.

Three days later, on January 18, a blizzard practically cut Scotland off from England, although there were people on both sides of the border who didn't think that was entirely a bad thing, and conditions continued to deteriorate over the next couple of days as severe gales and huge snowfalls caused roads to be blocked by abandoned vehicles and train services to grind to a halt in deep snowdrifts. Heathrow, then known as plain old London Airport, was also closed when an airliner skidded off an icy runway.

Incredibly, Marys managed to play a match the following day, at home against Ransome and Marles, when Gedling Road was surprisingly declared playable despite it being bone hard and covered in snow. Supporter Alf Askew, who had resorted to using a hammer and chisel to break up frozen soil in his garden when he was endeavouring to fix a fence post, must have been as shocked as anyone when he put through his regular telephone call to Syd Gray on the morning of the match and found out that it was on; one of the very few games in the district and which as a result attracted nearly twelve hundred football-starved spectators to KGV. The efforts of everyone concerned in staging the fixture were rewarded with a four-nil victory for the Saints, with Arthur Oldham bagging a couple and Joe Boucher and John Anthony getting on the scoresheet too. Unfortunately the new showers in the pavilion had frozen up and so it was back to the Baths for the post-match soak.

Not many people other than those who actually attended the match would have known much about the result because the lack of football anywhere had meant that production of the Football Post had been put on hold. Also in limbo were the Football Pools companies who depended upon fixtures being fulfilled for their businesses to survive. Rather than just sit out the bad weather they came up with a solution that still exists today; the Pools Panel. Consisting of a group of individuals with some knowledge of the game the panel predicted what the scores might have been had the games been played and punters bet on this hypothetical outcome just as they would have done on the real thing. Even with ex-players such as George Young, Ted Drake, Tommy Lawton, and Tom Finney featuring in the original panel it wasn't ideal, but everybody seemed to agree that it was better than nothing.

For Marys' players, fans, and committeemen alike, the game against Ransomes turned out to be a false dawn. It would be another seven weeks before a ball was kicked in anger as further falls of snow arrived and the country remained locked in near-freezing temperatures. In urban areas one of the biggest problems was in keeping warm and this often led to a number of ingenious schemes to keep water pipes from freezing solid. At Castleton Avenue we got off pretty lightly, even though my mother did have to resort on occasion to using a hair dryer to unfreeze blocked taps, but in upland areas conditions were particularly bleak. Two sets of climbers were killed by avalanches on moorlands in Lancashire and across on the North York Moors the Fylingdales Early Warning Station was completely snowbound for several days. The day after the Saints' rare fixture RAF helicopters had to evacuate nearly three hundred of its civilian workers in treacherous conditions with winds gusting up to eighty miles an hour. In one of the biggest airlifts ever to take place in this country the workers were ferried in groups of seven or eight, flown to nearby Whitby, only to find snowdrifts marooning them there too. At least there was no shortage of fish for them to eat.

The following month was marked by more snow arriving on south-easterly winds during the first week, with a thirty-six hour blizzard hitting western parts of the country. Drifts twenty feet deep formed in gale force winds and many rural communities found themselves cut off for no less than the tenth time since Christmas. A slight lull in the wintry proceedings happened around mid-month, but in the third week of February it was the turn of the north-west to suffer with Cumberland falling victim to what was reckoned to be the worst snowfall in living memory. With the mean temperature for the whole of the month never rising above freezing the country had suffered two consecutive months with the thermometer averaging sub-zero for the first time since records began. Thankfully a gradual thaw set in at the beginning of the following month and the morning of March 6 was the first day in the year that the entire country was frost free; the 'Big Freeze', the coldest winter since 1740, was finally over.

Life had been a little bit uncomfortable since the turn of the year but it hadn't stopped altogether. In January Marys' committee was told that a preliminary meeting had been arranged with the Council to discuss the new stand and the following month a request from the newly formed Arnold (Kingswell) Youth Club football team for an old Saints' touchline-marker was given the thumbs up.

For me personally, however, the most momentous happening in the early part of the frozen New Year was the release of the Beatles' second single 'Please Please Me' on January 11, a red letter day in the annals of British popular music. Far more upbeat than their first single, I was well and truly hooked the first time I heard it over the radio. Aided by the group's appearance on ITV's 'Thank Your Lucky Stars' a week later, their first on national network TV, the record soon shot to number one in every music paper that I was buying at the time; always the New Musical Express and more often than not one at least from the Melody Maker, Disc Weekly, or Record Mirror, such the total hold that the pop world had on me at the time. I'd remained loyal to the Shads and would soon even be shelling out for a future number one, 'Diamonds', by two of their ex-members Jet Harris and Tony Meehan, but the boys from Merseyside sounded like nothing I'd ever heard. They also sounded like nothing my mother had ever heard because when the song was being belted out at full volume on our radio soon after it had hit the top she turned to me and said "Turn it down. I can't stand that racket". I knew there and then that I loved them even more.

With the thaw came a return to regular footy and Marys were soon into their stride. Indeed they hardly performed like a side which had been without a game for seven weeks and one who'd only played once since before Christmas. They were due to meet Creswell but, with the Derbyshire side having a county cup-tie that took priority over the league fixture, another colliery side, Linby, stepped in at short notice to take their place. By the end of the ninety minutes they probably wished they hadn't bothered as the Saints ran up double figures for the third time this season. Finishing twelve-nil with four goals apiece from Mick Hornbuckle and Arthur Oldham and a hat-trick from Joe Boucher, the victory also took the maroon and golds to the top of the table for the first time since the start of the campaign. Having finally got there, the next three week's results showed that they were determined to stay there. Forest A were hammered eight-nil with hat-tricks from Joe Boucher and Alan Ball, the return match with Linby finished six-nil, and on the last Saturday in March Ericsson Athletic were seen off handsomely by the same score in a match that doubled as a league fixture and the quarter final of the Notts Senior Cup.

Thirty-two goals and what was effectively five wins from four matches was a splendid way to re-start the campaign following its unfortunate period of hibernation. With the reserves tearing into opponents in a similar fashion the club was enjoying one of its most successful spells for a long time and the only slightly negative aspect of the month's events was the loss of Terry Bell to Burton Albion. With the first team performing so well and Noel Simpson choosing not to deviate from a core group of players the youngster felt that the chance to play under Peter Taylor in the Southern League was too good an opportunity to turn down. In the event, his move was the making of him as he later followed his new manager to Hartlepool, played under Brian Clough, and eventually ended up making over three hundred appearances in the Football League and scoring over a century of goals. Terry wasn't the last Marys' player to be enticed away by the persuasive powers of the Albion manager either, but with him being tied to a professional contract the club did at least receive some financial recompense for the loss of a player with a bright future. With Peter Taylor involved however the 'deal' probably had one or two strings attached.

AM : Terry Bell's sale to Burton? That was a bit of a wangle an' all.

Apart from the enthusiasm generated by the Saints' high scoring play there was another event close by earlier in the month that had caused more than a ripple of excitement of its own, especially to those handful of people in the know. On Mar 7 the Beatles headlined an evening of 'Beat-le Music' at the Elizabethan Ballrooms above the main Co-op on Parliament Street. It was the group's first visit to Nottingham and they topped a bill that also included Gerry and the Pacemakers and Billy J Kramer. Tickets cost six shillings and sixpence and were remarkably good value considering that two nights later it would have set a fan back six bob to see Johnny Kidd and the Pirates at the Co-Operative Hall in Ilkeston. There was also the added attraction that the music could still be heard. Those Merseybeat fans astute enough to turn up on that Thursday evening might have caught a glimpse of the Fab Four, as they were soon to be known, loading up their own gear, but before long this mucking in would be a thing of the past. When the group next played in the city a couple of months later it was at the much larger Nottingham Odeon cinema, tickets were hard to get, and the boys themselves were cocooned inside a security blanket. They were at number one in the singles and LP charts with 'From Me To You' and 'Please Please Me' respectively, the screaming had started and the phenomenon known as 'Beatlemania' was well and truly underway.

The album came out on the very same day, March 22, that the Secretary of State for War, John Profumo, told the House of Commons that there was no impropriety in his relationship with model Christine Keeler. The truth, however, was rather different. He'd met the young lady at a party in early 1961 and soon afterwards they'd begun an affair. Ms Keeler, who led what was then euphemistically called a 'colourful' life, also had sexual relations with Yevgeny Ivanov, a senior naval attaché at the Soviet Embassy. With the so-called 'Profumo Affair' now having apparently serious implications regarding national security it was becoming more and more difficult to keep the lid on the scandal, even though this was a time when the private life of an MP was considered just that; private. Unfortunately Fleet Street had got the bit between their teeth and despite Profumo's denial his position was becoming more untenable by the day. Within three months of his first address to his fellow Members of Parliament he finally admitted that he had lied to them and as a consequence resigned from office, from the House, and from the Privy Council. A broken man, at least politically, he maintained a distinguished public silence on the matter for the rest of his life although he did redeem himself in many people's estimation through his tireless work for charity. Four tracks on the Fab Four's first album were 'I Saw Her Standing There', 'A Taste of Honey', 'Do You Want to Know a Secret', and 'Misery'; an apt, if entirely coincidental, chronological resume of the sordid affair.

Four days after Profumo had originally mislead the House of Commons it was the turn of another public figure, the Chairman of British Rail Dr Richard Beeching, to arouse controversy when reporting to the Government. In his case it wasn't what he'd personally done, or not done, that was causing a stir, but what he was recommending. In his report 'The Reshaping of British Railways' he advocated the wholesale closure of routes and stations within the national network as a means of reducing costs and concentrating resources on core services. The notoriety that the report gained was mainly due to the fact that the cost cutting element of the report focused on what it considered to be little-used and unprofitable routes, and these were usually suburban or rural lines served by passenger stopping trains. Beeching was also criticised for adopting an over-simplistic analysis of the economics of the routes under threat and failing to recognise how the branch lines contributed to the core network.

The Government accepted the recommendations and the closures went ahead. Pressure was brought to bear in certain regions and strategic routes were saved, in particular two in Scotland, but generally track was uplifted in indecent haste and station buildings boarded up and left to fall derelict. The whole *raison-d'etre* of the report seemed to be based around short-term thinking with no aspect of long-term demographics or potential changes in society being factored in. The possibility of any significant growth in tourism didn't seem to dawn on the authors so lines through parts of the country with significant natural beauty and the potential to carry large numbers of holidaymakers, such as the very scenic Scarborough to Whitby line, were given up to the surrounding flora and fauna.

Close to home the Beeching axe inevitably fell on Daybrook station and I, for one, was sad to see its demise, even though it had been closed to passenger traffic since Mapperley tunnel, known to all the kids around as 'Jonas', had become unstable a couple of years previously. Serious publications written almost fifty years later cast some doubt on this, suggesting that the instability might have been caused by deliberate sabotage from within British Rail, but whatever the truth there was no getting away from the fact that a significant part of my growing up would soon exist only in my memory and in old photographs and books about the history of the country's railways. A couple of 'day-trip' passenger excursions to Cleethorpes had been run from the station since the tunnel 'collapse' but these had exited from its western end. The daily school run carrying some of the district's brighter pupils to Henry Mellish Grammar School at Bulwell had also continued but now it too would soon be no more.

If the closure of Daybrook and many other similar stations had been deemed inevitable by the bureaucrats, their passing still triggers fierce debate, with the consensus view being that the current UK travel network would have been far better off had thousands of miles of track been mothballed for future generations rather than being ripped up and sold off for scrap, with the subsequent result that the track beds themselves were then allowed to fall into the hands of developers whose piecemeal projects would render the routes impossible to reinstate at a future date. The argument for closure might have been more popular had it actually achieved its stated aim of trying to restore the railway network to profitability but the savings targets were never met, leaving Dr Beeching's dubious reputation as a bogey-man rather than a benefactor still intact forty five years later.

A few days after the Beeching Report first appeared Marys' committee was being asked to consider a proposal too, one that would have far reaching implications not just for everyone connected with the club but for the rest of the town's inhabitants as well. The matter for consideration was the provision of the long awaited spectator stand at Gedling Road and the thorny issue of its financing. There were a number of people in Arnold, and not only those handful of known dissenters at the Council, who were quite put out by the fact that a couple of hundred pounds towards the installation of the showers in the pavilion had apparently been taken out of the public purse, so the prospect of additional ratepayer's money being channelled towards further development at KGV was likely to polarise opinion even more.

The cost of building the stand had originally been estimated at two and half thousand pounds as far back as April 1960 and a year later the figure had increased to three and a half thousand. The development had of course been put on the back burner as a result of 'concerns' about subsidence but now, with these fears seemingly allayed, the project had at last been given the green light, tenders had been sought for the stand's steel framework and sheeting and a quotation of nine hundred and sixty five pounds, the lowest received and a tremendous improvement on the last estimate, accepted by the Council. Hard standing would still need to be provided under cover of the stand but with Marys' committee willing to put in as much of their own labour as might be necessary the club were at last tantalisingly close to achieving its dream of Midland League membership.

Whilst the committee now had to sit down with the Council and try and thrash out a suitable deal regarding the stand's funding, not forgetting that they were still sharing the ground with Rovers, the team was due to face two of its nearest rivals in the race for the Central Alliance championship twice each in just twelve days. Both Kimberley and Eastwood were expected to provide a stern test of the Saints' credentials as the business end of the season was about to begin in earnest. This is how the top of the table looked at the beginning of April.

	P	W	D	L	F	A	P
Arnold St Marys	**17**	**15**	**1**	**1**	**104**	**16**	**31**
Gresley Rovers	17	13	2	2	56	24	28
Eastwood Town	15	13	0	2	53	21	26
Kimberley Town	18	12	2	4	59	32	26

The first of the four fixtures was a midweek home game against Kimberley on the first Wednesday of the month and which was, rather amazingly, the club's first non-Saturday match of the season. Buoyed by their tremendous run of form Marys were naturally full of confidence, but up against a much tougher side than they'd recently faced they weren't able to bully their Nottinghamshire neighbours like they had their recent opponents and had to settle for a three-nil victory. Apart from strengthening their own position it had effectively put paid to any lingering hopes that Kimberley might have had in engineering a late run for the title themselves.

More importantly from the Saints' point of view the win had set up the following Saturday's visit of Eastwood perfectly. The Badgers had also beaten Kimberley recently, in the Quarter-Finals of the Notts Senior Cup, so both teams were still in with a great chance of a league and cup double. With the added attraction of the match being a local derby a good crowd was in attendance at Gedling Road as Marys, unchanged for the seventh game in a row, quickly established the upper hand. Attacking straight from the kick-off in their usual quick and decisive style the Saints soon found themselves one up when right half Jack Davis headed home from a corner. Twelve minutes later Arthur Oldham added a second after good work from Alan Ball and from there on in the maroon and golds' attack harassed the Eastwood defence at will. The visitors held out gamely and it wasn't until the closing minutes of the contest that two late goals from Arthur Oldham and Alan Ball finally put the result beyond doubt. The victory had taken Marys' record in 1963 to seven wins out of seven with the fantastic goal differential of forty-three scored and none conceded. The seven clean sheets kept by Len Rockley and the defence was a club record, although Len did admit that there were passages of play over the previous few weeks where he could have kept goal in his dressing gown and slippers, such was the dominance of the Saints' forward line.

The return game with Eastwood took place over at Coronation Park the following week, Easter Saturday, in front of another good turn-out eager to see whether the Badgers could gain swift revenge for their defeat at KGV. Despite their disappointment in the first clash with Marys they'd picked themselves up sufficiently to beat second placed Gresley in mid-week by three goals to one and in doing so had made the Derbyshire side's chances of challenging for the title that much more difficult. For Town, however, a victory over the Saints would keep them well in the hunt for the championship as it would mean that the maroon and golds would have dropped five points in comparison to Eastwood's six with a long way still to go. In fact the game was only four minutes old when the home side showed their intent by claiming the first goal Len Rockley had conceded since December, and the contest quickly developed into a typical no quarter asked, no quarter given local derby with tackles flying in and bodies everywhere. When Mick Hornbuckle equalised for Marys in the seventeenth minute, scooping the ball into the net whilst lying on the ground after colliding with two defenders, the goal exemplified the physical nature of the game. Eight minutes later the same player added a second and as the Saints stepped up the pressure the hosts had to resort to some robust defending in trying to keep the scoreline at two-one. Of course the maroon and golds weren't short of players who could 'mix it' themselves but with the visitors quite clearly the more skilful of the two sides it was almost inevitable that this superiority in technique would tell. It did, minutes before the interval, when Arthur Oldham cleverly hooked a volley just inside a post to give his side a decisive three-one lead.

JOE BOUCHER IN THE THICK OF THINGS : EASTWOOD TOWN v MARYS 13 APR 1963

(Courtesy Football Post)

The second half saw no let up in Marys' domination of the play and although the home goal survived a number of narrow escapes two more strikes from the visitors put the game completely out of Eastwood's reach. Not only was the five-one final scoreline emphatic, it resulted in the Saints taking what seemed to be an unassailable lead at the top of the table.

	P	W	D	L	F	A	P
Arnold St Marys	**20**	**18**	**1**	**1**	**116**	**17**	**37**
Gresley Rovers	20	14	3	3	61	30	31
Eastwood Town	18	14	0	4	57	31	28
Kimberley Town	20	13	2	5	61	36	28

A closer look at the fixture list however showed that they didn't have that easy a run-in. They still had to meet Clay Cross, who they'd already lost to on two occasions this season, as well as having to play twice against Creswell Colliery, a side that had troubled them in recent years and who were currently lying fifth. Then there was the return game at Kimberley on Easter Monday, the outcome of which no-one at the club was expecting to be a foregone conclusion. The caution was well advised because in front of The Stag ground's biggest gate of the season the home side played much better than they had in the first match between the teams. Urged on by their supporters and with their defenders keeping Marys' much vaunted forward line in check, Kimberley actually led by two goals to one, and it was only a penalty, successfully converted by Arthur Oldham, that prevented them from gaining both points. There were no complaints in the Saints' camp, just a feeling of relief at picking up a point, especially as the next game the following mid-week was at Creswell, where the maroon and golds hadn't won since October 1959. The colliery team were having one of their better seasons too and even without the assistance of the man with the dog they managed to keep Marys' attack unusually quiet. Quiet enough, in fact, to become only the second side all season to prevent them scoring. Fortunately the Saints' defence was equally as parsimonious and the game ended goalless.

The post-match view was that, as against Kimberley, it had been a point well-earned and with the maroon and golds' unbeaten sequence now extending to ten matches there was no reason not to be confident, even with Midland League Retford Town as their next opponents four days later in the Semi-Final of the Notts Senior Cup. With Marys' exploits in the league now regularly dominating the headlines interest in the match was so great that the game kicked-off in front of one of the biggest crowds seen on the Gedling Road ground. Taking a little time to settle the Saints allowed the visitors the early initiative but once the maroon and golds got into gear it was the Shamrocks who came under pressure. Urged on by their vociferous supporters a goal for the home side was inevitable, and it came in the thirty-ninth minute when Joe Boucher latched onto a through ball from Arthur Oldham and beat the visiting keeper with some ease. Although Marys had a number of chances in the second half to put the result beyond doubt Retford never gave up the fight, staging a late rally that might have brought more success against a defence less rock solid than the Saints'. When the final whistle blew the maroon and golds left the field to a richly deserved ovation from their fans and once back inside the pavilion were complimented on their display by none other than the visiting team's manager. Committeeman Albert Moore would be the first to admit that any compliments towards Marys from anyone connected with the Midland League were pretty thin on the ground, so it made the comment from the Retford boss all the sweeter.

The Saints' hadn't had a fixture the previous Saturday but fans of football in the town had been treated, if that's the right word, to a most telling demonstration of exactly how well the maroon and golds had progressed in the past five years, and the extent to which their former arch rivals Rovers had declined. The occasion was the meeting of Marys' Reserves and Rovers in Division 1B of the Central Alliance. All that was needed to gauge how far the fortunes of Arnold's two leading clubs of the nineteen fifties had diverged was a glance at the league tables. Marys were top of the Premier Division, their reserves held a similar position in 1B, whilst poor old Rovers propped up the rest with only a couple of points to their name. It was a sorry sight, just as it was sad to see the red and whites take the field a man short in front of a decent sized crowd. If those gathered had come to see a re-run of the glorious days of old they would have been disappointed. With a Peterborough scout numbered amongst them, believed to be casting an eye over David Staples and Ray Knight, they saw the Saints' second eleven tear Rovers apart, rattling in five goals before the break and another five after it. It was painful for everyone associated with the losing side and a poignant reminder to any neutrals around of how fortunes can so quickly change.

Once upon a time a clash between Marys and Rovers was the top story in town but on this particular day that honour fell to an event that had taken place a few hours earlier at the top end of Front Street. Builder and businessman Bert Thomas, who had been responsible for the redevelopment of the Bonington cinema site, had recently completed the construction of Front Street Garage at the junction of that thoroughfare with Coppice Road, opposite where the Arnold Library now stands. Petrol station, service garage, MOT station, and Austin car dealership all rolled into one, it was a significant addition to the town's commercial resources and one that, in Bert's estimation, needed a grand opening.

The term 'celebrity' was seldom used back then but if it had been there was one person who would certainly have more than qualified for the accolade. She was actress Pat Phoenix, better known as Elsie Tanner of Coronation Street fame and acknowledged as one of the first sex symbols of British television. With the programme being seen twice a week and attracting audiences far larger than today, Pat's portrayal of the fiery Elsie captured the hearts of those watching, even that of future Labour Prime Minister James Callaghan, who described her as 'the sexiest thing on television'. She was the undoubted star of the show so who better then to open Bert's latest business venture? Whatever the cost it was still a massive coup for the Welsh born Arnold entrepreneur when she agreed to come down from Manchester to do the honours and her arrival, complete with police escort, was greeted by an excited crowd of well over a thousand people, all straining for a view of the Corrie star. For some reason which now escapes me I was among them, all of us squeezed closely together by a cordon of fifteen policemen, but unfortunately the nearest I got to her was a distant view of her head and shoulders.

Four days later another female who I also thought looked a bit of all right made her very first appearance in my life too. Having been at Castleton Avenue now for the best part of ten months I'd made a number of new friends, one in particular being George Nowak who lived halfway up the road. On this particular day, April 24, I'd gone with him to his house and in doing so met his family. One of them in particular caught my eye. It was his sister, Anna, who was sitting watching the wedding of Princess Alexandra on television. George introduced me, as a polite young man would, and as she turned her face towards me I wondered if she would sound as nice as she looked. Imagine my dismay when she shot me a look that could have frozen fire and went back to looking at the TV screen without so much as a word. I might as well have been a shadow on the wall for all the interest she had shown. Thankfully our relationship is a lot more cordial now, which is as it should be I suppose after thirty-eight years of marriage. Even so, I still don't dare interrupt her when she's watching her favourite television programmes.

Three days after my first brief glimpse of my future bride, Marys' great win over Retford had earned them a showdown with Sutton Town, yet another Midland League side, in the Notts Senior Cup Final due to take place at Meadow Lane on May 11. This would normally have been the last match of the season but the two months lost to the 'Big Freeze' had resulted in an extension of the fixture schedule to the end of the month. This meant that the Saints had three league matches to fit in before the final, and three after, and although they started the month as clear favourites, Eastwood had won their last three matches to keep the pressure on at the top of the table:-

	P	W	D	L	F	A	P
Arnold St Marys	22	18	3	1	118	19	39
Eastwood Town	21	17	0	4	67	38	34

Having come this far however Marys showed no signs of letting things slip and even though Aspley Old Boys proved surprisingly resilient in restricting the Saints to a two-nil victory, Ashbourne and Creswell Colliery were then both on the receiving end of a torrent of goals from the maroon and golds' formidable forward line, succumbing eight-two and nine-one respectively with Mick Hornbuckle helping himself to a hat-trick against the latter. Remarkably the title remained tantalisingly out of reach as another Eastwood victory saw Marys still requiring one more point from their last three matches before they could get their hands on the championship trophy.

No-one associated with the club doubted that the team would pick up the single point necessary and many of them were also of the opinion that Sutton Town would be the fourth Midland League side to fall to the all-conquering Saints this campaign. After all the boys had been unbeaten since the start of the year, winning twelve and drawing the other two of their fourteen matches, scored seventy goals and conceded only six, and all the time using the same eleven players: Len Rockley, Barry Molyneux, Vince Howard, Jack Davis, Derek Smith, John Anthony, Peter Williams, Mick Hornbuckle, Joe Boucher, Arthur Oldham, and Alan Ball. For one of their number however, a below par performance in the Senior Cup Final not only brought this sequence to an end, it also marked his final appearance for the club he loved.

Arnold through and through, goalkeeper Len Rockley was as distraught as anyone when his mistake gave Sutton the upper hand at Meadow Lane in front of almost three thousand fans and was instrumental in setting the Snipes on the way to a three-one victory. There is little sentiment in football, even in the Central Alliance, and manager Noel Simpson let his own displeasure be known by leaving Len out of the run-in for the championship. As it transpired, the title fell to the Saints just a few days later. Eastwood dropped another couple of points and the championship was Marys'. The last three matches were a stroll, with only one other major target in sight. Having scored an amazing one hundred and thirty seven goals so far in the league, could the maroon and golds amass another thirteen to reach a century and a half?

MARYS' SIDE THAT WENT UNCHANGED FOR FIFTEEN CONSECUTIVE GAMES JAN-MAY 1963 : Back Row (l to r); B Molyneux, V Howard, L Rockley, J Davis, D Smith, J Anthony. Front Row; P Williams, M Hornbuckle, J Boucher, A Oldham, A Ball. Mascot, T Gray. (Courtesy Football Post)

With Ernie Iremonger taking over from Len a three-one victory at Wilmorton was followed with a win by the same margin at home against Clay Cross. As might be expected the mood in the camp was jovial, exemplified by a little bit of dressing room banter recounted by the Saints' keeper.

EI : It was the last game of the season at Gedling Road and Pat, my wife to be, came to watch me with a friend. I was engaged to her at the time and our right-half Jack Davis, a good looking lad, always immaculate, said during the half-time break "Have you seen those two birds? They're a bit of all right." I said "You can keep your eyes off them, one's my fiancée". I can remember Simmo [Noel Simpson] saying to me "It's no good talking to him, he can't understand French".

All that was now required was to score seven times in an away match two nights later, a Friday at that. As the destination was Ashbourne, entailing a nice cross-country journey into the Derbyshire hills of around an hour, Marys' players could have been forgiven for thinking that this might have been a trip too far, but according to Arthur Oldham, the target of a hundred and fifty goals was incentive enough to turn in a performance.

AO : We knew what we needed and I was lucky enough to score four goals in seven minutes; three before the break and then another after it. We managed to get the score up to six but we just couldn't get that one extra goal.

The Saints had to settle for a mere six-nil victory and whilst a hundred and fifty goals would have been nice, a hundred and forty nine still looked pretty decent when the final tables were printed. The goals against tally wasn't that shabby either, just twenty-four conceded in twenty-eight matches but the manager was obviously not convinced by the numbers; Ernie Iremonger's tenure in Marys' goal was about to be ended as abruptly as his predecessor's had.

EI : After that last game, on the bus back home, I could hear them talking at the back of me about getting another goalkeeper. I think it was Syd Gray, talking about signing this goalkeeper from Derby. I must admit I was really disappointed.

The season might have ended sourly for the Saints' two goalies but for the rest of the team it had been one to savour; five of them had played in every game, two others had only missed one match, Joe Boucher had hit over fifty goals with Arthur Oldham not far behind on forty-odd and in his first full season in charge Noel Simpson had produced a championship winning side, Marys' first for thirteen years.

Only one question remained to be answered. Had the club done enough to secure a place in the Midland League?

Whilst the Central Alliance Championship Trophy was tangible proof of an excellent season it would be regarded as a mere bauble if it wasn't accompanied by the club's elevation to the higher level of Midland League football. Having also beaten three out of the four teams from that competition in the various cup ties they'd played over the past nine months there was little doubt that they could more than hold their own in such company but in reality there was no guarantee that the twenty existing members of the league would find a place for the Saints.

Crucially Gedling Road still had no covered accommodation for spectators, a pre-requisite for membership and without which there could be no hope of progress. Had the maroon and golds beaten Sutton in the Notts Senior Cup Final to make it a clean sweep of Midland League teams, they still wouldn't be admitted. The only way that this stumbling block could be removed was by the erection of a stand during the close season, a short time frame normally but one that had already been truncated following the extension of the campaign just ended.

Even if, and it was a very big 'if', the project might be able to be completed in time for the beginning of the new season, work couldn't start on it until the all important issue of its financing had been resolved. To this end preliminary discussions and exchanges of correspondence had already taken place between the three parties involved, the Council, Marys, and Rovers, in the final three or four weeks of the past season. To recover the cost of the project over a reasonable time span, an increase in the annual rent for the use of the ground and its improved facilities from its current twenty five pounds per annum per club to one hundred pounds each was suggested by the Council. This was obviously a hefty increase but the Saints' committee were effectively in a position where they had to agree. If they didn't accept the hike in rent they could kiss goodbye to their dream of Midland League football.

For Rovers, however, the situation was somewhat different. They had endured the worst season in their seventeen year history, picking up a paltry three points and finishing bottom of their division. In fact their only win had been achieved way back in the previous September. It was obvious that the red and whites would never revisit their glory days of the nineteen fifties and so it was of little surprise to the football followers of the town when news came through of the club's plans for the following season. Acknowledging that the writing was on the wall, certainly at the level of the Central Alliance, they notified the necessary parties that they wouldn't be taking up the Council's offer. Instead they would play in the Nottingham and District League Division One, in essence taking the place of their own reserve side which was subsequently disbanded, and return to their spiritual home at Nottingham Road; the Bottom Rec.

The field had been well and truly left to Marys, in more ways than one, and it was at this stage that the Saints' committee went into overdrive. Sensing an opportunity to cement their tenure at KGV the club agreed to pay the two hundred pounds per annum rent necessary to secure the exclusive use of Gedling Road for the forthcoming season. The only ground sharing from now on would be between the first team and the reserves. Next, a letter was sent to the Notts FA applying for the club's name to be changed to Arnold FC and a week later, only five days before the crucial Annual Meeting of the Midland League on June 22 to discuss the make-up of the competition for 1963-64, approval was received. All that remained now was for Marys' spokesman Bill Whittaker to be at his persuasive best. The combination of the dropping of the 'church' name, the provision of on-site changing and bathing facilities at KGV, and the Saints' impressive on-field performances, couldn't truthfully be argued against, but he still had to convince the league's management committee that the stand could be erected in two months. Should he succeed in that tough task, it was by no means a racing certainty that Marys would be admitted. Old enmities, as well as old friendships, ran deep, and it remained to be seen whether the Saints had more friends than foes around the table on that fateful Saturday.

Support might reasonably be expected from the league's champions Loughborough United, managed by former Arnold Rovers' and Notts Regent player Geoff Hazledine and featuring a former Marys' man, Norman Gough, at left back, but with Scarborough and Lockheed-Leamington also making a pitch for membership, the Saints would need all the help they could get. Like them, the other two applicants had both finished top of their respective competitions, the North Eastern League and the West Midlands (Regional) League, making it difficult to split them merely on their playing record, but Marys did at least have the advantage of being better placed geographically than the other two contenders, whose grounds were both around ninety miles from the league's administrative centre at Worksop and well outside its self-imposed fifty mile limit for membership. Scarborough, to their credit, had foreseen this problem and had taken steps to mollify any potential opposition to their bid by announcing they were prepared to offer five pounds to any Midland League club which found itself in financial difficulties from the travelling expenses to the seaside town. The league had of course stretched the fifty mile radius rule before and there was no doubt that they would do it again if it suited them but as Bill Whittaker put his club's case to the management committee and listened to the opening salvos of the other interested parties in the voting process all he could do was content himself with the fact that Marys had put a tick in every box on the application form.

Bill would also have had his hopes raised when it was decided to expand the league from its current twenty clubs to twenty-two, but first he had to await the outcome of the re-election contest of the bottom two teams Spalding United and Holbeach United. Quite how the latter failed to gain automatic re-election when they finished nine points above their rivals isn't known but Spalding it was who retained their place leaving Holbeach to join the three new applicants in the next stage of voting. The ballot consisted of the nineteen existing members casting three votes each, with the club receiving the fewest number being eliminated.

When the votes had been counted the results showed what an incredibly close run matter it had been. Each of the four applicants had won the approval of more than two-thirds of the delegates, with only three votes separating the clubs. Holbeach and Lockheed-Leamington received thirteen each, Scarborough fifteen, and despite having been unsuccessful in impressing three of the representatives present, Marys topped the poll with sixteen votes. The wait was over, the dream had been achieved. Holbeach missed out by a single vote when a second ballot was taken to decide which of them or Lockheed-Leamington would be the league's twenty-second member for the following season, and as soon as the meeting ended a call was put straight through to Syd Gray, waiting eagerly for news at his home in Redhill. Albert Moore recalls the reaction back in the town.

AM : Bill was appointed because he was a very good talker, no umming and arring with him. Our Charlie had gone with him and they let Syd Gray know that we were in as soon as possible. They left it to him to let everybody else know because they knew then that the news would spread like wildfire. It was a great feeling, just what we'd been waiting for because then we could start work on the stand.

At the Saints' committee meeting on the Monday night 'Mr Whittaker' was formally thanked by the Chairman, Walter 'Kegga' Parr, for 'doing a grand job' regarding the club's entry into the Midland League, and a plan of action prepared as to how best to ensure that the stand could be guaranteed to be ready for the start of the season, now only two months away. Everyone present was aware that any hiccups at this late stage could still jeopardise their presence in the competition, so the committee members did what they always did at a time like this; they decided to carry out as much of the work as they could themselves.

As soon as the contractors had finished installing the steel framework and sheeting they swung into action. With the assistance of a number of the club's supporters they spent as much of their spare time as they could mixing over a hundred tons of concrete for the hard standing terracing beneath the stand. Evenings and week-ends were given over to the task but with the work not being able to commence until well into July it was always going to be a race against the clock. Fortunately, some judicious rearrangement of the fixture list meant that Marys' first six matches would all be away, with Gedling Road not being used until the middle of September. It gave the club the breathing space that it needed and when Goole Town were the visitors for the Saints' very first home game in the Midland League, the brand new stand, concrete terracing and all, was firmly in place. It was a proud moment for all those associated with the club, none more so than Albert Moore.

AM : We used to work six nights a week putting it up, we only stopped on a Sunday, and it was very hard work, very tiring. In fact I can still feel it now! Still, it looked excellent really.

Without disclosing too much of what the future held for the club most people reading this will know that the stand was one of two demolished this very summer, 2008. For Albert, it was a very poignant moment.

AM : I went on to the ground the other day when they were knocking it all down and I got talking to a bloke there and I said to him "I spent weeks putting these stands up". He said "You didn't, did you?" I said "Yes, never had a hapeth of trouble, apart from sweat." I don't think I'll be going back there again though, I found it quite upsetting. It took us all that time and effort to put them up and only ten minutes to knock them down.

Albert needn't worry. The fact that the first stand was still there forty-five years after he and the others had helped put it up was testament enough to their efforts, especially when it had provided both shelter and an elevated view of proceedings for many thousands of appreciative spectators down the seasons.

With the large crowds that the Saints were attracting a good vantage point was important, especially if you were one of Marys' younger fans, but not all junior Saints settled for a place inside the ground. Martin Dermody was one such youngster when the maroon and golds were terrorising the defences of Aspley Old Boys and the rest.

MD : I was nine at the time and two or three of us from Smithy Crescent used to go down to the playground at KGV and we sort of realised that there were games taking place. The playground was situated behind one of the goals and it had a big, heavily constructed metal slide, probably a Wicksteed, that we used to go on. If it was summer then the metal got really hot and with us wearing short trousers it could be very painful. There was no safe landing area either. On match days we would get there about an hour before kick-off maybe and play on all the equipment. There was a rocking horse that you could easily lose your fingers on, a sand pit with no sand in it, swings, and a roundabout. At least this one wasn't like the roundabout on the Bottom Rec that always seemed to have a puddle of water around it. When we heard the players coming out for their warm up we used to climb to the top of the slide where there was a small platform big enough for the three of us and we would stay there because at that time you could just about get a view of the pitch. We thought this was good because we could stand there for the entire game. Quite often some older boys got the same idea and there was a hierarchy involved, a pecking order. We found ourselves threatened I suppose and we were bundled off down the slide. It was no use trying to go back up the steps because there was a hawthorn hedge and you couldn't see over it unless you were at the top of the slide.

If someone brought a football we used to be torn between watching and playing and we used to set up our game behind the goal at the cricket end but every time we heard the cheering of the crowd we'd stop our game, run to the goal and have a quick peek at who'd scored. Even though you usually missed the goals you still felt that you were part of it but at that time Marys were scoring so many that we used to go home not knowing what the final score had been.

Funnily enough we didn't seem to have a problem playing football on match days but at all other times the Groundsman or Park-Keeper seemed to think that there was no football allowed anywhere on KGV. We even tried playing on that bit near Castleton Avenue that wasn't part of either the football pitch or the cricket pitch but he still seemed to object.

Being chased off recreation fields was an occupational hazard for most kids, me included, especially if it happened to belong to a school with a particularly mean spirited caretaker, like the one at Kingswell. Most of us would climb over garden fences on Castleton to gain access to its football field and even though we were minding our own business he would suddenly make an appearance, standing on the school playground about a hundred yards away shouting and gesticulating and waving his fist. If he'd have made an attempt to come down towards us we would have scattered sharpish but he never did. All that usually happened was that a short while later a policeman, maybe even a police car, would appear alongside him and then we would all scarper back from where we'd come. Most days the police were too busy to bother and so we carried on until he ran out of steam and returned to his janitor duties.

That desire to be out in all weathers kicking a football around with some mates had been the one constant in my own life in the five years covered by this volume. I was nine at the start of the 1958-59 season and fourteen at the end of 1962-63, I'd 'progressed' from comics and toy cars to records and girls and ticked off all the stuff in between too, but despite the numerous changes that those five years had brought my love for football never altered.

The world in which the game was played however was a much different one in 1963 than it had been five years earlier; not better, just different. The USA had seen John F Kennedy become President and the country's Civil Rights movement win more bloody battles in its fight to end segregation, whilst the world had also looked on anxiously as JFK locked horns with Khrushchev over the Cuban Missile Crisis. In the UK life had speeded up enormously with the introduction of motorways and faster telecommunication systems whilst the un-banning of 'Lady Chatterley's Lover' had marked the beginning of a less buttoned up approach to matters of intimacy that would forever be associated with the sixties. This landmark case, together with the change in musical tastes that had seen skiffle replaced by Merseybeat via the early British rock 'n' roll of Cliff and the Shadows led poet Philip Larkin to famously remark that 'Sex began between the end of the Chatterley ban and the Beatles' first LP'.

I think that whatever 'sex' he had in mind reached Arnold quite some time later, but we had seen a bit of a revolution in other areas nonetheless. The slum clearance plan had been a success, new buildings were sprouting up around town, and with Fine Fare's arrival, for better or for worse, the supermarket era had finally begun. The biggest negative was the increase in the incidence of anti-social behaviour, with vandalism and hooliganism seemingly forever in the news. Nor was this phenomenon purely a local one; the whole of the country was witnessing a decline in self-discipline. The worst example had been when it involved people of different colour, as in the St Anns and Notting Hill race riots, but the malaise had started to spread into the sporting arena with disturbances amongst crowds at football matches and declining standards of respect on the pitch itself.

Happily for local football fans good things had taken place on the pitch too; Forest's Cup Win in 1959, Notts' promotion the following year, and of course the remarkable continuation of Marys' unrivalled consistency since the war, seventeen seasons in which they had only once finished outside the top five of the division they were playing in. It was a tremendous record and one of which everyone at the club had reason to be proud, but for the Saints' fans, players, supporters, and administrators, how best to sum up the last five of these years spent in the higher echelons of the Central Alliance?

Certainly the club had never had five consecutive years in which so much had happened. They'd progressed from being a purely amateur outfit to one that embraced professionalism in all its forms. The senior eleven had made its debut in the FA Cup and seen its name inscribed on the prestigious Notts Senior Cup for the first time. The club had acquired players of great pedigree from the Football League, such as ex-Foresters Colin Collindridge, Roland 'Tot' Leverton, and Noel Simpson, and then been instrumental in giving future participants in that competition their start in the game. Noel had also become the first coach in the club's history and then its first manager, and there was no doubt that his experiences as a full-time pro had rubbed off on his new charges. He certainly wasn't a soft touch.

PW : Not the easiest person Noel. I'd played against him a couple of times, a real nasty tackler.

AB : Noel was a very hard man. You thought you knew him but you didn't really.

DS : Noel was alright, I quite liked him, but he was a little bit strict. We were training at Redhill School one night and I hadn't paid my dues. I'd got changed into my kit and was going into the hall when he said, "I want a word with you. You haven't paid. I've been telling you for weeks that you've got to pay." It was five quid or something and I said "I'll bring it next week Noel, I haven't got it on me at the moment". "You're not", he said. "Until you bring it in you can bogger off". Arthur Oldham came in and said "Aren't you stopping" and I said "No, he won't let me".

Noel obviously kept high standards, making no exceptions even for one of the brightest talents in the club's reserve team that had won Division 1B of the Central Alliance as convincingly as the first eleven had won the Premier Division. In recognition of this tremendous achievement trophies were made for the players involved and presented to them at the AGM in July. What wasn't generally known was that Peter Taylor, future assistant to Brian Clough and current manager of Burton Albion, had made a daring raid on Marys' finest young players and managed to convince no less than five of them that their future held better prospects under his stewardship than Noel's.

END OF SEASON PRESENTATION EVENING JULY 1963 : Standing (l to r); - -, - -, A Ball, L Rockley, L Woollacott, D Smith, D Parr, T Watson, J Page, B Molyneux, - -, J Anthony, P Groome, M Hornbuckle, P Williams. Seated; R Knight, P Burton, D Staples, A Oldham.

(Alan Ball Collection)

DS : The first game after the frost the reserves played Forest A at Bestwood. Terry Bell was in the team then and his dad, who was a mate of Pete Taylor, came to watch us. He obviously mentioned me to him. At the end of the season we played in a semi or final against Heanor Town Reserves and I think we lost 3-2. I scored both our goals and I got a trial with

Grimsby Town I played three games for their reserves at the end of the season against Middlesborough, Lincoln, and then Newcastle in a final. It was a two legged game and we lost 4-1 in the first leg. I got injured and didn't play in the second leg. Our captain was Graham Taylor. I could have gone to Grimsby. I went to see manager Tommy Johnston after the game. I was doing an apprenticeship as a joiner and he said "We'll sign you on a full-time contract but if I was you I'd sign as an amateur, come to pre-season training and take it from there". Then Pete Taylor, who lived in Nottingham, said "Look, I've got a lot of contacts in football and if you make it with us I can shove you in different directions". So that's why I signed for Burton.

Burton were of course a Southern League side and the money on offer was quite attractive too. David's first contract was eight pounds per week plus a pound per point, rising to ten pounds per week the following season, so it's easy to see why he decided to make the move. Peter Taylor didn't stop there either. Before the summer was out he'd poached two other of Marys' outstanding youngsters, Ray Knight and Peter Burton, and then made an audacious swoop on the first team, signing two players who'd been ever-present all season, Arthur Oldham and John Anthony.

AO : I was going out with [my wife-to-be] Jenny at the time. She lived at Wilford and we went to the Ferry Inn for a lunch time drink one Sunday. Peter Taylor was there with Derek Pavis and he came over to me and said "You don't know who I am, do you?" and I said "No, I haven't got a clue." Then he introduced himself and said that he wanted me to sign for Burton. When we'd played their reserves I'd had a couple of really good games. I scored four in the first match and a couple more when they'd got a lot of first-teamers in the side and that's why he was interested in signing me. Noel Simpson was very good about it. He said to me "I won't stand in your way but if you decide that it's not what you want later promise me that you'll come back".

A few weeks later Arthur's new manager was telling him that the club was on the look out for a wing-half. Arthur mentioned the name of John Anthony, who he had become good friends with in his first season with the Saints.

AO : I told Peter Taylor that John was a terrific player but that I didn't think he'd want to move. He was a loyal lad and his dad had played for Marys as well, but I gave him his number and left it at that. Then John spoke to me and said he'd like to give it a go.

This latest exodus of players was made worse by the fact that it had come at a time when the club were faced with a step up in class to the Midland League but the fact of the matter was that players come and go and Marys had been in this position any number of times before. What they had managed to do so very successfully was to continually produce teams of excellent quality for whatever level of competition in which they were participating.

It had been a big jump back in 1958 from fifth in the second tier of the Central Alliance to the top division but they had ended that first season just a fraction of a goal away from the championship. Five years later they had won it, but now they would be faced with an even bigger challenge. However, with fresh players added to the squad, Noel Simpson still in charge, the changing rooms fully fitted out and a sparkling new stand running almost the length of the touchline, everyone involved with the club could look forward with optimism and excitement to the times ahead.

The years of the early fifties when Rovers' and Marys' rivalry was at its zenith had been a special time, but then so had the past five years. They represented another chapter in the town's rich footballing history that could never return. Neither of the teams would ever play in the Central Alliance again and there was certainly a sense of sadness that Rovers' glory days were officially over. For me, however, this wasn't the most poignant aspect of the parting of the ways. Rovers, back playing local league football in front of a handful of spectators, would at least be retaining their name, but Marys, as a price they had to pay to further their ambitions, would not. From now on, they would be known by the rather more prosaic title of Arnold FC.

The sixties were already off and running towards the heady mid-decade explosion of popular culture, with memories of the slower and gentler fifties, almost sleepy by comparison, already fading from the memory. The swinging sixties would be forever associated with sex, but I like to think that the fifties had a slightly more romantic feel about it, and what more attractive a tale in football could there be than a little 'church' team taking on and beating bigger and brasher sides from towns in Nottinghamshire and Derbyshire, Lincolnshire and Yorkshire, and on occasion even further afield than that, all the while playing on various Recs around the district; Top and Bottom at the beginning and KGV more recently.

None of them, on the face it, much more than a pitch, two goals, and some line markings, but for so many people they were magical, a place where you might see Colin Collindridge flying down the wing with his neckerchief trailing in the wind, Dennis Parr giving stalwart service at either centre-half or centre-forward, Barry Molyneux, Peter Williams, Len Rockley and Sid Thompson all racking up over a century of appearances, and the emergence of a new ace marksman by the name of Joe Boucher.

Dennis, Barry, Peter, and Joe would make the transition to the Midland League and in the process become just 'Arnold' players, but for many people they'd always be Marys' men first and foremost. In the last Central Alliance season they were also part of what many people thought was one of the most successful and entertaining sides the club had ever fielded.

PW : Good team that you know. In fact it may have been one of the best they ever had.

I for one wouldn't argue with Peter's assessment, a fitting summary at the close of yet another wonderful era, a time when the players were proud to pull on those maroon and gold striped shirts, a time synonymous with fast, attacking football, a time when any game involving the Saints drew bumper crowds both home and away and a time when Walter 'Kegga' Parr's beloved club finally came of age. It was a time never to be repeated, a very special time, that time.....

WHEN MARYS WERE KINGS!

STATISTICAL SECTION

Just as with KOTR! this section has again been the most difficult part of the book because even with Marys playing in the top division of the Central Alliance the newspaper coverage given to their matches was still far from comprehensive. Unlike towns such as Ilkeston, Belper, Matlock and the like, who had their own newspapers that usually carried a report of every match their teams played in, Arnold had no such resource. Despite this I am extremely pleased that every result in the period has been verified and that I have also been able to piece together complete appearance records for the five years covered by WMWK!

Performing a similar task with regard to goalscorers has unfortunately not been possible and I've had to settle on a success rate of around seventy percent. Generally speaking the identities of players scoring goals late in a match or those that were on the scoresheet in a game played in midweek or in some far flung place or, worse still, both, were hardly ever published. In addition quite a number of home games staged late in the season didn't seem to be of sufficient interest to local sports editors for them to even send a fledgling reporter out to cover.

Happily the situation improves noticeably after 1963 so here's to Volume 3 and beyond!

ARNOLD ST MARYS

1958-59 to 1962-63

HONOURS

1962-63
CENTRAL ALLIANCE PREMIER DIVISION

1960-61
NOTTS SENIOR CUP

SEASON BY SEASON SUMMARY : ALL GAMES

SEASON	P	W	D	L	F	A	%
1958-59	46	32	5	9	134	71	75.0
1959-60	37	25	4	8	108	56	73.0
1960-61	41	24	6	11	108	63	65.9
1961-62	38	19	8	11	102	64	60.5
1962-63	36	29	3	4	175	43	84.7
TOTAL	**198**	**129**	**26**	**43**	**627**	**297**	**71.7**
LEAGUE	162	110	21	31	534	227	74.4
CUP	36	19	5	12	93	70	59.7
TOTAL	**198**	**129**	**26**	**43**	**627**	**297**	**71.7**
HOME	98	70	10	18	361	131	76.5
AWAY	92	56	14	22	256	153	68.5
NEUTRAL	8	3	2	3	10	13	50.0
TOTAL	**198**	**129**	**26**	**43**	**627**	**297**	**71.7**
SEASON AVERAGE	**40**	**26**	**5**	**9**	**125**	**59**	**71.7**

ARNOLD ST MARYS

POST-WAR HONOURS

1949-50 NOTTM SPARTAN LEAGUE DIVISION 1
1962-63 CENTRAL ALLIANCE PREMIER DIVISION

1952-53 ARNOLD & DISTRICT BENEVOLENT CUP [TROPHY SHARED]
1953-54 NOTTS INTERMEDIATE CUP
1954-55 NOTTM SPARTAN LEAGUE CUP
1957-58 CENTRAL ALLIANCE DIVISION 2 CUP
1960-61 NOTTS SENIOR CUP

POST-WAR SEASON BY SEASON SUMMARY
ALL GAMES

SEASON	LEAGUE	P	W	D	L	F	A	%	POS
1946-47	NSL	23	14	2	7	87	65	65.2	03/14
1947-48	NSL1	22	8	2	12	56 +	88 +	40.9	07/09
1948-49	NSL1	39	30	2	7	156 +	64 +	79.5	02/13
1949-50	NSL1	37	31	3	3	171	56	87.8	01/15
1950-51	NSL1	41	27	5	9	154 +	66 +	72.0	04/16
1951-52	NSL1	29	17	4	8	141 +	79 +	65.5	05/12
1952-53	NSL1	33	23	5	5	128 +	48 +	77.3	02/12
1953-54	NSL1	34	30	1	3	121 +	32 +	89.7	02/12
1954-55	NSL1	28	23	1	4	118 +	44 +	83.9	02/09
1955-56	CA2	36	22	4	10	113	78	66.7	04/18
1956-57	CA2	36	23	6	7	166	78	72.2	03/18
1957-58	CA2	43	29	4	10	166	79	72.1	05/17
1958-59	CA1(N)	46	32	5	9	134	71	75.0	02/18
1959-60	CA1(N)	37	25	4	8	108	56	73.0	03/18
1960-61	CA1(N)	41	24	6	11	108	63	65.9	05/18
1961-62	CAP	38	19	8	11	102	64	60.5	05/17
1962-63	CAP	36	29	3	4	175	43	84.7	01/15
TOTAL		**599**	**406**	**65**	**128**	**2204 +**	**1074 +**	**73.2**	
SEASON AVERAGE		**35**	**24**	**4**	**7**	**130 +**	**63 +**	**73.2**	

NSL = NOTTINGHAM SPARTAN LEAGUE; CA = CENTRAL ALLIANCE

ARNOLD ST MARYS : 1958-59

#	DoW	Date	Opponents	v	Att	Res	Comp	Rockley	Molyneux	Gough	Hinson	Parr (D)	Thompson	Cripwell	Moore (K)	Collindridge	Smith (P)	Parr (G)	Lawton	Stalker	Barnes	Salmon	Wilkinson	Day	Woodhouse	Kitson	Burton (N)	Pike	Leverton	Williams	Scorers (Where known)
1	Sa	23-Aug-58	Wilmorton & Alvaston	a		4-2	CA1N	1	2	3	4	5	6	7	8	9	10	11													Parr (G) 2
2	Sa	30-Aug-58	South Normanton	a		2-1	CA1N	1	2	3	4	5	6	7	8	9	10	11													Thompson, Parr (G)
3	We	3-Sep-58	Heaner Town	h		2-4	CA1N	1	2	3	4	5	6	7	8	9	10	11													
4	Sa	6-Sep-58	Nottingham Forest A	a		3-1	CA1N	1	2	3	4	5	6	7	8	9	10	11													
5	We	10-Sep-58	Ilkeston Town	a		3-2	CA1N	1	2	3	4	5	6	7	8	9	10	11													
6	Sa	13-Sep-58	King's Lynn Res	h		5-2	CA1LC11L	1	2	3	4	5	6	7			10	11	9	8											Stalker, Parr (G)
7	Sa	20-Sep-58	Langwith MW	h		3-2	CA1N	1	2	3	4	5	6	7		8	10	11	9												Collindridge
8	We	24-Sep-58	Ollerton Colliery	h		2-3	CA1N	1	2	3	4	5	6	7		8	10	11	9												
9	Sa	27-Sep-58	Matlock Town	h		1-3	CA1N	1	2	3	4	5		7		8	10	11	9		6										Smith (P)
10	Sa	4-Oct-58	Burton Albion Res	a		5-2	CA1N	1	2	3	4	5		7		8	10	11	9		6										
11	Sa	11-Oct-58	King's Lynn Res	a		1-3	CA1LC12L	1	2	3	4	5		7			10	11	8		6	9									Salmon
12	Sa	18-Oct-58	Clay Cross MW	h		3-1	CA1N	1	2	3	4	5	6	7			10	11	8				9								Cripwell, Parr (G)
13	Sa	25-Oct-58	Langwith MW	a		3-2	CA1N	1	2	3	4	5	6	7			10	11	8				9								Cripwell, Wilkinson
14	Sa	1-Nov-58	Creswell Colliery	h		3-2	CA1N	1	2	3	4	5	6	7			10	11					9	8							Wilkinson
15	Sa	22-Nov-58	Ollerton Colliery	a		2-1	CA1N	1	2	3	4	5	6	7		10		11					9	8							Day
16	Sa	29-Nov-58	Sutton Town Res	h		1-1	CA1N	1	2	3	4	5	6	7		10		11					9	8							Parr (G), Cripwell 2
17	Sa	6-Dec-58	Matlock Town	a		3-1	CA1N	1	2	3	4	5	6	7		10		11					9	8							Collindridge, Cripwell
18	Sa	20-Dec-58	Nuneaton Borough Res	h		2-3	CA1N	1	2	3	4	5	6	7		10		11					9	8							Wilkinson 4
19	Th	25-Dec-58	Belper Town	h		5-1	CA1N	1	2	3	4	5	6	7		10		11					9	8							Cripwell
20	Fr	26-Dec-58	Belper Town	a		1-4	CA1N	1	2	3	4	5	6	7		10		11					9	8							Wilkinson, Parr (G), Day, Cripwell
21	Sa	3-Jan-59	Lenton Gregory	h		4-0	NSC4Q	1	2	3		5	6	7	4	10		11					9	8							Thompson 2, Wilkinson, Cripwell
22	Sa	17-Jan-59	Anstey Nomads	h		4-0	CA1N	1	2	3		5	6	7	4	10		11					9	8							Day
23	Sa	31-Jan-59	Ericsson Athletic	h		2-0	NSCQF	1	2	3		5	6	7		10		11					9	8	4						Collindridge
24	Sa	7-Feb-59	Cambridge City Res	a		2-2	CA1LC3	1	2	3		5	6	7	4	10		11						8	9						Parr (G) 2
25	Sa	14-Feb-59	Cambridge City Res	h		5-2	CA1LC3R	1	2	3		5	6	7	4	8	10	11								9					Parr (G), Collindridge, Smith (P) 2
26	Sa	21-Feb-59	Kettering Town Res	h		4-1	CA1LCQF	1	2	3		5	6	7	4	11	10	9						8							Day
27	Sa	28-Feb-59	South Normanton	a		1-2	CA1N	1	2	3		5	6	7	4	11	10						9	8							Wilkinson, Day
28	Sa	7-Mar-59	Creswell Colliery	a		4-1	CA1N	1	2	3		5	6	7	4	11	10						9	8							Smith (P)
29	Sa	14-Mar-59	Sutton Town Res	a		3-2	CA1N	1	2	3		5	6	7	4	11	10						9	8							Cripwell, Day, Smith (P), Collindridge
30	Sa	21-Mar-59	Burton Albion Res	a		7-0	CA1N	1	2	3		5	6	7	4	11	10						9	8							
31	Th	26-Mar-59	Ransome & Marles	a		2-0	CA1N	1	2	3		5	6	7	4	11	10						9	8							
32	Sa	28-Mar-59	Rushden Town	h		1-3	CA1LCSF	1	2	3		5	6	7	4	11	10						9	8							
33	Tu	31-Mar-59	Nuneaton Borough Res	a		1-0	CA1N	1	2	3		5	6	7	4	11	10						9	8							
34	Sa	4-Apr-59	Clay Cross MW	a		3-0	CA1N	1	2	3		5	6	7	4	11	10						9	8							Cripwell, Wilkinson
35	We	8-Apr-59	Shirebrook MW	h		6-2	CA1N	1	2	3		5	6	7	4	11	10						9	8							
36	Sa	11-Apr-59	Ilkeston Town	h		4-1	CA1N	1	2	3		5	6	7	4	11	10						9	8							Cripwell, Wilkinson
37	Sa	18-Apr-59	Anstey Nomads	a		6-3	CA1N	1	2	3		5	6	7	4	11	10						9	8							Gough, Wilkinson
38	Tu	21-Apr-59	Wilmorton & Alvaston	h		3-1	CA1N	1	2	3		5	6	7	4	11	10						9	8							
39	Th	23-Apr-59	Shirebrook MW	a		1-1	CA1N	1	2	3		5	6	7	4	11	10						9	8							
40	Sa	25-Apr-59	Nottingham Forest A	h		2-1	CA1N	1	2	3		5	6	7	4	11	10						9	8							
41	Tu	28-Apr-59	Ransome & Marles	h		9-2	CA1N	1	2	3		5	6	7	4	11	10						9	8							
42	Sa	2-May-59	Gedling Colliery	n		2-2	NSCSF	1	2	3		5	6	7	4	11	10						9	8							Collindridge
43	Tu	5-May-59	Heaner Town	a		1-0	CA1N	1	2	3		5	6	7	4	11	10						9	8							
44	Sa	9-May-59	Gedling Colliery	n		1-0	NSCSFR	1	2	3		5	6	7	4	11	10						9	8							
45	Sa	16-May-59	Retford Town	n	4000	1-1	NSCF	1	2	3		5	6	7	4		10	11					9					8			Parr (G)
46	Mo	7-Sep-59	Retford Town	n		1-3	NSCFR	1	2			5	6	7	4								9	8			3		10	11	Wilkinson
			Appearances				**506**	46	45	45	21	46	44	46	30	38	34	28	8	1	3	1	31	32	2	1	3	1	1	1	

158

1958-59

CENTRAL ALLIANCE DIVISION 1 (NORTH)

	P	W	D	L	F	A	P	H	A
BELPER TOWN	34	25	4	5	141	66	54	5-1	1-4
ARNOLD ST MARYS	**34**	**26**	**2**	**6**	**105**	**52**	**54**		
MATLOCK TOWN	34	21	4	9	109	59	46	1-3	3-1
HEANOR TOWN	34	22	1	11	100	58	45	2-4	1-0
SOUTH NORMANTON	34	15	9	10	80	70	39	1-2	2-1
CRESWELL COLLIERY	34	18	2	14	107	88	38	3-2	4-1
ILKESTON TOWN	34	14	9	11	74	59	37	4-1	3-2
SUTTON TOWN RESERVES	34	15	6	13	97	77	36	1-1	3-2
NOTTINGHAM FOREST A	34	14	5	15	72	84	33	2-1	3-1
SHIREBROOK MW	34	11	11	12	75	95	33	6-2	1-1
NUNEATON BOROUGH RESERVES	34	13	6	15	85	78	32	2-3	1-0
CLAY CROSS MW	34	12	7	15	81	87	31	3-1	3-0
OLLERTON COLLIERY	34	11	8	15	66	83	30	2-3	2-1
WILMORTON & ALVASTON	34	8	8	18	51	84	24	3-1	4-2
BURTON ALBION RESERVES	34	8	6	20	76	116	22	7-0	5-2
RANSOME AND MARLES	34	9	3	22	60	113	21	9-2	2-0
ANSTEY NOMADS	34	8	5	21	52	110	21	4-0	6-3
LANGWITH MW	34	4	8	22	57	109	16	3-2	3-2
	612	254	104	254	1488	1488	612		
MARYS HOME	17	11	1	5	58	29	23		
MARYS AWAY	17	15	1	1	47	23	31		

CENTRAL ALLIANCE DIVISION 1 CUP

R11L : KINGS LYNN RESERVES (H)	5-2
R12L : KINGS LYNN RESERVES (A)	1-3
R2 : bye	
R3 : CAMBRIDGE CITY RESERVES (A)	2-2
R3R : CAMBRIDGE CITY RESERVES (H)	5-2
QF : KETTERING TOWN RESERVES (H)	4-1
SF : RUSHDEN TOWN (H)	1-3

NOTTS SENIOR CUP

1Q : bye	
2Q : bye	
3Q : bye	
4Q : LENTON GREGORY (H)	4-0
QF : ERICSSON ATHLETIC (H)	2-0
SF : GEDLING COLLIERY (Meadow Lane)	2-2 (after extra time)
SFR : GEDLING COLLIERY (Meadow Lane)	1-0
F : RETFORD TOWN (Sutton Town FC)	1-1 (after extra time)
FR : RETFORD TOWN (Meadow Lane)	1-3

ARNOLD ST MARYS : 1959-60

#	Day	Date	Opponents	v	Att	Res	Comp	Rockley	Molyneux	Southwell	Moore (K)	Parr (D)	Thompson	Cripwell	Day	Wilkinson	Leverton	Williams	Burton (N)	Parr (G)	Hinson	Pike	Smith (P)	Collindridge	Barnes	Noone	Coombe	Mason	England	Simpson	Scorers (Where known)
1	Sa	22-Aug-59	Alfreton Town	a	3000	2-6	CA1N	1	2	3	4	5	6	7	8	9	10	11													Moore (K)
2	Sa	29-Aug-59	Belper Town	a	1250	2-4	CA1N	1	2		4	5	6	7		9	8	10	3	11											Leverton, Cripwell
3	We	2-Sep-59	Ollerton Colliery	a		4-2	CA1N	1	2			5	6	7		9	8	10	3	11	4										
4	Sa	5-Sep-59	Gresley Rovers	a		4-2	CA1N	1	2			5	6	7		9	8	11	3		4	10									
5	Sa	12-Sep-59	Ilkeston Town	h		0-0	CA1N	1	2			5	6	7	8	9		11	3		4	10									
6	Tu	15-Sep-59	Belper Town	h		2-1	CA1N	1	2			5	6	7		9		10	3	11	4		8								Parr (G) 2
7	Sa	19-Sep-59	Kimberley Town	a		5-1	CA1N	1	2			5	6	7				10	3	11	4		8	9							Parr (G), Cripwell
8	Sa	26-Sep-59	Stamford	h		1-2	CA1LC1	1	2			5	6	7				10	3	11	4		8	9							Cripwell
9	Sa	3-Oct-59	Langwith MW	a		5-1	CA1N	1	2				6	7				10	3	11	4		8	9	5						Smith (P)
10	Sa	10-Oct-59	Ollerton Colliery	h		3-0	CA1N	1	2				6	7				10	3	11	4		8	9	5						
11	Sa	17-Oct-59	Creswell Colliery	a		1-0	CA1N	1	2			5	6	7				10	3	11	4		8	9							
12	Sa	24-Oct-59	Heanor Town	h		2-1	CA1N	1	2			5	6	7	8			10	3	11				9							Thompson, Williams
13	Sa	31-Oct-59	Shirebrook MW	a		4-0	CA1N	1	2		4	5	6	7	8			10	3	11				9							Collindridge
14	Sa	7-Nov-59	Heanor Town	a		0-3	CA1N	1	2		4	5	6	7	8			10	3	11				9							
15	Sa	14-Nov-59	Alfreton Town	h		3-3	CA1N	1	2		4	5	6	7	8			10	3	11				9							Day, Collindridge
16	Sa	5-Dec-59	South Normanton	h		3-0	CA1N	1	2		4	5	6	7	8			10	3	11				9							Collindridge 2, Parr (G)
17	Sa	12-Dec-59	Ilkeston Town	a	891	0-2	CA1N	1	2		4	5	6	7				11	3			10		9		8					
18	Sa	19-Dec-59	Nottingham Forest A	h		2-1	CA1N	1	2		4	5	6	7	8	9		11	3					10							Cripwell, Williams
19	Sa	26-Dec-59	Wilmorton & Alvaston	a		1-0	CA1N	1	2		4	5	6	7	8	9		11	3					10							
20	Mo	28-Dec-59	Wilmorton & Alvaston	h		1-1	CA1N	1	2		4	5	6	7	8	9		11	3					10							
21	Sa	2-Jan-60	Gresley Rovers	h		4-1	CA1N	1	2		4	5	6	7				11	3					10			8	9			Mason, Williams, Collindridge, Cripwell
22	Sa	9-Jan-60	South Normanton	a		5-3	CA1N	1	2		4	5	6	7				11	3					10			8	9			Williams, Cripwell
23	Sa	16-Jan-60	Matlock Town	h		0-1	CA1N	1	2		4	5	6	7				11	3					10			9	8			
24	Sa	30-Jan-60	Matlock Town	a		1-4	CA1N	1	2		4	5		7				11	3					10	6		8		9		Collindridge
25	Sa	6-Feb-60	Nottingham Forest A	h		3-1	CA1N	1	2		4	5	6	7				11	3					10			8		9		
26	Sa	13-Feb-60	Nottingham University	h		4-1	NSCQF	1	2		8	5	6	7				11	3					10	4				9		England 3, Collindridge
27	Sa	27-Feb-60	Sutton Town Res	a		4-1	CA1N	1	2		8	5	6	7				11	3					10	4				9		Williams 2, Collindridge, Moore (K)
28	Sa	5-Mar-60	Langwith MW	h		5-0	CA1N	1	2		8	5	6	7				11	3					10	4				9		England, Williams, Moore (K)
29	Sa	12-Mar-60	Burton Albion Res	h		2-0	CA1N	1	2		8	5	6	7				11	3					10	4				9		Cripwell
30	Sa	19-Mar-60	Burton Albion Res	a		5-0	CA1N	1	2		8	5	6	7				11	3					10	4				9		Moore (K), England
31	Sa	2-Apr-60	Sutton Town Res	h		3-3	CA1N	1	2		8	5	6	7				11	3					10	4				9		
32	Sa	16-Apr-60	Clay Cross MW	h		7-0	CA1N	1	2		8	5	6	7				11	3					10					9	4	Collindridge, Moore (K) 2, England 3
33	-	tbc	Clay Cross MW	a		3-2	CA1N	1	2		8	5	6	7				11	3					10					9	4	
34	Sa	23-Apr-60	Kimberley Town	h		6-4	CA1N	1	2			5	6	7	8			11	3					10					9	4	England
35	Th	28-Apr-60	Shirebrook MW	h		10-0	NSCSF	1	2			5	6	7	8			11	3					10					9	4	England 2, Collindridge, Cripwell 4, Burton 2, Day
36	Sa	30-Apr-60	Sutton Town	a		0-5	CA1N	1	2		8	5	6	7				11	3					10					9	4	
37	Th	5-May-60	Creswell Colliery	h		1-0	CA1N	1	2		8	5	6	7				11	3					10					9	4	
			Appearances				407	37	37	1	24	35	36	35	14	9	4	37	36	13	10	4	6	32	9	1	5	3	13	6	

160

1959-60

CENTRAL ALLIANCE DIVISION 1 (NORTH)

	P	W	D	L	F	A	P	H	A
MATLOCK TOWN	34	27	2	5	106	34	56	0-1	1-4
HEANOR TOWN	34	26	0	8	107	40	52	2-1	0-3
ARNOLD ST MARYS	**34**	**24**	**4**	**6**	**103**	**48**	**52**		
ALFRETON TOWN	34	24	3	7	118	52	51	3-3	2-6
ILKESTON TOWN	34	22	5	7	88	42	49	0-0	0-2
BELPER TOWN	34	21	5	8	121	68	47	2-1	2-4
WILMORTON & ALVASTON	34	15	7	12	73	58	37	1-1	1-0
KIMBERLEY TOWN	34	16	5	13	93	82	37	6-4	5-1
SOUTH NORMANTON	34	13	7	14	81	76	33	3-0	5-3
CRESWELL COLLIERY	34	15	3	16	63	66	33	1-0	1-0
NOTTINGHAM FOREST A	34	13	5	16	93	75	31	2-1	3-1
CLAY CROSS MW	34	13	3	18	67	89	29	7-0	3-2
SUTTON TOWN RESERVES	34	11	7	16	77	90	29	3-3	4-1
BURTON ALBION RESERVES	34	9	5	20	59	83	23	2-0	5-0
SHIREBROOK MW	34	9	4	21	53	128	22	10-0	4-0
GRESLEY ROVERS	34	6	8	20	41	80	20	4-1	4-2
LANGWITH MW	34	2	2	30	28	162	6	5-0	5-1
OLLERTON COLLIERY	34	2	1	31	41	139	5	3-0	4-2
	612	268	76	268	1412	1412	612		
MARYS HOME	17	12	4	1	54	16	28		
MARYS AWAY	17	12	0	5	49	32	24		

CENTRAL ALLIANCE DIVISION 1 CUP

R1 : STAMFORD (H)   1-2

NOTTS SENIOR CUP

1Q : bye
2Q : bye
3Q : bye
4Q : bye
QF : NOTTINGHAM UNIVERSITY (H)   4-1
SF : SUTTON TOWN (A)   0-5

ARNOLD ST MARYS : 1960-61

#	Day	Date	Opponents	v	Att	Res	Comp	Rockley	Molyneux	Burton (N)	Simpson	Parr (D)	Thompson	Williams	Day	England	Moore (K)	Collindridge	Barnes	Jackson	Leverton	Mason	Iremonger	Moore (J)	Gough	Cunningham (B)	Brady	Clarke	Martin	Cripwell	Haynes	Wright (E)	Parr (G)	Anthony	Coombe	Scorers (Where known)
1	Sa	27-Aug-60	Kimberley Town	a		1-0	CA1N	1	2	3	4	5	6	7	8	9	10	11																		
2	Sa	3-Sep-60	Kimberley Town	h		2-1	CA1N	1	2	3	4	5		7	8	9	10	11	6																	Collindridge
3	Sa	10-Sep-60	Wilmorton & Alvaston	a		2-0	CA1N	1	2	3	4	5	6	10	7	9		11		8																
4	Sa	17-Sep-60	Worksop Town	a		1-1	CA1N	1	2	3	4	5	6	7	10	9		11		8																England
5	Sa	24-Sep-60	Nottingham Forest A	h		6-1	CA1N	1	2	3	4	5	6	7		9		11			10	8														Mason 2, Williams, Leverton
6	Sa	1-Oct-60	Alfreton Town	a		1-1	CA1N		2	3	4	5	6	11		9		7			10	8	1													Leverton
7	Sa	8-Oct-60	Clay Cross MW	a		4-0	CA1N		2		4	5	6	11		9		7			10	8	1		3											England 2
8	Sa	15-Oct-60	Clay Cross MW	h		6-1	CA1LC1		2		4	5	6	11		9		8			10	7	1		3											Mason 3, Williams
9	Sa	22-Oct-60	Gainsborough Trinity	a		1-3	CA1N		2		4	5	6	11		9		7			10	8	1		3											England
10	Sa	29-Oct-60	Worksop Town	h		5-0	CA1N		2		4	5	6	7		9		11			10		1		3		8									og, Leverton, Williams, England, Brady
11	Sa	5-Nov-60	Alfreton Town	h		5-0	CA1N		2		4	5	6	7		9		11			10		1		3		8									Brady 3, Williams, England
12	Sa	12-Nov-60	Creswell Colliery	a		3-3	CA1LC2		2		4	5	6	7		9		11			10		1		3		8									Brady
13	Sa	19-Nov-60	Gainsborough Trinity	h		2-2	CA1N		2			5		7		9		11	6		10		1		3	4	8									Collindridge 2
14	Sa	26-Nov-60	Sutton Town	a		2-1	CA1N		2			5	6	7		9		11			10		1		3	4	8									Parr (D), England
15	Sa	3-Dec-60	Denby United	h		3-2	CA1N		2		4	5	6	7		9		11			10		1		3		8									Collindridge, Brady, England
16	Sa	10-Dec-60	Denby United	a		5-3	CA1N		2		4	5	6	7		9		11			10		1		3		8									Brady 4, Parr (D)
17	Sa	17-Dec-60	Sutton Town	h		3-2	CA1N		2		4	5	6	7		9		11			10		1		3		8									Leverton, England 2
18	Sa	24-Dec-60	Nottingham Forest A	a		6-2	CA1N		2		4	5	6	7		9		11			10		1		3		8									Brady 2, Collindridge 2, England 2
19	Sa	7-Jan-61	Goole Town	h		1-1	CA1N		2		4	5	6	7		9		11			10		1		3		8									Leverton
20	Sa	14-Jan-61	Shirebrook MW	a		4-2	CA1N		2		4	5	6	7		9		11			10		1		3		8									Brady, Williams
21	Sa	21-Jan-61	Creswell Colliery	h		3-1	CA1LC2R		2			5	6	7		9		11			10		1		3	4	8									Thompson, England, Williams
22	Sa	28-Jan-61	Belper Town	a		1-2	CA1N		2		4	5	6	7		9		11			10		1		3		8									England
23	Sa	11-Feb-61	Ericsson Athletic	a		6-2	NSCQF		2			5	6	7		9		11					1		3	4	8	10								Williams 2, Thompson, Brady
24	Sa	18-Feb-61	Worksop Town	h	450	0-2	CA1LC3		2		4	5	6	7		9		11			10		1		3		8									
25	Sa	4-Mar-61	Shirebrook MW	h		3-0	CA1N		2		4	5	6	7		9		11			10		1		3		8									England, Williams
26	Sa	11-Mar-61	South Normanton	a		2-1	CA1N		2		4	5	6	7		9		11			10		1		3		8									Williams, Collindridge
27	Sa	18-Mar-61	Matlock Town	a		0-3	CA1N		2		4	5	6	7		9		11			10		1		3		8									
28	Sa	25-Mar-61	Matlock Town	h		1-3	CA1N		2		4	5		7		9		11			10		1		3			8	6							Williams
29	Sa	1-Apr-61	Creswell Colliery	h		3-4	CA1N		2		4	5						11			9		1		3			8	6	7	10					Haynes, Cripwell 2
30	Mo	3-Apr-61	Wilmorton & Alvaston	h		5-0	CA1N		2		4	5				9					10		1		3				6	7		8	11			England 4, Simpson
31	Sa	8-Apr-61	Goole Town	a	550	3-4	CA1N		2		4	5				9					10		1		3				6	7		8	11			England
32	We	12-Apr-61	Ilkeston Town	h		1-1	CA1N		2		4	5		7		9		11			10		1		3				6			8				
33	Sa	15-Apr-61	Clay Cross MW	h		4-2	CA1N		2		4	5		7		9		8			10		1		3				6				11			England 2, Collindridge, Williams
34	Th	20-Apr-61	Ransome & Marles	n		2-1	NSCSF		2		4	5		7		9		8			10		1		3				6				11			England, Collindridge
35	Sa	22-Apr-61	Heanor Town	a		1-2	CA1N		2		4	5		7		9		11			10		1		3		8		6							Brady
36	Mo	24-Apr-61	South Normanton	h		5-3	CA1N		2		4	5		7				11			9		1		3		8		6					10		
37	We	26-Apr-61	Belper Town	h		1-0	CA1N		2		4	5				7		11			9		1		3		8		6					10		
38	Sa	29-Apr-61	Heanor Town	h		2-3	CA1N		2		4	5						11			9		1	7	3		8		6					10		
39	Tu	2-May-61	Ilkeston Town	a		1-2	CA1N		2		4	5		11							9		1		3	6	8			7				10		
40	We	3-May-61	Creswell Colliery	a		0-1	CA1N		2		4	5		11							9		1		3	6	8			7				10		Anthony, Leverton
41	Sa	6-May-61	Retford Town	n	2550	1-0	NSCF		2		4	5		11									1	7	3	6	8							10	9	Williams
		Appearances						5	41	6	37	41	26	36	4	35	2	36	2	2	33	5	36	3	35	7	25	2	11	6	1	3	4	6	1	451

1960-61

CENTRAL ALLIANCE DIVISION 1 (NORTH)

	P	W	D	L	F	A	P	H	A
MATLOCK TOWN	34	24	6	4	126	51	54	1-3	0-3
SUTTON TOWN	34	23	6	5	103	46	52	3-2	2-1
GOOLE TOWN	34	23	5	6	122	54	51	1-1	3-4
HEANOR TOWN	34	21	4	9	87	67	46	2-3	1-2
ARNOLD ST MARYS	**34**	**19**	**5**	**10**	**87**	**53**	**43**		
WORKSOP TOWN	34	20	3	11	96	60	43	5-0	1-1
GAINSBOROUGH TRINITY	34	17	8	9	77	38	42	2-2	1-3
ILKESTON TOWN	34	17	7	10	91	57	41	1-1	1-2
BELPER TOWN	34	19	2	13	106	79	40	1-0	1-2
ALFRETON TOWN	34	18	3	13	94	60	39	5-0	1-1
DENABY UNITED	34	15	3	16	98	73	33	3-2	5-3
KIMBERLEY TOWN	34	12	4	18	72	88	28	2-1	1-0
CRESWELL COLLIERY	34	12	2	20	66	103	26	3-4	0-1
NOTTINGHAM FOREST A	34	10	4	20	57	110	24	6-1	6-2
SOUTH NORMANTON	34	6	3	25	59	102	15	5-3	2-1
CLAY CROSS MW	34	5	5	24	61	123	15	4-2	4-0
WILMORTON & ALVASTON	34	4	5	25	48	115	13	5-0	2-0
SHIREBROOK MW	34	2	3	29	34	207	7	3-0	4-2
	612	267	78	267	1484	1486	612		
MARYS HOME	17	11	3	3	52	25	25		
MARYS AWAY	17	8	2	7	35	28	18		

CENTRAL ALLIANCE DIVISION 1 CUP

R1 : CLAY CROSS MW (H)	6-1
R2 : CRESWELL COLLIERY (A)	3-3
R2R : CRESWELL COLLIERY (H)	3-1
R3 : WORKSOP TOWN (H)	0-2

NOTTS SENIOR CUP

1Q : bye	
2Q : bye	
3Q : bye	
4Q : bye	
QF : ERICSSON ATHLETIC (A)	6-2
SF : RANSOME AND MARLES (Meadow Lane)	2-1
F : RETFORD TOWN (Meadow Lane)	**1-0**

ARNOLD ST MARYS : 1961-62

No	D	Date	Opponents	v	Att	Res	Comp	Fremonger	Molyneux	Gough	Wright (R)	Parr (D)	Anthony	Leverton	Page	England	Wright (E)	Williams	Groome	Cann	Watts	Martin	Moore (J)	Simpson	Radford	Raynor	Collindridge	Bell	Jeffries	Thompson	Staples	Mann	Knight	Davis	Roberts	Burton (P)	Rockley	Smith (Derek)	Mason	Scorers (Where known)
1	Sa	19-Aug-61	Boston United	a	1883	2-2	CAP	1	2	3	4	5	6	7	8	9	10	11																						Anthony, Williams
2	Sa	26-Aug-61	South Normanton	a		0-0	CAP	1	2		4	5	6	10	8	9		11	3	7																				
3	Sa	2-Sep-61	South Normanton	h		3-0	CAP	1	2		4	5	6		8	9		11	3	7	10																			Cann
4	Sa	9-Sep-61	Matlock Town	h		1-5	FAC1Q	1	2		4	5	6		8	9		11	3	7	10																			Cann
5	Sa	16-Sep-61	Aspley Old Boys	h		4-3	CAP	1	2		4	5	6		10	9		11	3	7	8																			Watts 2, Page, England
6	Sa	23-Sep-61	Creswell Colliery	h		5-0	CAP	1	2		4	5	6		10	9		8	3	11		7																		England 2, Page, Cann, Williams
7	Sa	30-Sep-61	Boston United	h	1556	3-3	CAPC1	1	2		4	5	6		10	9		8	3	11		7																		England, Cann, Williams
8	Sa	7-Oct-61	Gresley Rovers	a	500	2-3	CAP	1	2		4	5	6		10	9		8	3	11		7																		England 2
9	Sa	21-Oct-61	Clay Cross MW	a		4-0	CAP	1	2			5	6		8	9		7	3			4			10		11													Radford 2, Page 2
10	Sa	28-Oct-61	Ransome & Marles	h		2-3	CAP	1	2			5	6		8	9		7	3			4			10		11													England, Page
11	Sa	4-Nov-61	Ashbourne Town	a		10-2	CAP	1				5	6		8	9			3			4	7		10	2	11													Moore (J), Anthony, Collindridge, England 4, Radford 2, Page
12	Sa	11-Nov-61	Boston United	h		1-3	CAPC1R	1				5	6		8	9			3			4	7		10	2	11													England
13	Sa	18-Nov-61	Aspley Old Boys	a		7-1	CAP	1	2			5	6		10		8	7	3			4	9				11													Collindridge 3, Moore (J), Anthony, Wright (E) 2
14	Sa	25-Nov-61	Eastwood Town	a		3-2	CAP	1	2			5	6		10		8	7	3			4	9				11													Wright (E), Moore (J), Collindridge
15	Sa	2-Dec-61	Burton Albion Res	a		1-1	CAP	1	2			5	6		8			7	3			4	10		11		9													Page
16	Sa	16-Dec-61	Shirebrook MW	a		3-1	CAP	1	2			5	6		8				3			4	10	7	11		9													og, Simpson, Page
17	Sa	23-Dec-61	Clay Cross MW	h		3-1	CAP	1	2			5	6		10			7	3			4			11		9	8												Page, Bell, Collindridge
18	Sa	13-Jan-62	Kimberley Town	a		2-2	CAP	1	2			5	6					7	3			4			11		9	8	10											og, Collindridge
19	Sa	20-Jan-62	Shirebrook MW	h		8-1	CAP	1	2				6		11				3			4					9	8	10	5	7										Bell, Collindridge, Jeffries 3, Page 2, Staples
20	Sa	27-Jan-62	Wilmorton & Alvaston	a		2-1	CAP	1	2			5	6		11				3			4					9	8	10		7										Collindridge, Page
21	Sa	3-Feb-62	Anstey Nomads	a		0-2	CAP	1	2			5	6		11			7	3			4						8	10			9									
22	Sa	10-Feb-62	Eastwood Town	a		3-0	NSCQF	1	2			5	6		7				3								11	8	10			9	4								Jeffries, Mann, Page
23	Sa	17-Feb-62	Gresley Rovers	h		3-2	CAP	1	2			5	6		7				3						9		11	8	10				4								Jeffries, Page
24	Sa	24-Feb-62	Linby Colliery	a		1-2	CAP	1	2						8			7	3			4			9		11		10	5			6							
25	Sa	10-Mar-62	Wilmorton & Alvaston	h		0-0	CAP	1	2			5	6		8			7	3								11		10					4	9				
26	Sa	17-Mar-62	Anstey Nomads	h		2-1	CAP	1	2			5	6		8			7	3								11		10					4	9					Page
27	Sa	24-Mar-62	Ransome & Marles	a		2-4	CAP	1	2			5	6		8			7	3								11		10					4						Page
28	Sa	31-Mar-62	Eastwood Town	h		2-5	CAP	1	2			5	6		10			9	3								11	8						4		7				Page, Bell
29	Sa	7-Apr-62	Burton Albion Res	h		0-0	CAP		2			5	6		10			9	3			4					11							8		7	1		
30	We	11-Apr-62	Creswell Colliery	a		1-1	CAP		2			9	6		10			7	3			4					11							8			1	5		
31	Sa	14-Apr-62	Nottingham Forest A	a		3-0	CAP		2			9	6		10			7	3			4						11						8			1	5		Bell, Davis, Page
32	Tu	17-Apr-62	Boston United	h		2-4	CAP		2			9	6		10			7	3			4						11						8			1	5		Parr (D), Bell
33	Sa	21-Apr-62	Nottingham Forest A	h		1-3	CAP		2			9	6		10			11	3			4												8		7	1	5		Anthony
34	Mo	23-Apr-62	Ashbourne Town	h		5-1	CAP		2			9	6		10			11	3															4		7	1	5	8	
35	Fr	27-Apr-62	Ericsson Athletic	h		3-0	NSCSF					9	6		10			11																4		7	1	5	8	
36	Sa	28-Apr-62	Kimberley Town	h		3-2	CAP					9	6		10			11								2								4		7	1	5	10	Page 2
37	We	2-May-62	Linby Colliery	h		4-0	CAP		2			9	6		8			10									11							4		7	1	5		Page 2
38	Sa	5-May-62	Sutton Town	n		1-3	NSCF		2			9	6		8			10									11							4		7	1	5		Page, Anthony, Burton (P), Parr (D)
			Appearances				418	28	34	1	8	30	37	2	37	12	3	33	33	7	3	28	9	4	11	3	21	10	10	2	2	2	3	14	2	7	10	9	3	

164

1961-62

CENTRAL ALLIANCE PREMIER DIVISION

	P	W	D	L	F	A	P	H	A
BOSTON UNITED	32	26	3	3	107	48	55	2-4	2-2
RANSOME AND MARLES	32	23	2	7	115	68	48	2-3	2-4
GRESLEY ROVERS	32	20	7	5	97	44	47	3-2	2-3
EASTWOOD TOWN	32	20	5	7	105	50	45	2-5	3-2
ARNOLD ST MARYS	**32**	**17**	**7**	**8**	**90**	**50**	**41**		
WILMORTON & ALVASTON	32	15	6	11	60	47	36	0-0	2-1
KIMBERLEY TOWN	32	15	5	12	88	70	35	3-2	2-2
ASPLEY OLD BOYS	32	15	4	13	79	76	34	4-3	7-1
SOUTH NORMANTON	32	11	8	13	81	64	30	3-0	0-0
BURTON ALBION RESERVES	32	12	6	14	72	71	30	0-0	1-1
CRESWELL COLLIERY	32	13	4	15	64	72	30	5-0	1-1
CLAY CROSS MW	32	11	4	17	58	79	26	3-1	4-0
NOTTINGHAM FOREST A	32	7	8	17	52	88	22	1-3	3-0
ASHBOURNE TOWN	32	4	10	18	54	101	18	5-1	10-2
LINBY COLLIERY	32	4	8	20	36	103	16	4-0	1-2
ANSTEY NOMADS	32	4	8	20	41	92	16	2-1	0-2
SHIREBROOK MW	32	6	3	23	57	133	15	8-1	3-1
	544	223	98	223	1256	1256	544		
MARYS HOME	16	10	2	4	47	26	22		
MARYS AWAY	16	7	5	4	43	24	19		

CENTRAL ALLIANCE PREMIER DIVISION CUP

R1 : BOSTON UNITED (A)	3-3
R1R : BOSTON UNITED (H)	1-3

FA CUP

1Q : MATLOCK TOWN (H)	1-5

NOTTS SENIOR CUP

1Q : bye	
2Q : bye	
3Q : bye	
4Q : bye	
QF : EASTWOOD TOWN (A)	3-0
SF : ERICSSON ATHLETIC (H)	3-0
F : SUTTON TOWN (tbc)	1-3

ARNOLD ST MARYS : 1962-63

No.	Day	Date	Opponents	v	Att	Res	Comp	Rockley	Molyneux	Howard	Davis	Parr (D)	Anthony	Burton (P)	Hornbuckle	Boucher	Oldham	Williams	Iremonger	Watson	Smith (Derek)	Ball	Page	Scorers (Where known)
1	Sa	18-Aug-62	Burton Albion Res	h		7-1	CAP	1	2	3	4	5	6	7	8	9	10	11						Hornbuckle 3, Oldham 4
2	Sa	25-Aug-62	Gresley Rovers	a		3-2	CAP	1	2	3	4	5	6	7	8	9	10	11						Oldham, Howard, Boucher
3	Sa	1-Sep-62	Aspley Old Boys	h		16-1	CAP	1	2	3	4	5	6	7	8	9	10	11						Boucher 7, Oldham 4, Anthony 2, Hornbuckle, Williams, Burton
4	Sa	8-Sep-62	Matlock Town	h		3-2	FAC1Q	1	2	3	4	5	6	7	8	9	10	11						Hornbuckle, Burton 2
5	Sa	15-Sep-62	Ashbourne Town	a		5-4	CAPC1	1	2	3	4	5	6	7	8	9	10	11						Boucher 2, Williams, Oldham
6	Sa	22-Sep-62	Alfreton Town	a	2371	4-0	FAC2Q	1	2	3	4	5	6	7	8	9	10	11						Boucher, Oldham 2, Williams
7	Sa	6-Oct-62	Buxton	a		3-6	FAC3Q	1	2	3	4	5	6	7	8	9	10	11						Hornbuckle, Burton, Boucher
8	Sa	13-Oct-62	Ericsson Athletic	a		7-3	CAP	1	2	3	4	5	6	7	8	9	10	11						Boucher 3, Oldham 3, Burton
9	Sa	20-Oct-62	Clay Cross MW	a		3-4	CAPC2	1	2	3	4	5	6	7	8	9	10	11						Boucher 3
10	Sa	27-Oct-62	Ransome & Marles	a		0-0	CAP		2	3			6	7	8	9	10	11	1	4	5			
11	Sa	3-Nov-62	Gresley Rovers	h		6-1	CAP		2	3	4		6	7		9	10		1		5	11	8	Boucher 3, Ball 2, Anthony
12	Sa	10-Nov-62	Anstey Nomads	h		12-3	CAP		2	3	4		6	7		9	10		1		5	11	8	Boucher 5, Ball 2, Oldham 2, Page 2, Williams
13	Sa	24-Nov-62	Anstey Nomads	a		7-1	CAP		2	3	4		6	7		9	10		1		5	11	8	Boucher 2, Oldham, Howard, Ball, Page, og
14	Sa	1-Dec-62	Nottingham Forest A	a		3-0	CAP	1	2	3	4		6	7		9	10				5	11	8	Oldham
15	Sa	8-Dec-62	Burton Albion Res	a		3-1	CAP	1	2	3	4		6	7		9	10				5	11	8	Oldham 2, Boucher
16	Sa	15-Dec-62	Wilmorton & Alvaston	h		2-0	CAP	1	2	3	4		6	7		9	10				5	11	8	Page, Ball
17	Sa	22-Dec-62	Clay Cross MW	a		2-3	CAP	1	2	3	4		6	7	8	9	10				5	11		og, Ball
18	Sa	19-Jan-63	Ransome & Marles	h	1160	4-0	CAP	1	2	3	4		6		8	9	10	7			5	11		Oldham 2, Boucher, Anthony
19	Sa	9-Mar-63	Linby Colliery	h		12-0	CAP	1	2	3	4		6		8	9	10	7			5	11		Ball, Boucher 3, Hornbuckle 4, Oldham 4
20	Sa	16-Mar-63	Nottingham Forest A	h		8-0	CAP	1	2	3	4		6		8	9	10	7			5	11		Boucher 3, Ball 3, Williams, Anthony
21	Sa	23-Mar-63	Linby Colliery	a		6-0	CAP	1	2	3	4		6		8	9	10	7			5	11		Williams 2, Ball 2, Howard, Boucher
22	Sa	30-Mar-63	Ericsson Athletic	h		6-0	NSCQF&CAP	1	2	3	4		6		8	9	10	7			5	11		Hornbuckle 2, Oldham 2, Howard, Boucher
23	We	3-Apr-63	Kimberley Town	h		3-0	CAP	1	2	3	4		6		8	9	10	7			5	11		
24	Sa	6-Apr-63	Eastwood Town	h		4-0	CAP	1	2	3	4		6		8	9	10	7			5	11		Davis, Oldham 2, Ball
25	Sa	13-Apr-63	Eastwood Town	a		5-1	CAP	1	2	3	4		6		8	9	10	7			5	11		Hornbuckle 2, Oldham
26	Mo	15-Apr-63	Kimberley Town	a		2-2	CAP	1	2	3	4		6		8	9	10	7			5	11		Oldham
27	Tu	23-Apr-63	Creswell Colliery	a		0-0	CAP	1	2	3	4		6		8	9	10	7			5	11		
28	Sa	27-Apr-63	Retford Town	h		1-0	NSCSF	1	2	3	4		6		8	9	10	7			5	11		Boucher
29	Th	2-May-63	Aspley Old Boys	a		2-0	CAP	1	2	3	4		6		8	9	10	7			5	11		Williams, Boucher
30	Sa	4-May-63	Ashbourne Town	h		8-2	CAP	1	2	3	4		6		8	9	10	7			5	11		Oldham 2, Hornbuckle 2, Boucher 2
31	We	8-May-63	Creswell Colliery	h		9-1	CAP	1	2	3	4		6		8	9	10	7			5	11		Hornbuckle 3, Boucher, Oldham 2, Howard, Williams
32	Sa	11-May-63	Sutton Town	n	2859	1-3	NSCF		2	3	4		6		8	9	10	7	1		5	11		Williams
33	Sa	18-May-63	Wilmorton & Alvaston	a		3-1	CAP		2	3	4		6		8	9	10	7	1		5	11		Oldham, Ball, Boucher
34	We	22-May-63	Clay Cross MW	h		3-1	CAP		2	3	4		6		8	9	10	7	1		5	11		Hornbuckle 2, Williams
35	Fr	24-May-63	Ashbourne Town	a		6-0	CAP		2	3	4		6		8	9	10	7	1		5	11		Oldham 4, Davis
			Appearances				385	27	35	35	34	9	35	11	29	35	35	34	8	1	26	25	6	6

166

1962-63

CENTRAL ALLIANCE PREMIER DIVISION

	P	W	D	L	F	A	P	H	A
ARNOLD ST MARYS	**28**	**24**	**3**	**1**	**149**	**24**	**51**		
GRESLEY ROVERS	28	19	5	4	91	38	43	6-1	3-2
KIMBERLEY TOWN	28	19	3	6	78	44	41	3-0	2-2
EASTWOOD TOWN	28	19	0	9	74	51	38	4-0	5-1
CRESWELL COLLIERY	28	14	5	9	46	46	33	9-1	0-0
BURTON ALBION RESERVES	28	13	7	8	55	56	33	7-1	3-1
RANSOME AND MARLES	28	11	9	8	58	45	31	4-0	0-0
WILMORTON AND ALVASTON	28	14	3	11	62	54	31	2-0	3-1
CLAY CROSS MW	28	11	1	16	58	57	23	3-1	2-3
ASHBOURNE TOWN	28	9	5	14	52	69	23	8-2	6-0
LINBY COLLIERY	28	9	4	15	55	77	22	12-0	6-0
NOTTINGHAM FOREST A	28	10	2	16	46	77	22	8-0	3-0
ERICSSON ATHLETIC	28	7	1	20	53	81	15	6-0	7-3
ANSTEY NOMADS	28	4	4	20	33	86	12	12-3	7-1
ASPLEY OLD BOYS	28	0	2	26	24	129	2	16-1	2-0
	420	183	54	183	934	934	420		
MARYS HOME	14	14	0	0	100	10	28		
MARYS AWAY	14	10	3	1	49	14	23		

CENTRAL ALLIANCE PREMIER DIVISION CUP

R1 : ASHBOURNE TOWN (A)	5-4
R2 : CLAY CROSS MW (A)	3-4

FA CUP

1Q : MATLOCK TOWN (H)	3-2
2Q : ALFRETON TOWN (A)	4-0
3Q : BUXTON (A)	3-6

NOTTS SENIOR CUP

1Q : bye	
2Q : bye	
3Q : bye	
4Q : bye	
QF : ERICSSON ATHLETIC (H)	6-0
SF : RETFORD TOWN (H)	1-0
F : SUTTON TOWN (Meadow Lane)	1-3

MISCELLANEOUS RECORDS : MARYS 1958-59 to 1962-63

MATCHES UNBEATEN FROM START OF SEASON

ALL GAMES	8	1960-61
LEAGUE	11	1962-63

CONSECUTIVE WINS

ALL GAMES	8	1962-63
LEAGUE	10	1958-59

CONSECUTIVE MATCHES UNDEFEATED

ALL GAMES	14	1962-63		
LEAGUE	18	1959-60	to	1960-61

BIGGEST MARGIN OF VICTORY

HOME	16-1	v	ASPLEY OLD BOYS	1962-63
AWAY	10-2	v	ASHBOURNE TOWN	1961-62

BIGGEST MARGIN OF DEFEAT

HOME	1-5	v	MATLOCK TOWN	1961-62
AWAY	0-5	v	SUTTON TOWN	1959-60

HIGHEST SCORING MATCH

17 GOALS	16-1	v	ASPLEY OLD BOYS	1962-63

INDIVIDUAL GOALS IN A GAME (WHERE PUBLISHED)

JOE BOUCHER	7	v	ASPLEY OLD BOYS	1962-63

PLAYERS PROGRESSING TO THE FOOTBALL LEAGUE

	APPS	GOALS	CLUB(S)
TERRY BELL	328	103	HARTLEPOOLS UNITED, READING, ALDERSHOT
JOHN MOORE	30	5	LINCOLN CITY

FORMER FOOTBALL LEAGUE PLAYERS JOINING THE CLUB

	APPS	GOALS	CLUB(S)
COLIN COLLINDRIDGE	327	103	SHEFFIELD UTD, NOTTM FOREST, COVENTRY CITY
PAT GROOME	40	0	NOTTS COUNTY
JIMMY JACKSON	113	47	NOTTS COUNTY
ROLAND 'TOT' LEVERTON	165	44	NOTTM FOREST, NOTTS COUNTY, WALSALL
FRED MARTIN	64	0	ACCRINGTON STANLEY
NOEL SIMPSON	338	11	NOTTM FOREST, COVENTRY CITY, EXETER CITY
AUBREY SOUTHWELL	328	2	NOTTS COUNTY
SID THOMPSON	22	8	NOTTM FOREST
PETER WILLIAMS	15	4	DERBY COUNTY, CHESTERFIELD

MISCELLANEOUS RECORDS

LEADING APPEARANCES FOR MARYS 1958-59 to 1962-63

BARRY MOLYNEUX	192 *
DENNIS PARR	161 *
PETER WILLIAMS	141 *
COLIN COLLINDRIDGE	127
LEN ROCKLEY	125
SID THOMPSON	108
MICK CRIPWELL	87
NORMAN GOUGH	81
JOHN ANTHONY	78 *
ERNIE IREMONGER	72
BILLY ENGLAND	60
KEITH MOORE	56
DENNIS DAY	50

PLAYERS APPEARING FOR ARNOLD CLUBS IN FIVE OR MORE SEASONS : 1946-47 to 1962-63

DENNIS PARR	REGENT & MARYS	15 *
GEOFF PARR	REGENT & MARYS	15
ROY 'FLY' CARTER	REGENT, ROVERS & MARYS	12 +
BILL WHITT	REGENT, ROVERS & MARYS	12 +
RON HINSON	MARYS	12
LEN ROCKLEY	MARYS	11
SAM ARCHER	ROVERS & MARYS	10 +
FRANCIS 'FRANNY' GREENSMITH	ROVERS	10 +
JACK BRACE	ROVERS & MARYS	9
JOHN CUNNINGHAM	REGENT, ROVERS & MARYS	9
JACK SURGEY	REGENT & ROVERS	9
ALEC CASTERTON	ROVERS	8 +
RON MADDOCKS	ROVERS	8 +
LES PEEL	ROVERS & MARYS	8 +
KEITH MOORE	MARYS	8
JOHN PIKE	ROVERS & MARYS	7 +
KEN ATHERLEY	ROVERS & MARYS	7
ERNIE BARBER	ROVERS & MARYS	7
CHARLIE MOORE	MARYS	7
HARRY 'JACK' WHARTON	MARYS	7
JIM ATKINSON	ROVERS & MARYS	6
KEN CUNNINGHAM	ROVERS & MARYS	6
DOUG HODGSON	ROVERS & MARYS	5 +
RAY BENNETT	MARYS	5
NORMAN BURTON	MARYS	5
TOMMY DICKINSON	MARYS	5
KEN DOVE	ROVERS	5
DON HAZLEDINE	REGENT & ROVERS	5
BILL HORTON	ROVERS & MARYS	5
CYRIL MIDDLETON	MARYS	5
BARRY MOLYNEUX	MARYS	5 *
REG ROCKLEY	MARYS	5
HERBERT 'DUKE' RYAN	REGENT, ROVERS & MARYS	5
JACK TULLEY	ROVERS	5
PETER WILLIAMS	MARYS	5 *

(*played for Marys beyond 1962-63)

SOURCES

WEBSITES

CHURCHILL SOCIETY
NEWARK ADVERTISER
CLIFTON SUSPENSION BRIDGE
BBC
THE TIMES
ROCKABILLY (NL)
UK ONLINE
EARLESTOWN
SCREEN ONLINE
TELEGRAPH
ETTA (ENGLISH TABLE TENNIS ASSOCIATION)
EUROPEAN CUP HISTORY
UK TV
THE PEOPLE HISTORY
FREEDOM RIDERS FOUNDATION
BERLIN-LIFE
AMNESTY INTERNATIONAL
STUART FREW
MET OFFICE
THE RAILWAYS ARCHIVE
YOUTUBE
WIKIPEDIA

BOOKS

A HISTORY OF NOTTINGHAM HIGH SCHOOL by Adam W Thomas
THE WEEK THE WORLD STOOD STILL by Sheldon M Stern
STEAM MEMORIES : 1950s – 1960s : AROUND NOTTINGHAM by John Cowlishaw

NEWSPAPERS

NOTTINGHAM GUARDIAN JOURNAL
NOTTINGHAM EVENING POST
FOOTBALL POST
NOTTINGHAM ADVERTISER
NUNEATON OBSERVER
BELPER NEWS
RETFORD, GAINSBOROUGH AND WORKSOP TIMES
BURTON DAILY MAIL